# *Colonial Virginians at Play*

*Shooting. Engraved after an original painting, artist unknown.*

# Colonial Virginians at Play

by
Jane Carson

The Colonial Williamsburg Foundation
Williamsburg, Virginia

Library of Congress Cataloging in Publication Data

Carson, Jane.
    Colonial Virginians at play / by Jane Carson.
      p.   cm.
    Reprint. Originally published: 1965.
    Includes bibliographical references.
    ISBN 0-87935-122-5
      1.  Recreation—Virginia—History.   2.  Play—Virginia—History.
   3.  Virginia—Social life and customs—Colonial period, ca.
   1600–1775.   I.  Colonial Williamsburg Foundation.   II.  Title.
   GV54.V8C3   1989
   790'.09755—dc20                                   89-27034
                                                     CIP

Printed in the United States of America

Cover: *The End of the Hunt. Courtesy, National Gallery of Art, Gift of Edgar William and Bernice Chrysler Garbisch.*

Back cover: *"Boys of the Grymes Family" by Charles Bridges.*

# Contents

## Contents

# Illustrations

Research for this report was limited to the conventional historical record; it covers the readily available manuscript and printed sources—diaries and letters, account books and inventories, newspaper advertisements and county court records. The illustrations, taken from the archaeological, curatorial, and research collections of Colonial Williamsburg, suggest ways in which surviving objects such as toys, children's books, and game equipment complement the written record.

Colonial Virginians at play were the same people who engaged in more serious pursuits. The man who was his own lawyer and his own doctor also made his own fun: it was a do-it-yourself age, and amusements were uncomplicated and spontaneous. On the frontier, and among the middling and meaner sort everywhere, the Virginia colonists found their diversion in their work—hunting and fishing, riding and boating, shooting matches, social gatherings at home and church and county court. Once the wilderness was tamed, there was more time for play. Yet the gentry remained a working aristocracy, and even among the great tidewater planters there were no playboys and no organized games in the modern sense. There were no spectator sports except horse racing and cock fighting, and the colonial Virginian rode his own horse and fought his own cocks after breeding and training them.

Colonial Virginians' ideas of amusement were associated with the outdoors. Indoors, at night or in bad weather, pastimes were simple and sociable. Their convivial nature, like their hospitality, was rooted in the social isolation of the plantation. Good food, good drink, good company, good conversation—components of their social grace—were cultivated as arts and practiced with flair.

Jane Carson
1965

### EDITORIAL NOTE

*Colonial Virginians at Play* was originally published in 1965. The Colonial Williamsburg Foundation decided to reprint this classic research report so that today's readers will be better able to understand the amusements that Virginians of two centuries ago enjoyed. Unfortunately, the untimely death of Dr. Carson prevented the Foundation from preparing the second edition under her direction. For this reason, changes have been kept to a minimum. Several of the illustrations have been replaced with more recent or more appropriate ones, and a few new examples have been added. In cases where names of manuscript repositories and libraries have changed the notes have been amended accordingly.

The updating of this book also provides an opportunity to acknowledge the contribution of several people who did not participate in the preparation of the first edition. Cary Carson, Vice President of Research, provided ongoing support for the project. In the Department of Collections, Graham S. Hood, Margaret Pritchard, and Laurie Suber suggested more recent and more appropriate illustrations. Suzanne Brown and Jim Garrett in the Library provided new photographs. Finally, designer Vernon Wooten created a layout that complements the spirit of the author's text.

*1. A Family Group. Painting by Charles Philips.*

# I. HOME ENTERTAINMENTS

## VISITING

Visiting was the favorite amusement of colonial Virginians.[1] Their hospitality was already traditional while life on the plantation was still simple and luxuries were rare. At the end of the seventeenth century a native planter-historian, Robert Beverley, explained:

> Here is the most Good-nature, and Hospitality practis'd in the World, both towards Friends and Strangers. . . . The Inhabitants are very courteous to Travellers, who need no other Recommendation, but the being Human Creatures. A Stranger has no more to do, but to inquire upon the Road, where any Gentleman, or good Housekeeper lives, and there he may depend upon being received with Hospitality. . . . The Gentry when they go abroad, order their Principal Servant to entertain all Visitors, with every thing the Plantation affords. And the poor Planters, who have but one Bed, will very often sit up, or lie upon a Form or Couch all Night, to make room for a weary Traveller, to repose himself after his Journey.[2]

By the middle of the eighteenth century wealthy tidewater planters were entertaining so eagerly and so lavishly that guests were sometimes overwhelmed and decided that their hosts—and Virginians in general—were idle and vain, ostentatious and pleasure loving.[3] The extravagance of their welcome and of the plantation itself was easily misinterpreted. Englishmen who were accustomed to the relatively small estates of the gentry at home did not always understand that land was plentiful in America and a prosperous colonial planter had to have large holdings in order to provide the new fields demanded by tobacco culture. Family units were isolated by the long distances between plantation houses, and visitors were greatly valued as a relief to the loneliness and monotony of daily social life. Servants were numerous if not always efficient, food was abundant and varied, and entertaining was informal and easy.

Travelers who stayed long enough to feel at home appreciated the spontaneity and sincerity of their welcome and understood the fact that their hosts were normally busy people who were themselves enjoying a vacation in the company of their guests. The Reverend Hugh Jones, after living among them for five years, wrote, "No people can entertain their friends with better cheer and welcome; and strangers and travellers are here treated in the most free, plentiful, and hospitable manner."[4] Another visiting English clergyman, the Reverend Andrew Burnaby, was generally critical of American manners, but he spent an "agreeable" year in Virginia, where the people were "extremely fond of society and much given to convivial pleasures."[5] The popular actor, John Bernard, found their "conviviality . . . like their summers, as radiant as it was warm."[6]

When guests were few in number, they were taken into the family group and became part of the daily routine. Gentlemen might enjoy a morning ride over the home quarters, accompanying the master on his regular tour of inspection, while the ladies attended to household affairs and personal appearance—and gossiped, of course. Everyone gathered around the dinner table early in the afternoon to enjoy the company and the food and drink for several hours. Toward evening they strolled through the gardens in good weather or devoted the remainder of the day to cards and billiards, dancing and music, eating and drinking. Running through the entire day was spirited conversation, which was practiced as a social art and a practical substitute for newspapers, books, and the other intellectual fillips of cosmopolitan life.

If the guest was a neighbor or kinsman or old friend, social and political gossip added a note of sprightliness to discussions of the tobacco trade. If he came from London,

2.  *Mama Reading. Mezzotint by Philip Mercier, 1756.*

he was plied with eager questions about events "at home"—in mercantile houses and the Houses of Parliament, at court and in the City, in Drury Lane and Fleet Street. If he was young and eligible, flirtation—whether polite formality or serious pursuit—was an important part of social exchange.[7]

The home took on a house party atmosphere when guests were numerous enough and young enough to have the leisure for long, carefree visits. A lively account of a series of frolics of this kind has survived in the journal of young Lucinda Lee,[8] who made a three-month round of visits in the lower Northern Neck in 1782, stopping at the homes of Washington, Lee, and Turberville relations. The girls gave the usual feminine allotment of time to dressing for a long succession of callers, who dropped in for tea or dinner or an evening of dancing.

Customary strolls through the gardens or down to the river were seldom uneventful. Intimate conversations about their beaux—whether they were already enslaved or only "lately commenced lovers"—punctuated raids on peach and fig trees, grape vines and flower beds, or clumps of thistles "to try" their sweethearts in the love-me-love-me-not ritual. The sudden appearance of the "impertinent" gentlemen ended in a merry chase through the gardens. On one occasion two "horred Mortals" seized two of them and kissed them a dozen times in spite of all they could do.

One of the most faithful beaux, Mr. Pinkard, sometimes read aloud to a feminine audience enthralled by plays and novels of his selection. On other quiet evenings guests played on the spinet or the new pianoforte while the company sang, or they all played cards and forfeit games like "grind the bottle" and "hide the thimble." One evening all the girls went to a baptismal ceremony where six people were "dipt"—a very solemn sight, Lucinda thought, but they remembered to bring two beaux home with them.

Most evenings there was dancing. Mr. James Thomson, Lucinda's favorite partner, was often the best dancer present—a distinction indeed because everyone danced well except Captain Grigg, whose minuet was "really the most ludicrous thing" Lucinda ever saw. "And what makes it more so," she explained, "is, he thinks he dances a most delightful one."[9]

Frolic did not always end at bedtime. One night at Bushfield after the girls had gone to their room, Lucinda related,

> We took it into our heads to want to eat; well, we had a large dish of bacon and beaf; after that, a bowl of Sago cream; and after that, an apple pye. While we were eating the apple pye in bed—God bless you! making a great noise—in came Mr. [Corbin] Washington, dressed in Hannah's short gown and petticoat, and seazed me and kissed me twenty times, in spite of all the resistance I could make; and then Cousin Molly. Hannah [Mrs. Corbin Washington] soon followed, dress'd in his Coat. They joined us in eating the apple pye, and then went out. After this we took it in our heads to want to eat oysters. We got up, put on our rappers, and went down in the Seller to get them; do you think Mr. Washington did not follow us and scear us just to death. We went up tho, and eat our oysters. We slept in the old Lady's room too, and she sat laughing fit to kill herself at us.[10]

Larger and more formal parties were customary on special days and special occasions—Christmas, Twelfth Night, birthdays, weddings. Great houses and small ones alike were crowded with house guests, and neighbors living nearby drove in each day for the merrymaking that lasted several days. These were essentially family parties, and yet the number of guests might be very large indeed because of close family ties among all members of the gentry.

By mid-century three hundred tidewater families made up the ruling class; all these were closely related after generations of intermarriage within the class. Any group of guests composed of neighbors and friends were largely kinsmen, therefore, and nearly everyone addressed everyone else as "Cousin."[11] This close kinship is one of the reasons for the frequency and informality of Virginia visits and for the circumstance—so strange to modern experience—that even in the great houses there was at least one bed in every room except the kitchen.[12] Guests who lived within easy riding distance slept at home and frequently offered sleeping accommodations to others when the host could not care for them all.

## CHRISTMAS PARTIES

Although Christmas in colonial Virginia was primarily a religious festival, it was also a convivial season.[13] Early in December 1773 Philip Fithian explained that at Nomini Hall "Nothing is now to be heard of in conversation, but the *Balls,* the *Fox-hunts,* the fine *entertainments,* and the *good fellowship,* which are to be exhibited at the approaching *Christmas.*"[14] Guests for a Christmas ball in 1771 at Toulston, Bryan Fairfax's plantation farther up the Northern Neck in Fairfax County, included ten gentlemen, two ladies, and a Mrs. Gunnell, who "brought her sucking child with her." Mrs. Fairfax herself prepared some of the refreshments; those of special interest to her little daughter Sally were six mince pies, seven custards, twelve tarts, one chicken pie, and four puddings.[15]

Thirty-five years later a similar Christmas house party in Mecklenburg County was described by one of the guests, Sally Skipwith Kennon, daughter of General Richard Kennon. The hosts were Major John Nelson of Oak Hill and his wife, Anne, daughter of the Williamsburg merchant John Carter. It was "a most delightful Christmas," Sally thought, because "we, that is Nancy Nelson, Helen Skipwith [daughter of Sir Peyton of Prestwould] and myself had all the beaux in the county with us." For amusement:

> In the morning we played at cards, then dressed for dinner, after that was over, we rode out and then again at night, we either played at cards, at romps, or at pawns, just as the fancy struck our wavering minds, our notions were as fickle as the winds, don't you think we spent our time quite a la mode de Paris? . . . Nancy Nelson will be at the races and Helen Skipwith says, that she will endeavour to prevail on her incorrigible mother to let her also come over to see me at that time.[16]

The holiday season closed on Twelfth Night, often with a ball. Nicholas Cresswell attended one in Alexandria in 1775 and recorded this description of it:

> *Saturday, January 7th, 1775.* Last night I went to the Ball. It seems this is one of their annual Balls supported in the following manner: A large rich cake is provided and cut into small pieces and handed round to the company, who at the same time draws a ticket out of a Hat with something merry wrote on it. He that draws the King has the Honor of treating the company with a Ball the next year, which generally costs him Six or Seven Pounds. The Lady that draws the Queen has the trouble of making the Cake. Here was about 37 ladies dressed and powdered to the life, some of them very handsome and as much vanity as is necessary. All of them fond of dancing, but I do not think they perform it with the greatest elegance. Betwixt the Country dances they have what I call everlasting jigs. A couple gets up and begins to dance a jig (to some Negro tune) others comes and cuts them out, and these dances always last as long as the Fiddler can play. This is sociable, but I think it looks

more like a Bacchanalian dance than one in a polite assembly. Old Women, Young Wives with young children in the lap, widows, maids and girls come promiscuously to these assemblies which generally continue till morning. A cold supper, Punch, Wines, Coffee and Chocolate, but no Tea. This is a forbidden herb. The men chiefly Scotch and Irish. I went home about two o'clock, but part of the company stayed, got drunk and had a fight.[17]

Landon Carter usually marked the close of the Christmas season with a feast, which he enjoyed as much as the guests at Sabine Hall. In 1770, he wrote,

My annual entertainment began on Monday, the 8th, and held till Wednesday night, when, except one individual or two that retired sooner, things pleased me much, and, therefore, I will conclude that they gave the same satisfaction to others. The oysters lasted till the third day of the feast.[18]

The next year it was a larger affair:

From the 1st day of this month till this day we have had prodigious fine weather indeed, so that I have enjoyed my three days' festival to-wit: The 10, 11 and 12, with great cheerfulness to everybody; in all about 60 people.[19]

## BIRTHDAYS

Birthday parties, too, were annual customs with Landon Carter and several of his friends in the Northern Neck. On his sixty-second birthday, August 18, 1772, dinner guests included many of those who attended Twelfth Night feasts. In his old age Colonel Carter enjoyed his own eccentricities and recorded personal squabbles with great relish. On this occasion:

[Parson] Giberne would not come, and old Captain Beale came not. I fancied the reason. In my invitation I excepted also a son of his, whose behavior I shall ever remember, and tho' I excused that in my invitation, yet he did not come; his son made some excuse about the change of weather. I complaisantly admitted of it, tho' I think the cause was as before. If it is so, I am quite easy. Such things I pass by thro' old age.[20]

Two years later he wrote:

God be praised that I have seen this my 64th birthday. My son Landon got here about 11 in the night. Very well all this day; and as it was my 64th birthday I received the compliments of most of my better sort of neighbors around me, except Colo. Tayloe who had the gout, besides Colo. Corbin was sick at home. Tom Beale, indeed, did not come, he alone knows the reason why.[21]

Fithian, too, mentioned the party this year. "Colonel Carter," he wrote, "gave an Entertainment Yesterday to celebrate his Birth-Day; and had a numerous and gay Company."[22]

## WEDDINGS

Birthday parties and holiday feasts might provide occasions for home entertainments, but the best excuse for a big house party was a wedding. Throughout the colonial period the ceremony was performed by an Anglican minister, usually in the home of the bride,[23] and the entertainment consisted of cards and dancing, an elegant supper, a cheerful glass, and a convivial song.[24] Unfortunately for the social historian, the colonial newspaper did not feature descriptions of the wedding party, the music, and the accompanying festivities; the regular editor—a man—wrote the social column. Announcements of marriages did describe the bride in terms of the qualities most desirable for a woman to have. She was usually a young lady of independent fortune and great beauty; lacking these virtues, she might be accomplished or genteel or amiable or a young lady of great merit. At times she was praised with startling frankness. Mrs. Sarah Ellyson, who married young William Carter in 1771, was the "Relict of Mr. Gerard Ellyson, deceased, aged eighty five; a sprightly old Tit, with three Thousand Pounds Fortune."[25]

Lacking newspaper stories, one turns to travel accounts and diaries for information about colonial weddings. The earliest surviving description of Virginia wedding festivities is that of Durand, the Huguenot who visited the colony in 1686. The groom in this case was a Frenchman from Picardy who had come to Virginia as an indentured servant and then worked as an overseer, saved his money, and was now marrying a girl "of a very decent family."

On his wedding-day [Durand continued] he sent two of his father-in-law's negroes for me in a boat and I went by water. The Indians [i.e., colonists born here] make a great festival of a wedding. There were at least a hundred guests, many of social standing, and handsome, well-dressed ladies. Although it was November, we ate under the trees. The day was perfect. We were twenty-four at first table. They served us so copiously with meats of all kinds that I am sure there would have been enough for a regiment of five hundred soldiers, even entirely made up of men from Languedoc, Provence, or Dauphiné. The Indians eat almost no bread, seldom drink during meals; but they did nothing afterwards, for the rest of the day and all night, but drink, smoke, sing and dance. They had no wine; they drank beer, cider, and punch, a mixture prepared in a large bowl. They put in three jugs of beer, three jugs of brandy, three pounds of sugar, some nutmegs and cinnamon, mix these well together and when the sugar has melted they drink it,

and while making away with the first, they prepare another bowl of it. . . . It is the custom to take only one meal upon such occasions, at two o'clock in the afternoon. They do not provide beds for the men; those available are for the women and girls, so that about midnight, after much carousing, when some were already lying on the floor, I fell asleep in a chair close by the fire. . . . They caroused all night long and when it was day I got up. I did not see one who could stand straight. A little later the bridegroom arose, gave me a good breakfast, and had me taken back to my lodgings by his slave.[26]

When Nancy Gordon married Richard Chichester in 1759, the ceremony was performed at her home, Merry Point. Her father, Colonel James Gordon, recorded these details in his diary:

This day my daughter Anne was married to Mr. Richd. Chichester about 11 o'clock forenoon; had a very agreeable company—viz.: Col. Conway, Mrs. C. and her children, Col. Tayloe, Dr. Robertson and his wife, Mrs. Chin, Mr. Armistead, Mr. Dale Carter and his wife, Mrs. Doget and Sally, Bridger Haynie, Col. Selden, and Miss Betty Selden, Richd. Spann, Robt. Hening. We invited several others who did not come. The Parson, Mr. Currie, went off first.[27]

The quarrelsome eccentric, Colonel Landon Carter, indirectly attested the convivial spirit of Virginia weddings in a diary entry for April 18, 1776:

This day we are to attend the solemnity of Mr. Mann Page, jun's. wedding to Miss Mary Tayloe, and this by invitation. I hope a little innocent mirth will produce no harm, and I will entertain the most lively expectations that I will be assisted according to my most hearty and devout Prayer that I may keep my tongue even from good words, rather than offend even the most Perverse, most licentious and most inveterate guest.[28]

Two travelers who visited Norfolk at the end of the century commented on the jollity and feasting characteristic of weddings there. The Frenchman Moreau de St. Méry wrote in 1794:

> Norfolk weddings are extremely gay. A dear female friend of the bride prepares pastries of all kinds for the occasion, and does the honors at the fete which follows the consecration of the marriage which the minister celebrates in the house. At this repast, as at all others, the women seat themselves first, but always leave the table the moment the men announce they prefer Bacchus to Venus.[29]

Mrs. Anne Ritson's husband was a merchant in Norfolk, where she lived for a year or so. Her interest in social customs and her keen eye for ordinary details of daily living redeem the literary quality of her poetry. The wedding described took place in 1799 or 1800:

> A wedding in our family;
> My husband's brother's daughter fair,
> Was to assume the matron's care:
> With winter she was to forsake
> Her father, and a husband take.
> The rooms were dress'd with flow'rets gay,
> The company, in best array,
> Converse, and pass the time away,
> Till Sol withdraws his brilliant ray;
> When, entering the drawing-room
> The parson shows the hour is come;
> The parents then fetch in the bride,
> The bridegroom walking by her side,
> Attended by the bride-maids fair,
> And bridegroom's-men, in all three pair.
> One would suppose this preparation,
> Led to a solemn celebration;
> The matrimonial form well said,
> With serious tone devoutly read:
> But no such thing, tho' they confess,
> And protestants themselves profess,
> Yet at the revolution made
> No law by which the clergy pray'd,
> That when they christen or they marry,
> They never on the service tarry;
> The ceremony soon is o'er,
> The preacher saying little more,
> Than you take John and John take thee,
> I give my blessing heartily.
> The contract o'er, the company
> Wish the young couple health and joy;
> Then all unite in cheerful mirth,
> The laugh, the dance, the song, goes forth;
> Till late th' evening hours advance,
> When they all quit the song and dance,
> Ent'ring the supper-room to eat
> Some of a light refreshing treat;
> The table elegantly is spread,
> With the young couple at the head;
> Where chickens, oysters, tarts, and fruit,
> With cakes and syllabubs to suit;
> Confections, trifles, floating cream,
> All there in high perfection seem,
> Well frosted o'er, in fact they show
> A table cover'd with sweet snow.
> Th' effect is pleasing to the sight,
> Bright sparkling with the glare of light;
> The bridegroom's men and bridemaids wait
> Upon the company in state;
> Who, when retiring, wish repose,
> And ev'ry good the world bestows.
> But true enough it's often said,
> The brightest prospects soonest fade:
> So was it with this blushing bride,
> For ere the year was o'er she died.[30]

A more elegant affair was described by young Robert Hunter, an Englishman visiting Virginia cousins at Tappahannock, when he attended a wedding at Blandfield in 1785. The host was Robert Beverley, grandson of the historian, his daughter Maria was the bride, and Richard Randolph of Curles was the groom.[31] Hunter and his McCall cousins set out from Tappahannock at eleven o'clock, driving in a coach-and-four, and two hours later arrived at Blandfield, where, he wrote,

[We] were fortunate in finding the ceremony was not begun, as we understood it was to have been at twelve.[32] About two the company became very much crowded. We were now shown into the drawing room and there had the pleasure of seeing Miss Beverley and Mr. Randolph joined together in holy matrimony. The ceremony was really affecting and awful. The sweet bride could not help shedding tears, which affected her mother and the whole company. She was most elegantly dressed in white satin, and the bridegroom in a lead color, lined with pink satin. After the ceremony of saluting, the ladies retired.

At four we joined them to a most sumptuous and elegant dinner that would have done honor to any nobleman's house in England. We were about a hundred in company.

After dinner we danced cotillions, minuets, Virginia and Scotch reels, country dances, jigs, etc. till ten o'clock. . . . The bride and bridegroom led off the different country dances. . . . After supper, which was elegant as the dinner—it's in vain to attempt describing it—we continued dancing till twelve. The bride, however, slipped away at eleven, and the happy bridegroom soon followed. Mr. McCall and I were under the necessity of turning in together, in the same room with Dr. Brockensburg, and thought ourselves very fortunate in getting so good a bed where there was such a large company.

For three days the company continued to enjoy sumptuous meals and almost constant dancing, with an occasional horseback ride for variety. The ladies appeared each day in different dresses, all of them elegant, and they wore out a pair of satin slippers every night dancing. All the guests were congenial, everything went smoothly, Hunter thought, and the whole affair did great honor to Colonel Beverley.

Soon after breakfast Sunday morning the guests drove off in their phaetons, chariots, and coaches-and-four with two or three footmen in attendance.[33]

Sometimes there were special refreshments at the wedding supper, notably the wedding cake. A young lawyer, William Wirt, who lived in Williamsburg at the turn of the century, attended a wedding there and described the affair in a letter to his absent wife, who, he knew, would be especially interested in the arrangement of the supper table:

*3. The Cotillion Dance. Colored engraving by James Caldwell from a painting by John Collet.*

And a very superb one it was, I assure you. The tree in the centre cake was more simply elegant than any thing of the kind I remember to have seen. It was near four feet high: the cake itself, the pedestal, had a rich—very rich—fringe of white paper surrounding it: the leaves, baskets, garlands, etc., etc., were all very naturally done in white paper, not touched with the pencil, and the baskets were rarely ornamented with silver spangles. At the ends of the tables were two lofty pyramids of jellies, syllabubs, ice-creams, etc.—*the which* pyramids were connected with the *tree* in the centre cake by pure white paper chains, very prettily cut, hanging in light and delicate festoons, and ornamented with paper bow-knots. Between the centre cake and each pyramid was another large cake *made for use:* then there was a profusion of meats, cheese-cakes, fruits, etc., etc.[34]

Not all refreshments were so lavish as these, nor were all hostesses so openhanded in their free distribution of them. Robert Wormeley Carter has left us an example of the exception to the rule of traditional Virginia hospitality. On May 25, 1769, he wrote:

Colo. F. Lightfoot Lee was married this day to Miss Rebecca Tayloe, second daughter to the Hon. John Tayloe. I received a very slight Invitation, but went that I might give no Offence to the Bride and Bridegroom. Drank no wine; because I was expresly within the Statute made by *Mrs.* Tayloe, who said at her Table that She wondered how Persons who were paying Interest for money and kept no wine of their own; could come to her House and tope it in such a manner as they did; that for the future it should not be so.[35]

Although the lesser folk had less to do with, they made as much of weddings as their betters.[36] During the morning of the wedding day, friends of the groom gathered at his father's house and accompanied him to the bride's home in time for the ceremony at noon. On the way they amused themselves with a headlong race, started with an Indian yell and finished at the bride's door, where the winner received and shared the prize, "black Betty," a bottle of liquor.

The wedding breakfast was a hearty meal of beef, venison, pork, chicken, and perhaps bear steak with plainly cooked vegetables and pie, served by the bride's attendants. During the meal the bridesmaids performed another function—protecting the bride's slipper from theft. If a guest got possession of the slipper, he received a prize of a bottle of liquor, and the bride could not dance until she had paid the forfeit. Dancing began immediately after the meal and lasted until dawn. If a tired dancer tried to hide out for a brief nap, he was hunted up, paraded onto the floor, and required to dance to a special tune, "Hang out till morning."

Before midnight the bride and her attendants were supposed to steal away to the bedroom provided for the young couple, and the groom and his attendants followed. Then came the ceremony of "throwing the stocking." The bridesmaids, one at a time, stood at the foot of the bed with their backs turned toward it and threw a rolled-up stocking over their shoulders at the bride. The first to hit the target was to be the next one married. The groomsmen then took turns throwing the stocking at the groom's head. Toward morning black Betty appeared again and a toast was drunk to the couple: "Here's health to the groom, not forgetting myself, and here's to the bride, thumping luck and big children."[37]

## DANCING

In the composite picture drawn by travelers, their Virginia hostesses were not always beautiful and accomplished, lively and graceful, amiable and industrious. But all of them loved to dance,[38] and they gave formal balls on the slightest excuse—or none at all. While Philip Fithian was living at Nomini Hall, he attended a ball at Lee Hall that lasted from Monday through Thursday, and even then Colonel Richard Lee entreated the wearied-out guests to stay on another day. Back home in New Jersey such protracted revelry was unheard of, and Fithian expressed amazed wonder at the presence of seventy guests, all of them "genteel," and the variety of refreshments and amusements. Although he did not dance or play cards or join in the drinking songs, he enjoyed the music of French horns and violins, the conversation, the elegant dinner, and the splendid appearance of the ladies, whose silks and brocades rustled and trailed behind them as they danced minuets, reels, country dances, and jigs.[39]

That was the customary order of an evening of dances as taught by dancing masters, who instructed the sons and daughters of the gentry in this important phase[40] of their training in manners and deportment. These special tutors held classes in their homes if they lived in a town, and they taught other groups of pupils by moving about in a circuit of convenient plantations.

One of the earliest dancing schools in Williamsburg was conducted by William Levingston and Charles and Mary Stagg, who built and operated on Palace Green the first theater in British America. For two decades the Staggs taught dancing classes in town and in homes throughout tidewater Virginia. Stagg's business arrangements with "King" Carter of Lancaster County were the customary ones: Once a month he made a circuit of the lower Northern Neck peninsula, stopping regularly at Corotoman, where five Carter children received a full day of dancing instruction. Another patron, Colonel James Ball, lived just across Corotoman Creek, and Stagg often taught both groups of children gathered into one home.[41] After the formal lessons were done, everybody joined in the dancing.[42]

Fortunately it is possible to determine Stagg's teaching methods. When his estate was inventoried in 1736, along with prints, maps, and a Bible were two copies of *The Art of Dancing*, one by J. Weaver, the other by J. Essex.[43] Both of these are translations of *the* French authority, Raoul A. Feuillet.

John Weaver, London dancing master, made his first translation of Feuillet in 1706; a later edition (about 1715) in the Library of Congress bears this title: *Orchesography of the Art of Dancing by Characters, and Demonstrative Figures. Wherein The whole Art is explain'd; with compleat Tables of all Steps us'd in Dancing, and Rules for the Motions of the Arms, &c. Whereby Any Person (who understands Dancing) may of himself learn all manner of Dances. Being An Exact and Just Translation from the French of Monsieur Feuillet.*[44] Weaver acknowledged Feuillet's mastery of dance forms and praised his method of notation—an original combination of shorthand and musical notes that show in one diagram the overall pattern of the dance, the successive steps and positions of each participant, and even the corresponding bars of music that accompany the dance.[45] If Stagg followed Weaver's example and studied Feuillet's designs carefully, he could teach his students to perform all the popular dance forms.

Englishmen everywhere danced country dances in great variety. It is not always remembered that the strictest Puritans approved of dancing because it improved manners and morals. Although elaborate court dances were frowned upon and abolished during the Commonwealth period, old English dances with traditional tunes replaced them. The Puritan John Playford brought out his *English Dancing Master* in 1651; when the seventeenth edition was published in 1728, it contained 918 dances.[46] These were the dance forms taught by New England dancing masters like Peter Pelham, father of Williamsburg's organist. When the elder

Pelham first came to Boston, he taught dancing, writing, reading, painting on glass, and needlework.[47]

Fithian noticed that Virginians preferred minuets and French dances, while country dances were more popular to the North. Immediately after the Revolution, when Baron Von Closen was stationed in Williamsburg with Rochambeau, he, too, commented on this difference in tastes. On December 15, 1781, he wrote in his journal:

> M. de Rochambeau gave a large dinner for the leading residents of Williamsburg, and a ball to which all the Ladies were invited; everyone very pleased with it.
>
> The fair sex in this city like minuets very much. It is true that some of them dance them rather well, and infinitely better than those up North; to make amends for this, the latter dance the Scottish [reels] better. All of them like our French quadrilles, and in general, they find French manners to their taste. That is all I will take the liberty of saying on this subject.[48]

It might well be said, speaking further on this subject, that Feuillet directed dancing in Virginia while New Englanders followed the gospel according to Playford.

After Charles Stagg's death, Mary Stagg stayed on in Williamsburg, teaching dancing and giving assemblies. In the late 1730s the town could boast several other dancing masters. Madame Barbara DeGraffenriedt, daughter-in-law of the founder of New Bern, North Carolina, was recommended by no less an authority than William Byrd II, who wrote to his friend Sir John Randolph:

> Upon the news of Mr. Stags death Madame la Baronne de Graffenriedt is in hopes to succeed to part of his business in town and were it not for making my good Lady Jealous (which I would not do for the World)—I would recommend her to your favour. She really takes abundance of pains and teaches well.[49]

Another friend of Byrd was the dancing master William Dering, a frequent guest at Westover especially valued for his musical talents and good conversation.[50] When he was a young man, Byrd loved to dance; in his middle sixties, however, the young people danced at Westover, and only twice in the years 1739–1741 could he be persuaded to join them in a quadrille.[51]

Other dancing masters in Williamsburg at mid-century included an indentured servant, Stephen Tenoe, whose circuit of classes extended to Yorktown and Hampton;[52] Richard Coventon, whose student balls in the courthouse were open to adults on payment of a half-pistole fee;[53] and the Chevalier de Peyroney, whose repertoire included fencing and the French language.[54]

The subsequent history of this group of teachers is blank except in the case of Peyroney, whom we find at Fort Necessity, wounded. George Washington, writing to Dinwiddie from Great Meadows on June 12, 1754, recommended the Chevalier for promotion and summarized his Virginia career:

> If merit, Sir, will entitle a gentleman to your notice, Mr. Peyrouny may justly claim a share of your favor. His conduct has been governed by the most consummate prudence, and all his actions have sufficiently testified his readiness to serve his country, which I really believe he looks upon Virginia to be. He was sensibly chagrined, when I acquainted him with your pleasure, of giving him an ensigncy. This he had twelve years ago, and long since commanded a company. He was prevailed on by Colonel Fry, when he left Alexandria, to accept the former commission, and assist my detachment, as I had very few officers, till we all met on the Ohio, which commission he would now have resigned, and returned to Virginia, but for my great dissuasion to the contrary. I have promised to solicit your Honor to appoint him adjutant, and continue him ensign, which will induce a very good officer to remain in the regiment.[55]

Two months later the Frenchman came to Williamsburg to petition the General Assembly for an allowance for loss of clothes and other expenses in the Ohio campaign and to carry Washington's personal plea to Dinwiddie for relief for his naked, unpaid soldiers. While he was in town, Peyroney wrote this letter to his commanding officer:

As I imagine you By this time, plung'd in the midst of Dellight heaven can aford: and enchanted By Charms even Stranger to the Ciprian Dame. I thought it would Contribute a litle to the variety of yours amusemens to send you few lines to peruse.

I Shan't make Bold to Describe the procedings of the house, which no doute you have had already Some hint of. I only will make use of these three expressions related to those of the oracle: furtim venerunt invane Sederunt and perturbate Redierunt

But all that is matere of indifference to the wirginia Regiment Collo. Washington will still Remain att the head of it, and I spect with more esplendor than ever: for (as I hope) notwithstanding we will Be on the British stablishment, we shall be augmented to Six houndred and by those means entitle you to the Name not only of protector of your Contry But to that of the flower of the wirginians, By the powers you'll have in your hands to prove it. So.—

Many enquired to me about Muses Braveries; poor Body I had pity him han't he had the weakness to Confes his coardise him self, and the impudence to taxe all the rest of the oficiers withoud exeption of the same imperfection. for he said to many of the Consulars and Burgesses that he was Bad But th' reste was as Bad as he:—

To speak francly had I been in town at that time I cou'nt help'd to make use of my horse's wheap for to vindicate the injury of that vilain.

he contriv'd his Business so that several ask me if it was true that he had challeng'd you to fight: my answer was no other But that he should rather chuse to go to hell thand doing of it, for had he had such thing declar'd: that was his Sure Road—

I have made my particular Business to tray if any had some Bad intention against you here Below: But thank God I meet allowais with a good wish for you from evry mouth each one entertaining such Caracter of you as I have the honnour to do my Self who am the Most humble

And Obedient of your Servants
Le Chevalier De Peyroney

September 5, 1754
his honour the Governor did Grand me the Capt. Comission after having being recomand to him from the house of Burgess and parlement and you Sir to whom I am infinitly oblig'd if th' was your pleasure I should stay some few dais more here below I should take it as a great favour not beeing yet well relaevd from my wond I beg'd it already from the governor which granted. I hope the same indulgence from you when you'll be pleased to send me your orders my adress is at Williamsburg at Mr. finis?[56]

"George Muse, late Lieutenant-Colonel," was specifically excepted from the burgesses' vote of commendation to the officers of the Virginia forces,[57] but Peyroney received his captain's commission in August.[58]

The following summer Washington sent in his terrible report of Braddock's engagement on the Monongahela. Out of his three Virginia companies, he wrote, only thirty men remained alive: "Captn. Peyrouny and all his Officer's, down to a Corporal, were killed. . . . I luckily escap'd with't a wound tho' I had four Bullets through my Coat and two Horses shot under me."[59]

It is to be regretted that so little is known of the gallant young Frenchman, so like Lafayette, who was staying at the Raleigh Tavern when he advertised for dancing students and again when he was Washington's emissary to Dinwiddie. Whether he stayed on in town, teaching, until he went to the Ohio is not known. He joined Colonel Joshua Fry in Alexandria early in 1754; perhaps he was living there at the time when he decided to "serve his country. . . . Virginia."

In the decade of the 1770s at least five other dancing teachers were available for instruction: Francis Russworm,[60] Sarah Hallam,[61] William Fearson,[62] John K'Dore,[63] and Francis Christian. Of these Mr. Christian is the best known because some of his patrons in the Northern Neck kept diaries that have survived to our time.[64] About twenty young people in the Carter, Lee, Fauntleroy, Booth, and Corbin families formed one of his classes, which met for two days each month in rotation among their homes in Richmond and Westmoreland counties. In the mornings and again in the afternoons Christian gave formal instruction to his students, singly and in groups; in the evenings adult hosts and guests joined the young people in regular ballroom dancing. A similar but smaller group made up the class that met at Mount Vernon, Gunston Hall, and other plantations near Alexandria.

## MUSIC

A social ornament of the female sex second only to dancing was musical skill. Gentlemen who recognized its enhancing values sometimes wrote poems in praise of the performer; a typical one, printed in the *Virginia Gazette*, follows:

*On Miss* ANNE GEDDY *singing,* and *playing on the* SPINET

WHEN Nancy on the spinet plays
I fondly on the virgin gaze,
    And wish that she was mine;
Her air, her voice, her lovely face,
Unite, with such excessive grace,
    The nymph appears divine!

A smile or kiss, or amorous toy,
To me can give but little joy,
    From any maid but she;
Corelli, Handel, Felton, Nares,
With their concertos, solos, airs,
    Are far less sweet to me!

Ye fates, who cause our joy, or grief,
Oh! give my wounded heart relief,
    Let me with her be blest;
Oh! Venus, soften the dear maid,
Oh! Cupid, grant thy powerful aid,
    And pierce her youthful breast.[65]

The second ornament was closely allied to the first, for the music so necessary to dancing was usually provided by members of the family. And, of course, it was an art cultivated for its own sake. A German officer who visited Monticello during the Revolutionary War later observed that "all Virginians are fond of music."[66] All the daughters of the gentry and some of the sons received some kind of formal training. Music teachers, like dancing masters, traveled about from plantation to plantation; sometimes the same person taught both dancing and music.[67]

Ladies usually played on the spinet or harpsichord; gentlemen preferred the violin, French horn, or flute. Other popular instruments were the piano, organ, banjo, guitar, and German flute; also recorded were the harmonica, barrel organ, bassoon, bugle, clarinet, clavichord, drum, fife, pedal-harp, oboe, tabor, trumpet, viola, and virginals.[68] Negroes often played fiddles and French horns for their masters' entertainment and dancing, but the banjo was their favorite instrument for their own amusement.[69]

Many an evening passed pleasantly in ensemble playing and group singing with instrumental accompaniment: catches, duets, sonatas, concertos, and selections from the classics. Popular English songs were quickly adopted in

Virginia. The music for Thomas A. Arne's "Love in a Village," for example, composed in 1762, was on sale in Williamsburg by 1765.[70] Other Arne favorites included "Water Parted from the Sea," from *Artaxerxes,* and "Rule Britannia," from *Alfred.*[71]

The Honorable John Blair's daughter Anne described such an evening in Williamsburg shortly after the arrival of a new governor, Lord Botetourt:

> We spent a cheerful afternoon yesterday. Mrs. Dawson's Family stay'd the Evening with us, and the Coach was at the door to carry them Home, by ten o'clock; but every one appearing in great spirits, it was proposed to set at the Steps and Sing a few Songs which was no sooner said than done. While thus we were employ'd, a Candle & Lanthorn was observed to be coming up Street; (except Polly Clayton censuring their ill taste, for having a Candle such a fine Night) no one took any notice of it—till we saw, who ever it was, stop to listen to our enchanting Notes—each Warbler was immediately silenced; whereupon, the invader to our Melody, call'd out in a most rapturous Voice, Charming! Charming! proceed for God sake, or I go Home directly—no sooner were those words utter'd, than all as with one consent sprung from their Seats, and the Air eccho'd with "pray, Walk in my Lord"; No—indeed, he would not, he would set on the Step's too; so after a few ha, ha's, and being told what all knew—that it was a delightful Evening, at his desire we strew'd the way over with Flowers etc. etc. till a full half hour was elaps'd, when all retir'd to their respective Homes.[72]

## BARBECUES

In good weather outdoor fish feasts and barbecues[73] were popular with Virginians of all classes and ages. The men and boys went fishing in the morning, and all the guests gathered under trees by the riverside for dinner. While servants cooked the fish or roasted the pigs, the young people danced to the music of fiddles and banjos. Already the plentiful supply of toddy had been put into circulation, and the party was often boisterous by the time the feast was ready.[74]

Their elders did not always approve of the free-and-easy manners that characterized these outdoor feasts by the end of the colonial period.[75] Landon Carter spoke for the critics when he complained:

> September 2, 1772. . . . This is our third Barbecue day. I think it an expensive thing. I confess I like to meet my friends now and then, but certainly the old plan of every family carrying its own dish was both cheaper and better, because then nobody intruded, but now every one comes in and raises the club, and really many do so only for the sake of getting a good dinner and a belly full of drink.[76]

## LITTLE PLAYS

More sedate groups played charades—acting out proverbs or "little plays," as they described the amusement. Word games of this kind had seized cultured Europeans like a malady in the sixteenth century, especially in the French province of Picardy, and by the eighteenth century the upper classes everywhere were playing them with enthusiasm. In contrast to today's "The Game" and nineteenth-century parlor charades, where each syllable of the word or each word of the phrase is one act of a little pantomime, the eighteenth-century "amusement à la mode" was a simple pantomime of the entire proverb. Special costumes, props, and musical accompaniment were permitted then, as well as action and facial expression.[77]

William Byrd learned to enjoy the pastime in England. During the Twelfth Night celebrations in 1719 the large company at Lord John Percival's "drew king and queen" in

4. *Children Playing Charades. Painting by Joseph Francis Nollekens.*

the traditional cake-cutting ceremony and then "played little plays and were merry" until eleven o'clock. Other evenings in merry company at Tunbridge Wells, at the country home of the Earl of Orrery, and on a boat trip up the Thames were spent in the same amusement. Byrd probably introduced it to Virginia friends after he came home, for he mentioned playing it on seven occasions during the next year. A Twelfth Night party at Westover in 1721—a merry company of about a dozen neighbors—acted proverbs until one o'clock. When he was in Williamsburg on public business, he played with friends at the Ludwell–Paradise House and at Green Spring.[78]

Occasionally, longer plays were read aloud and acted out by the company. The first recorded dramatic performance in British America was of this kind. On August 27, 1665, *The Bear and the Cub* was presented in Accomack to an audience of Eastern Shore people. The actors—Cornelius Watkinson, Philip Howard, and William Darby—were arrested in November on information furnished by a neighbor, Edward Martin, and were required to repeat the performance in costume before the Accomack justices. The court found the actors not guilty and required Martin to pay the costs. The precise charge was not stated in the court record; it was probably treasonable speech, since the actors were asked to repeat all their lines exactly as delivered in August. The traditional scene of the performance is the village of Pungoteague.[79]

More than a century later, when the Englishman Nicholas Cresswell was visiting friends in Maryland, some young ladies from Virginia were also guests of the family. After supper the company amused themselves with "several diverting plays." To Cresswell this seemed very strange. "But," he concluded, "it is common in this Country."[80]

Addison's *Cato* was a favorite vehicle for amateurs because it requires little acting ability; the characters simply strike attitudes and declaim noble sentiments in high-flown oratory. The elevating effects of the play made is especially suitable for young people like the students at William and Mary who invited the public to a performance in 1736.[81] The boys enrolled in the Reverend Mr. Warrington's school at Hampton gave a similar performance in 1767. Little Camilla Warrington spoke the epilogue written for that occasion. After expounding Addison's moral lessons, she pronounced the players' apology with special reference to the utility of the dramatic experience in her future social life in Virginia:

> For I, in exercising smiles and frowns,
> To gain my Prince, have scarce a thought of crowns
> But hope to make a better wife, when I
> Obtain my Princely Colonel by and by.[82]

Out on the Ohio in 1758 the thoughts of Colonel George Washington were dwelling on the social uses of a *Cato* performance when he laid aside military duties long enough to write a personal letter. Sally Fairfax had informed him of the doings of friends at Belvoir, and he replied: "I should think my time more agreable spent believe me, in playing a part in Cato, with the Company you mention, and myself doubly happy in being the Juba to such a Marcia, as you must make."[83]

## READING ALOUD

Sometimes the company spent an agreeable evening reading selections from plays and novels. If there was a gentleman present, he did the reading, and the ladies listened with eager attention, their "sensibilities" greatly moved while their hands lay idle, holding neglected needlework. When Lucinda Lee was at Chantilly, the faithful beau Mr. Pinkard read an entire play one evening; it was *The*

*Belle's Stratagem,* either a sequel to Farquhar's popular comedy, *The Beaux' Stratagem,* or an adaptation of it.[84] Later he read a novel.[85]

William Byrd often entertained ladies by reading aloud to them, sometimes from his own writings.[86] Once when heavy rains forced him to stay several days at Tuckahoe, another guest, Mrs. Fleming, asked him to read Gay's *Beggar's Opera* to the company. Since the only available copy of the libretto began with Part II, Byrd "acquainted the Company with the History of the Play," told some anecdotes about its successful run in London, and then read three acts of it, leaving "Mrs. Fleming and Mr. Randolph to finish it, who read as well as most Actors do at a Rehearsal." Thus they "kill'd the time, and triumpht over the bad Weather."[87]

Instructive and improving literature was usually chosen for ladies; novels were considered a pernicious influence because they warmed the imaginations, weakened the modesty, and disordered the hearts of persons of delicate sensibility and sometimes precipitated them headlong into error.[88] Left alone, girls of course read popular romances, wept over them, and discussed them—not only *Pamela* and *Clarissa,* but also the many imitations of Richardson's heroines that flooded the bookseller's market in the latter half of the century.[89] Mrs. Frances Brooke's tearjerkers were especial favorites. Lucinda and her friends agonized with Lady Julia Mandeville, whose modest lover nobly fought his way through innumerable obstacles to win her father's approval of his suit; then, success within his grasp, he was killed in a useless duel, and the fair heroine died of a broken heart. The girls enjoyed Pope's "Eloisa to Abelard," too. The poetry was beautiful and uplifting, Lucinda thought, but she questioned some of the sentiments of Eloisa—they were "too Ammorous for a female."[90]

Young Robert Hunter often read to members of the McCall household in Tappahannock. The library was a good one, and he selected sermons and other religious works, histories, letters of Lord Chesterfield and Madame de Sévigné, and a few novels. Reading aloud became a courting device when Catharine McCall was in the company. Her favorite stories were Fanny Burney's *Evelina* and Goethe's *Sorrows of Werther;* Hunter read from his own copy of Goethe and then gave her the volume.[91]

John Marshall used this same device when he was courting Mary Ambler in Yorktown. Years later, her sister Elizabeth recalled that he "used to read to us from the best authors, particularly the Poets, with so much taste and feeling, and pathos too, as to give me an idea of their sublimity,which I should never have had an idea of. Thus did he lose no opportunity of blending improvement with our amusements."[92]

Not all gentlemen held a very high opinion of ladies' reading habits when left to their own devices. James Parker, a Norfolk loyalist, with his usual cynicism reported to his friend Charles Steuart, back home in England:

> You must know that I was a subscriber for Mr. Sterns Works printed at Phila. by Jas. Humphrys jun. The books were Sent me latly. Our Women at that time were in what they call a round of Working, that is goeing to each others houses in the afternoon, with a needle thread and a bit of Rag just to make a show. 6 or 7 speak at a time scandel and half pa [Parker's expression for subjects of doubtful propriety]. Mrs. Aitchison by Way of Variety took to reading the above books.[93]

The more convivial pastimes at home did not have to be improving. Virginians played games that reflected their sociable nature: card games of all kinds except solitaire, simple dice games, and table games in which luck was as important as skill.

5. *Playing the Game at Quadrille. Artist unknown.*

# II. GAMES

## GAMING

As Virginia women loved to dance, so Virginia men loved to gamble. The gentry set the fashion in their homes and at public gatherings in taverns, laying bets on the fall of a card or a die, on sporting events, trials of strength, changes in weather, and politics.[1] No topic of idle conversation was too frivolous to call forth the most familiar of all retorts: "I'll lay you ten to one." Only at court and in fashionable London clubs—White's, Brooks's, the Cocoa Tree—was the passion for gaming stronger or more respectable than in a Virginia planter's home.

The gambling mania had seized the Restoration court and gradually spread through all classes of English society. Eighteenth-century London became a gambler's paradise—in clubs and gaming houses, at court, and in the slums. Public lotteries for state and church were common. An extreme example of the prevalence of the gaming spirit is the Pultney–Walpole wager on a quotation from Horace, a wager made and settled on the floor of the House of Commons.[2]

London preachers, playwrights, and poets railed against gambling addicts, and even Casanova was shocked at the recklessness and cold-bloodedness of English gamesters. Horace Walpole wrote that in his conservative circle young men lost five, ten, fifteen thousand pounds in an evening at White's. At Brooks's, he declared, "a thousand meadows and cornfields are staked at every throw, and as many villages lost as in the earthquake that overwhelmed Herculaneum and Pompeii."[3] Perhaps the heaviest plunger was the Duke of Cumberland, who did not always pay his losses. Charles James Fox, when he was twenty-four years old, had run up gambling debts amounting to £140,000. Another youth of Walpole's acquaintance, Lord Stavordale, playing cards at White's, once recovered the evening's losses of £11,000 in one turn at hazard; his only comment was an expression of regret that he had not been playing *deep*.[4]

This was the atmosphere in which young Virginians completed their education in polite society. The best known example is William Byrd III. Tradition has it that he learned to gamble while he was a student at the Middle Temple. According to his neighbor, David Meade:

> Before he reached his majority he went to England, where, it appears he engaged in all the gayeties, prodigalities and dissipations to which young men of rank and fortune were addicted. . . . Gaming, as followed in the higher circles of society, Mr. Byrd gave into as a fashionable amusement merely—avarice being then, and ever after, a passion alien to his breast. . . . The habit thus acquired followed him to the last period of his life. A story was current in Virginia . . . that at one of the most noted gaming tables at the west end of the town he lost ten thousand pounds at a single sitting to the Duke of Cumberland.[5]

Nearly a century later Benjamin Ogle Tayloe adopted the incident as a favorite anecdote. Now Byrd was *successfully* taking a bet of ten thousand *guineas* on *a card* offered by the Duke, who later tried to welsh and paid up only after Byrd had strongly intimated that he was ready to meet him in the field at any time.[6]

Back in Virginia, Byrd's prodigality led him into bankruptcy, but gambling was only one of several spendthrift habits; careless management cost him part of his patrimony. Local gossip was repeated by the French traveler who visited Williamsburg in 1765. At Mrs. Vobe's tavern he found a group of "professed gamesters, Especially Colonel Burd, who is never happy but when he has the box and Dices in

6. *Arrested for Debt. Plate IV of William Hogarth's* The Rake's Progress.

hand. This Gentleman from the greatest property of any in america has reduced himself to that Degree by gameing that few or nobody will Credit him for Ever so small a sum of money."[7] Specific evidence of his gambling, in contrast to traditions, is seldom found. John Blair made a memorandum in 1753 of winning £19.7 from Byrd at Westover and £192.8.6 at Williamsburg.[8]

Perhaps a more typical example is that of Jeffery Grisley, "a young wild raw Lad" when he first came to Hanover County at mid-century and said to be of a good family.

> After some Time he went to England, and shortly return'd to Virginia with a small cargoe, with which he open'd Store at Newcastle, the then Scene of Horse racing and all kinds of Gambling. How could a young Man, not accustomed to self Denial, resist the Temptation? He fell in with the thickest of the sport; bought Horses, ran Horses, and in short was not the Hindmost in all this Dissipation and Expence. In a little time, he became enamour'd with the Daughter of Majr. Harry Gaines, the Leader in all these Amusements; married her, and hath Several Children by her.

Now, in 1771, he had been for some months confined in the King William County gaol for debt. His estate was worth at best £400, his debts amounted to about £1,000, and Virginia friends were trying to find English relations who would be willing to supply "a Morcell of Bread" for "his Innocent Offspring."[9]

A more tragic case was that of John Custis, Williamsburg butcher, who was found in bed one Sunday morning in November 1753 with his throat cut. He had been gaming the night before and lost all his money, his horse, "etc." The coroner's jury "sat on the Body, and brought in their Verdict *Falo de se*."[10]

Gaming was not considered an evil in itself; it became a vice only when "inordinate" pursuit of the amusement led one to neglect his business or lose more money than he could afford. Professional gamesters were condemned for cheating if caught red-handed, but controlled "deceit" was only a mark of the skillful player.[11] In Virginia, as in England, gaming was a gentleman's privilege, forbidden by law to those who were supposed to be working: apprentices, artificers, fishermen, husbandmen, laborers, mariners, servants of all kinds, and watermen. During the Christmas season, even these persons were permitted to play the usually forbidden games in their own houses or in the master's house with his consent. The "unlawful games" were bear-baiting, bull-baiting, bowling, cards, cockfighting, coits, dice, football, ninepins, and tennis.[12] Students at the College of William and Mary were governed by similar restrictions,[13] for they were minors as irresponsible as servants and apprentices.

Throughout the colonial period conservative Virginians preached against the evils of inordinate gaming and tried to discourage it as a vice similar to drunkenness. The General Assembly set up legal restrictions on the "baneful practice," first in 1619 with a ten-shilling fine for gaming with dice and cards; later statutes were designed to prevent "unlawful, crafty, and deceitful Gaming, and the inordinate haunting of Alehouses, and Tipling Places."[14]

Anecdotal preachments against the habit sometimes appeared in the *Virginia Gazette*. This one is typical:

### THE GAMESTERS

A GENTLEMAN, after having travelled through different Parts of the Globe, returned at length to his own Country. His Friends, as usual in such Cases, flocked round him with eager Expressions of Welcome. "Bless me, how happy I am to see you (cried one and all

of them) come, do tell us some of your Adventures."
After relating to them a Number of miraculous Circumstances, "You know, Gentlemen (added he) what a prodigious Distance it is from this Country to that of the Hurons! Well, about twelve Hundred Leagues farther off, I met with a very strange Set of Men, who often sit round a Table the whole Night, and even till the Morning is well advanced; but there is no Cloth laid for them, nor is there any Thing to gratify the Appetite. The Thunder might rattle over their Heads, two Armies might engage beside them, Heaven itself might threaten an instant Chaos, without making them stir, or in the least disturbing them; for they are both deaf and dumb. At Times, indeed, they are heard to utter inarticulate Sounds. Sounds which have no Connexion with each other, and very little Meaning; yet will they roll their Eyes at each other in the oddest Manner imaginable. Often have I looked at them with Wonder. . . . Sometimes they appear furious, as Bedlamites; sometimes serious and gloomy, as the infernal Judges; and sometimes gasping with all the Anguish of a Criminal, as he is led to the Place of Execution." "Heavens (exclaimed the Friends of our Traveller) what can be the Object of these unhappy Wretches? Are they Servants of the Publick?" "No." "Then they are in Search of the Philosopher's Stone?" *"No."* "Oh! now we have it; they are sent thither in Order to repent of, and to atone for, their Crimes." *"No, you are much deceived, my Friends, as ever."* "Good God! then they must be Madmen. Deaf, dumb, and insensible! What in the Name of Wonder can employ them?" "Why, *Gaming*."[15]

## CARDS

In Virginia homes card playing was a favorite indoor amusement that ladies might share with their husbands and guests. Governor William Gooch's sister-in-law, Anne Staunton, described colonial life in a letter to Thomas Gooch. She explained that the family planned to visit friends up the James River, where she expected their stay to be all too short because "they all love Cards so well."[16] If Virginia women imitated the "female Gamesters" at court in England, we have no recorded instance of it and no gossip about it. They rarely went to London—Evelyn Byrd's education there is unique—and there was no colonial equivalent of the sophisticated court society that encouraged feminine idleness or full-time gaiety; however, they did play cards for small stakes.[17]

Changing fashions in games,[18] as in costumes, were quickly noted and followed by the gentry, who learned to play them in London, or heard of them from English correspondents, or purchased the latest books of rules released from British presses.

When William Byrd II was living in London, he often played cards at court, in clubs, and in private homes, where the other players were usually men. But at Tunbridge Wells most of the players were women. His diary for the years 1717–1719 specifically mentioned piquet, basset, ombre, commerce, loo, ace of hearts, faro, and slam.[19] Back home at Westover twenty years later he learned of a new development in fashionable card playing from one of his English friends, who wrote:

> You must understand that a Sertain game upon the Cards call'd Whisk (much in vogue these last three or four years) has engaged the Men of all ages to keep company with Women more than ever any thing did before; 'tis apparent there are much stronger charms belonging to Cards, than any of the female sex can boast of, for till Whisk came in fashion a reasonable Man would have thought his character forfeited for ever had it been known that he spent six evenings in a week in the company of Women.[20]

More than a century later whist playing was still the rage in London clubs. In 1872 the French novelist Jules Verne satirized it as a national characteristic of the British. Phileas Fogg, "one of the most perfect gentlemen of good English society," played whist throughout his eighty-day tour of the world—on shipboard, on transcontinental trains, even while waiting for his second to arrange the details of a duel. The tour itself was made on a wager laid at a whist game in the Reform Club. The heroine of the story, Mrs. Aouda, a young Indian widow rescued from a suttee ceremony, explained later that of course she understood whist because it had been an important part of her English education.[21]

By mid-eighteenth century there were two standard treatises on games—Cotton's and Hoyle's—and the Williamsburg Printing Office stocked both of them during the 1750s, 1760s, and 1770s.[22] Charles Cotton's *The Compleat Gamester: or, Instructions How to play at Billiards, Trucks, Bowls, and Chess. Together with all manner of usual and most Gentile Games either on Cards or Dice. To which is added, The Arts and Mysteries of Riding, Racing, Archery, and Cock-fighting* was first published in 1674, and new games were added with new editions.[23] Cotton was a country gentleman writing about games and sports he loved to play, warning the reader against unscrupulous gamesters who would cheat the unwary and spoil the game.

Edmond Hoyle brought out his *Short Treatise on the Game of Whist* in 1742. He had been using it for a year in manuscript as a text for his whist students, who excelled in play because they had been taught how to value their hands and apply mathematical laws of probability with precision. Hoyle's book, the first scientific study of a card game, was a guide to expert play and the persons who used it already knew the basic elements of the game. This first manual was so successful that he prepared others on backgammon, piquet, quadrille, and brag. By 1770 fifteen of his own

*7. All Fours. Cartoon by Henry W. Bunbury.*

editions had been published, and numerous pirated editions appeared after 1743. French, German, and Italian translations were made in the 1760s, and an American Hoyle appeared in 1860. The phrase "according to Hoyle" has become an international idiom.[24]

All these games were played in Virginia homes and taverns when time was passing heavily and more active amusements were not practical—at night, in rainy weather, when the company was too small for dancing or too dull for good conversation. Byrd, who was a skillful player when he was not sleepy, often whiled away an evening at Westover playing cards and billiards with friends or with his wife when they had no guests; on other occasions he "killed the Time, by that great help to disagreeable Society, a Pack of Cards."[25]

Some people disapproved of the all but universal waste of spare time at the card table. Readers of the *Virginia Gazette* sometimes sent in to the editor stringent criticisms of the fashion; one of these, printed in 1751 as a "Burlesque worthy of public View," began:

### MODERN CONVERSATION

I SICKEN at the Nonsense of the Croud,
Where noisy Folly talks and laughs aloud,
Still of her own applauded Nonsense proud.
Insipid Trifles occupy the Tongue,
And the eternal silly Chat prolong:
Th' unthinking Laugh, the Fleer, the scornful Eye
The rare, short intervals of Chat supply.
The calm and solemn Ev'ning Hours, design'd
For Contemplation by the noble Mind,
In marshalling a Pack of Cards they waste,
And, like their Fellow-Children, play themselves to Rest.[26]

In old age Landon Carter of Sabine Hall no longer enjoyed gambling himself and violently criticized "excessive" play in others, notably his son Robert Wormeley Carter and the gaming companions who played with him. The elder Carter's diary contains many comments like the following:

"They play away and play it all away."
". . . tho' I publickly decided agst any more card playing, [Robert Wormeley] got a gang after I went to bed etc—".[27]

## WHIST

After Hoyle demonstrated how to play whist scientifically, this ancestor of modern bridge became the favorite four-handed card game. Older forms had long been popular. "*Ruff and Honours* (alias *Slamm*) and *Whist*," Cotton wrote in 1674, "are games so commonly known in England in all parts thereof, that every child almost of eight years old hath a competent knowledg in that recreation." Already the score included both honors and tricks, and the rules of play were similar to those of bridge, but modern bidding was unknown, for the trump suit was determined by turning up the last card. The chief attraction of these games was explained by Cotton:

In playing your cards you must have recourse altogether to your own judgment or discretion, still making the best of a bad market; and though you have but mean cards in your own hand, yet you may play them so suitable to those in your partners hand, that he may either trump them, or play the best of that suit on the board.

To play skillfully, one had to concentrate on the play and remember what cards had been played out; therefore, *whist* was named "from the silence that is to be observed in the play."[28]

In Virginia, whist playing was specifically mentioned by the planter-diarists William Byrd, George Washington, and Robert Wormeley Carter. John Mercer's account books record occasional purchases of whist cards, as distinguished from ordinary packs of cards. Two visitors mentioned the game: Robert Hunter played whist with his McCall cousins at Tappahannock, and the tutor John Harrower played it at Colonial Daingerfield's Belvidera plantation. Two similar Spanish games, ombre and quadrille, were known in Virginia,[29] but, like ruff and slam, they gave way to whist.

## PIQUET

All his life William Byrd played piquet, a two-handed game similar to modern rummy but scored somewhat like cribbage and played like whist. It was a popular gambling

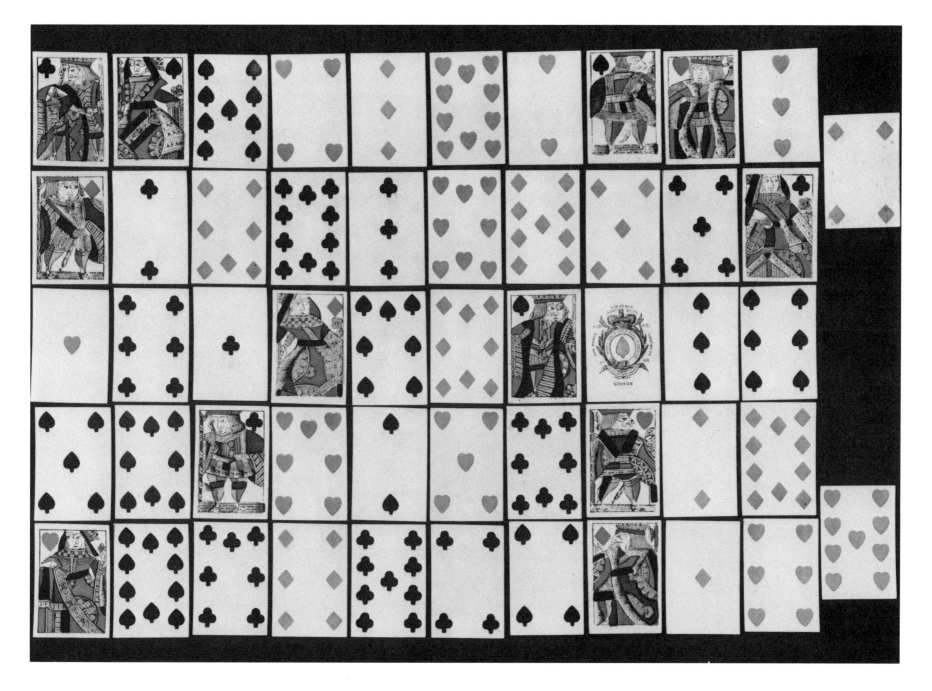

*8. Playing Cards. Eighteenth century.*

game because it is fast, scores pile up rapidly for the player with the better hand, and skill may improve chance because the large "widow" permits a nice use of discretion in discarding.[30]

## ALL-FOURS

Another good two-handed game, all-fours or pitch, is still played today as seven-up or setback. Success in this game is largely a matter of luck, and so all-fours was a favorite pastime of the middling sort, who often played it in taverns. For example, when Daniel Fisher, a Williamsburg innkeeper, took a trip to Philadelphia in May 1755, his first stop was at Chiswell's Ordinary,[31] where two planters were playing all-fours to the exclusion of all other interests.[32]

Earlier in the century a game in Richard Josslin's tavern at Norfolk had a tragic ending. Samuel Rogers, Nathaniel Newton, James Hustings, Henry Jenkins, and William Finiken were having a gay old time around a bowl of sangaree with jigs, friendly tussels, and horseplay. Then Finiken and Rogers began a game of all-fours, in which Rogers won several bowls of sangaree. During a scuffle around the bowl Finiken was thrown violently backward on the floor. The others put him to bed comfortably, and, finding that his pulse was normal, left him to sleep off the effects of the sangaree. The next morning he was dead.[33]

Another game of all-fours with startling results, played in Charleston in 1732, was reported in the *South Carolina Gazette*:

> On Saturday last, a certain Gentleman, belonging to his Majesty's Ship the Aldborough, met a jolly Widow at a publick House in this Town, where after a Full Bowl or two, and a little Courtship in Form, they came to a Resolution to decide the Matter by a Game of All-Fours:

Their Bodies and all their worldly Goods for Life, were the Stakes on each Side. Fortune favour'd the Fair, and she insisting on the Wager, nothing remained but for the Parson to tye the sacred Knot, which was accordingly done that very Afternoon.[34]

In Virginia, too, all-fours was held in contempt by the gentry. Philip Fithian expressed the attitude of the social group in the Nomini Hall neighborhood when he was ashamed of an aunt who played "at that vulgar game fit only for the meanest gamblers 'all Fours.' "[35]

## PUT

Another card game popular with the lower classes was a primitive ancestor of modern poker called put. Cotton had a low opinion of the game because its whole interest lies in the stakes and skillful play is only bold bluff. "Putt," he wrote, "is the ordinary rooking game of every place, and seems by the few cards that are dealt [three to a hand] to have no great difficulty in the play."[36] In one short paragraph he described the rules of play, but an essay of eleven paragraphs could explore only the more obvious rooking methods in common practice.

Cotton's "every place" included Virginia, where in one year—1685—two arguments growing out of games of put were settled in court: In Henrico County Captain William Soane won fifteen pounds of tobacco from Richard Dearlove,[37] and in York County a servant, John Marshall, won by fraud £5 sterling from his master's friend, Joseph Bascome.[38] Five years later Allanson Clerk won £4 sterling in a game with Peter Rowlett, who refused to pay his losses, and Clerk sued to collect them. The Henrico Court refused to pass judgment against Rowlett because the wager had no legal standing as a contract without a stakeholder and a formal agreement about payment.[39] The exact form of rooking was not recorded in any of these suits.

## LOO

More genteel than put and a faster gambling game was lanterloo or loo,[40] which could be played with three cards or five, and with either limited or unlimited stakes. In all its variations it was a round game suitable for any number of players but best for five or seven. By mid-century a special round table had been devised for the use of loo players. Small pits or grooves near the edge of the table held the counters, which in fashionable homes or clubs were little fish made of ivory or mother-of-pearl; hence the name "fish ponds" for counter grooves.[41]

In three-card limited loo, each player puts a stake into the "pool" before the deal. After he has looked at his hand, he may decide whether he wishes to play that round. If he passes, he loses his original stake. If he plays and does not take one of the three tricks, he is "looed," and after the pool is divided among the winners, he and the other losers stake the entire pool for the next hand in the same total count. Each person who "stands in" plays his three cards as in whist, one at a time beginning to the left of the dealer, and scores on tricks alone.

In the unlimited game, each loser is looed the whole amount of the pool; thus when five persons stand in, at least two are looed, and the pool doubles in value in the second round and quadruples in the third. If seven persons play, there are at least four losers, and the pool immediately quadruples, then becomes sixteen times the original size.

In the five-card game, there is a wild card (the knave of clubs) called *pam,* and the pace is quickened further by the rule that a flush (which may include pam) will sweep the board; that is, its holder loos all the other players simply by showing his hand. Skill in playing loo, as in poker, consists in understanding the other players, for the play is simple enough, and its fascination lies in the high stakes.[42] Readers of the *Virginia Gazette,* therefore, would not have been surprised in 1768—as we are today—to learn that a London lady of quality once lost a thousand guineas in an evening of play at loo.[43] In Virginia the game was usually a part of customary social exchange and stakes were more modest. For example, young George Washington's losses for an evening of loo in 1749 totaled five shillings—an average expenditure from a sum that he periodically devoted to cards, theater tickets, and other amusements.[44] John Mercer played for higher stakes. In November 1731 he lost £1.3.6 to James Markham playing "Liew at Mrs. Dent's."[45]

*9. Playing Cards. Eighteenth century.*

## CRIBBAGE

Whist and cribbage were favorite games of the group who played with Robert Wormeley Carter at Sabine Hall and neighboring plantations in the Northern Neck: Lees, Balls, Beales, Carters, Beverleys, Fitzhughs, Robinsons. One of the most inveterate players in the group was the witty and learned Reverend William Giberne, rector of Lunenburg Parish. In spite of his social charm and Christian benevolence, he was sometimes criticized for his gambling habits.[46] Wormeley Carter's elderly father, Landon, once remarked in his diary:

> August 14 [1774]. Sunday. Mr. Giberne came here on Thursday noon, and never went away till last night. At cards all the time, but at meals and in bed. . . . I hate such vulgarity.[47]

Giberne was a good loser rather than a good player.[48] But Colonel Carter could not criticize him on that score because he himself sometimes lost to his son when they were playing two-handed games.

Robert Beverley and the younger Carter often played cribbage when they met at Blandfield or Sabine Hall and sometimes at Todd's Ordinary when they were in Tappahannock on business. Over the years, winnings balanced losses, which seldom amounted to more than £5 at a time.[49]

John Mercer, too, played cribbage, but not so often. In 1725 his accounts show £1.5.0 lost to Benjamin Robinson at cribbage, and in 1731 Colonel George Mason was indebted to him for "your Part of £7.5.2 lost at your house with Phil. Key at cribbage, £3.12.7."[50]

The cribbage these men were playing was a five-card game of sixty-one holes invented by the seventeenth-century courtier, dramatist, and poet, Sir John Suckling. Today we prefer the six-card game of 121 holes, but the rules of play are essentially the same, and the count for both hands and melds is unchanged.[51]

## FARO

Games like faro, for large groups of players who bet against the dealer and won or lost on each card turned up, were known in colonial Virginia but not often played. Faro banks and roulette tables were found here more frequently after the Revolution, when their popularity was attributed to the influence of Rochambeau's soldiers.

James Bailey of Staunton was fined twenty dollars in 1799 for playing at faro while serving as a grand juror.[52] Four years later a Staunton merchant, Robert Bailey, was indicted for keeping a faro bank, convicted, and ordered to be hired out under the vagrancy law.[53]

In 1796 two travelers in Virginia commented on faro and roulette tables. Isaac Weld, stopping at a Richmond tavern, was asked whether he wished to go to the room with a faro table, one with a hazard table, or a third with a billiard table.[54] The architect Benjamin H. Latrobe found a roulette game in progress at Armstead's tavern in Richmond; also a whirligig carrying seventy-two boxes marked A, B, or C. When the whirligig was set in motion, he explained, a ball was thrown into it and bounced round and round until it settled in one of the boxes and those who had bet on that letter won the stake.[55]

Two games of this kind, basset and lasquenet, which Byrd learned to play in London, he sometimes but not often played at Westover.[56] Basset was very popular at court in England and in France, Cotton tells us, because the elaborate equipment and high stakes made it "fit for Kings and Queens, great Princes, Noblemen etc to play at."[57] Virginia planters preferred simpler and more sociable games like whist.

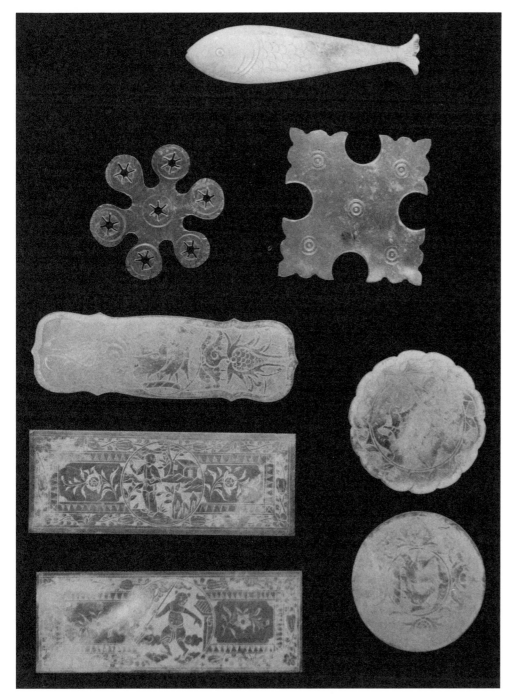

10. *Gaming Counters or Fish.*

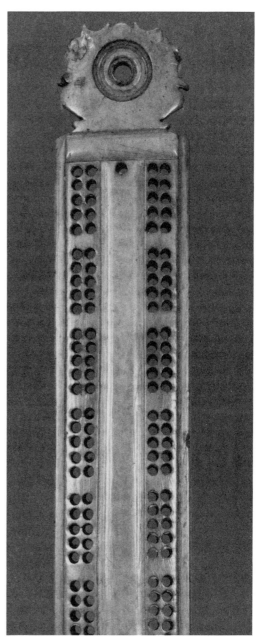

11. *Cribbage Board, dated 1735.*

29

## CHESS

Probably for this reason, the ancient game of intellectuals and introverts—chess—had little appeal to their convivial tastes. In Cotton's opinion, the chief drawback of the game was its tediousness; furthermore, he thought, it is "more difficult to be understood than any other game whatever."[58] Richard Seymour, who edited the 1734 edition of *The Compleat Gamester,* enjoyed chess. In his opinion, its chief charm was its peculiarity "that the Incidents and Turns are so many, and so various, that it will be found both delightful and entertaining, even where People play for nothing; which can hardly be said for any other Game."[59] Seymour's point is echoed by Hoyle, whose "Rules and Observations for playing well at Chess" appear as a minor part of the volume on piquet; his special interest was the application of the calculus of probabilities to popular games, and chess gave him no scope for this talent because it is a game of skill with no chance involved. At that time there were no standardized gambits, no "chess games" in the modern sense, and he described the play in the most general terms with rules for manipulating pieces and pawns.[60]

Although a number of colonial Virginians may have owned chessmen, only Thomas Jefferson's have survived. He bought them on a number of occasions[61] and two sets are now owned by the Thomas Jefferson Memorial Foundation. Furthermore, Jefferson mentioned playing the game. Writing to Jack Walker in the fall of 1769, he suggested that they play chess at the spring meeting of the college society.[62] Governor Francis Fauquier's inventory listed chessmen and a board that were purchased by Thomas Everard;[63] unfortunately, we have no record of its use. Richard Charlton's inventory included a chess board but no men; where he got it and what it was used for we do not know.[64] Governor Fauquier, young Jefferson, and their circle of friends doubtless enjoyed the intellectual challenge of chess and were willing to devote the necessary time to its mastery, but the typical planter was a busy man who seldom had the amount of leisure that chess playing requires. The earliest ardent chess player known to Virginia history was John Randolph of Roanoke; he was atypical in this taste, no doubt, as in almost all others.

## DRAUGHTS

Draughts, like chess, had a limited following in the colony. Checkers, as we know the game today, is essentially the English form of draughts developed by William Payne in 1756. A simpler form was being played in Spain in the sixteenth century, and a similar one in France in the seventeenth. The grand jury of Henrico County that presented John Edwards and one of Mr. Isham's servants for playing draughts on a Sunday in 1679[65] was probably condemning the French form of the game. Scientific play of the English version of draughts was a nineteenth-century development growing out of Joshua Sturges's *Guide to the Game of Draughts, Containing 500 Select Games,* published in 1800.[66]

## BACKGAMMON

Another board game, backgammon, had greater appeal in Virginia, probably because it is an easy game to learn and the use of dice immediately suggests a greater element of chance in the play. Backgammon tables were listed in inventories,[67] and they were advertised for sale in Williamsburg. One diarist, John Blair of Williamsburg, once won £1.10 playing backgammon with Burwell Bassett of Eltham.[68] Thomas Jefferson played, winning or losing as much as seven shillings at a time.[69] There was a table in the dining room closet at Corotoman,[70] but "King" Carter in his letters and diary never mentioned using it; he had no time for frivolities and played cards only once during the period of his extant diary—and this was when he was too ill with gout to get around.

In eighteenth-century play, there were several variations on backgammon. Irish was a slower version played with the same thirty men, which moved in the same pattern. In the French version, tric-trac or tick-tack, all the men started from the ace-point and penalties were different. Sice-ace was a modification for five players, each using six men. In dubblets the fifteen men used were placed differently on the tables, and in ketch-dolt all the men were piled in the center of the board.[71]

At mid-century Hoyle explained how to govern one's choice of moves by a table of thirty-six possible chances or combinations of spots on the two dice. Then all these "games within the tables" began to give way to the standardized backgammon we play today.

## DICE

Of the many dice games "without the tables," hazard was far and away the most "bewitching." Cotton explained: "*Hazzard* is a proper name for this game; for it speedily makes a man or undoes him; in the twinkling of an eye either a man or a mouse."[72]

American craps is a simplified form of hazard with a language all its own. Two hundred years ago the "caster," or player holding the dice, first announced his choice of "main," which might be any number from five to nine, and then he threw the dice. He immediately won the stakes if he "nicked"—cast his main on the first throw. (Several mains had alternate winning numbers; if the main was seven, for example, the nick was either seven or eleven.) He lost if he cast "crabs," any one of several unfavorable com-

*12. Chessmen. Seventeenth century.*

binations. If his initial cast was neither a winning number nor a losing one, it was established as his "chance," and he continued to throw until either his chance or his main came up; he won on the chance and lost on the main. Stakes were set up before he made his initial cast and again after his chance number was established.

In Cotton's day, it was already understood that seven was the easiest number to throw, but until Hoyle explained the precise frequency of each of the thirty-six possible combinations, the odds in betting were not set, even in gambling houses. After Hoyle's day, the second bet was standardized according to his table of probabilities and hazard in formal play became suitable only for gambling houses.

On the other hand, once everyone understood that he had six chances of casting a seven combination against five chances for a six or eight, seven became the only sensible choice of main when bets were even and the game was greatly simplified for informal play. Now the player won the stakes on an initial throw of seven or eleven (a "natural" in craps). He lost on crabs ("craps"), now confined to a two or three, the losing numbers formerly common to all choices of main. The chance became his "point," and now the odds in the second stake and in side bets could be determined by a few simple mathematical calculations.[73]

Throughout the colonial period, hazard and other dice games were favorites of the middling sort, and occasionally the gentry played them.[74] Dice were common items in inventories of house furnishings all over the colony, and they were standard equipment in ordinaries. They could be purchased in Williamsburg stores, and at least one craftsman, Samuel Galt of Elizabeth City County, made them to order or mended them on request.[75]

Dice games in ordinaries were sometimes rowdy affairs, and rooking was not uncommon. One fall night in 1745 two well-to-do citizens, George Holden and John James Hughlett,[76] were playing backgammon in the Williamsburg tavern we now call Shields Tavern. A visiting Maryland lawyer, George Douglas, joined them and they started a game of hazard, using new dice belonging to their host, James Shields. For some reason Shields removed the dice and Hughlett replaced them with a badly worn pair that someone outside handed him through a window. In a short time Douglas had lost six or seven pistoles and Holden had emptied his purse. Hughlett then took his winnings and his dice next door to the Hatter's Shop and started a new game with new victims. Later that night Holden and Douglas passed the open door of the Hatter's Shop and stopped to see the play. A bystander, James Littlepage, seized one of the dice, declaring his opinion that it was loaded, whereupon Hughlett refused to give him the other one and threw it into a corner of the room. Littlepage, Holden, and Douglas carried off the captured die, examined it carefully in private, and picked pieces of metal out of several of the spots. Holden later sued Hughlett for £38 fraudulently won at hazard; the court awarded him £28.15.[77]

In the new frontier town of Staunton in 1762 a group of men were playing dice at Tyler's Ordinary. The games were hazard and pass and no pass.[78] The latter game was probably an adaptation of Cotton's passage, played with three dice; the player throws until he "passes" with doublets over ten or until he loses on doublets under ten.[79]

Dice-playing members of the gentry do not often appear in the record of private games in private homes. John Mercer lost £5.7.6 to Harry Turner of King George County in June 1743 at hazard;[80] this debt probably represents a series of games while Mercer was practicing law in the county court. In London Byrd played hazard more frequently than anything else except piquet, and he sometimes played passage there. But in Virginia his dice games were confined to his earliest visits to Williamsburg during Publick Times. An experience in November 1711 all but put a stop to that. One night after a busy day in the Council Chamber he spent some time carousing in "King" Carter's room, then went to the coffeehouse almost drunk and played at dice, losing £12. The next morning, after only four hours' sleep, he made a "solemn resolution never at once to lose more than 50 shillings and to spend less time in gaming."[81] This resolution he kept moderately well with respect to dice games. Hazard does not appear in Robert Wormeley Carter's almanac diaries or in Jefferson's or Washington's account books. "King" Carter's diary contains no reference to it, but his inventory included nine pairs of dice in a chest. Probably the game was not genteel unless it was played in a fashionable London club—just as in today's social standards, dice tables at Monte Carlo or Las Vegas have an éclat conspicuously lacking in a pair of "bones" surrounded by a group of kneeling men.

## DOMINOES

Although dominoes is a very old game that was popular in France in the seventeeth and eighteenth centuries, it did not make an effective appeal to British tastes until later. Strutt declared in 1801 that it was then considered "a very childish sport, imported from France a few years back, and could have nothing but the novelty to recommend it to the notice of grown persons in this country."[82] Toward the end of the eighteenth century it became the favorite game in Paris cafés,[83] and its popularity may have spread to England at that time—too late to become a pastime in the British colonies. For this reason, probably, no reference to the game has been found in the historical record of colonial Virginia.

## BILLIARDS

Billiard tables were part of the standing furnishings in taverns and in planters' homes throughout the Virginia colony.[84] Travelers and diarists often mentioned billiards, which was popular because it was a game of skill with simple rules, easy to understand but rewarding to practice. Two persons could play it, while any number of spectators could enjoy it. Furthermore, it had a strong appeal to the sportsman who enjoyed betting on his own skill or his judgment of the skill of others. Cotton loved the game because it was "genteel, cleanly, and most ingenious," a recreation for the mind and exercise for the body.[85]

The colonial game of billiards was an adaptation of an ancient out-of-doors form of bowls, brought indoors and raised from the ground to a table.[86] The table was oblong, surrounded by a low railing, and covered with green cloth. At one end stood a sort of wicket made of ivory, called the port, and at the other end a pointed ivory peg called the king. There were six pockets or "hazards"—one at each corner and one in the middle of each of the long sides. Two small ivory balls and wooden sticks shaped like miniature hockey sticks completed the equipment.[87]

The player held the stick between his forefingers and thumb and struck his ball smartly with the flat side of the curved end. He scored for sending his ball first through the port, for touching the king without knocking it over, or for sending his opponent's ball against the king or into a hazard. Fine points of play included keeping his adversary out of the port by blocking or by turning the port with a light, glancing touch on one side; in later stages of the game there was opportunity for skillful cushion shots.

Since this was a "cleanly" pastime, there were special penalties against the slovenly player to reduce him to regularity and decency. If ashes fell from his pipe and burned a hole in the cloth, he paid a forfeit. A sleeve dragging across the table cost him a point.[88]

William Byrd loved the game as much as Cotton did, and he played it all his life—mornings, afternoons, and evenings—with his wife or son or guests.[89] George Washington alternated billiards with card playing when he was young, before public office eliminated his leisure time.[90] John Blair played for higher stakes; after he inherited the estate of his uncle, Commissary Blair, he could afford this luxury as well as a seat on the Council. Once in 1753 he lost £17.3 to Thomas Swann at billiards.[91]

Neither Robert Wormeley Carter nor Jefferson mentioned billiard play. Jefferson's great-granddaughter Sarah

*13.  Billiards. Engraving by Watson and Dickinson from a drawing by Henry W. Bunbury.*

Nicholas Randolph related the family tradition that the central room at Monticello was originally intended for a billiard room but before it was finished a state law had been passed prohibiting billiard play.[92] The Carters at Nomini Hall, too, preferred more intellectual amusements than billiards, although they did not care for chess. Fithian's only reference to billiards was made at Port Tobacco. In the ordinary where he spent the night on his return trip to Virginia in May 1774 he was kept awake by two nuisances—bed bugs, and several noisy fellows in the next room playing billiards.[93]

## LOTTO

In Virginia, as in England, lotteries were popular devices for selling property and raising money for worthy causes.[94] The Virginia Company was permitted several public lotteries in the early promotion of the new colony, and in eighteenth-century Virginia church and state and college used this method of raising funds on special occasions. If one needed to sell his slaves, lands, houses, furnishings, tools, or store goods to pay his debts, a lottery could be depended upon to bring in more money than a forced sale would do.

The ratio of prizes to tickets—usually about one to five—was gambling odds favorable enough to guarantee wide purchase of chances. Drawings were usually held on court days to insure good attendance, and they were great fun.[95] It is not surprising, therefore, that a popular gambling game was built on the principle of the lottery.

For a private game all the equipment needed was a set of lotto cards, a set of numbered lotto tiles or slips, and counters. Each card in the set (usually twenty-four) was ruled off into twenty-seven squares and numerals ranging from 1 to 100 occurred in fifteen of the squares, arranged in different patterns; for example:

Titles bore corresponding numbers from 1 to 100. Players put up stakes to form a pool, and the dealer shuffled and distributed the cards, one or more to each player. Then the dealer shook up the numbered tiles in a bag and drew one from it, calling out the lucky number as he drew it. The players having that number on their cards repeated it aloud and scored it on the cards by placing a counter over it. The drawing and scoring continued until one player covered all the numbers on his card, thus winning the game and the pool.[96]

It was a simple game, any number could play, and its gambling features made it a popular pastime. One summer evening in 1720 a group of Colonel Benjamin Harrison's guests at Berkeley played lotto and piquet until midnight.[97] Half a century later Jefferson, who was never a frivolous person or a gamester, lost eighteen shillings at lotto.[98]

*14. Lotto Cards. Italian, hand painted.*

## TOSSING COINS

In colonial times even simpler games were enjoyed by adults. Several ways of matching and pitching coins were employed. In cross-and-pile, one person tossed a coin into the air, and the other "called" it as it fell to the ground—"cross" for "heads" because very old English coins were stamped on one side with a cross, and "pile" for "tails," the reverse side of the coin. In the eighteenth century cross-and-pile was no longer a courtly game, but this had not always been so: King Edward II once entered for payment from the national budget sums due his barber and usher for money borrowed and lost playing cross-and-pile.[99] At Henrico, Virginia, in 1682 Mr. John Pygott won three hundred pounds of tobacco from Martin Elam and John Milner at cross-and-pile.[100]

There were other ways of tossing coins. Hustle cap (or hussel-cap) was a popular pastime for children in which coins were "hustled" or shaken up in a cap before they were tossed in the heads-or-tails routine or thrown at a target.[101] These were amusements associated with idleness and rowdiness in public rooms of taverns, but gentlemen sometimes played. The "pitchers" Mercer and Jefferson gambled on when they were at court in the counties of the backcountry may have been coins or quoits.[102] General Washington's officers, as well as his soldiers, were forbidden to play toss-up, pitch-and-hustle, or any other game of chance in the General Orders of October 3, 1775.[103]

An earlier example of people's attitudes toward others who spent their time in this way may be seen in an open letter to Lord Botetourt published in the *Virginia Gazette* in 1769. A Mecklenburg magistrate, David Christopher, was not deemed "fitten"[104] for public office because

Drunkenness is his open and daily practice; gaming of every kind, with any, or at any time, will he deny, even

at the common ordinaries, sitting upon his breech in the ashes, from Saturday evening until the rising of the sun on the Sabbath morning, playing at the same time the blackguard game called hussel cap, with five coins, with his nose bent down within six inches to a parcel of chunks, to give him light, and whilst engaged in these ungenteel practices, his conversation is filled with filth and the highest corruption. . . .[105]

## GOOSE

Other simple games that today would be considered suitable only for children were enjoyed by colonial adults as gambling devices. A board game similar to parcheesi, called "The Royall and Most Pleasant Game of the Goose," was played all over western Europe in one form or another.[106] It was invented in Italy, where the London printer John Wolfe discovered it in the sixteenth century. In 1597 he recorded in the *Stationer's Register* his exclusive right to print and sell his English version. It was still popular in the nineteenth century, when Lord Byron observed in *Don Juan* that "good society is but a game, 'The royal game of Goose,' as I may say." Oliver Goldsmith in *The Deserted Village* referred to

The Pictures plac'd for ornament and use,
The Twelve good rules, the Royal Game of Goose.

In Virginia, the Spotswood brothers John and Robert were playing the game in 1755 and Robert won 10/9.[107] Ten years later Robert Wormeley Carter lost to Mr. Page £11.17.6 at Goose.[108] The game is a race between two or more players, who move their men along a track as the throw of the dice directs. There are sixty-three numbered spaces on the track; most of the spaces are blank, but fifteen have pictures "for ornament and use." When his man lands on a goose, the player "doubles his chance forward." All other picture numbers are hazards that he pays in various ways: an extra stake, moving backward on the next play, losing a turn, or more. Death, the greatest hazard of all, requires a fresh start. The game ends when a man lands on Number 63, and the player wins both the game and the stakes.[109]

## TOYS

Although colonial children looked like miniature adults and were expected to behave like their elders, they played many of the age-old games that still appeal to youngsters. Little girls had many kinds of dolls that could be dressed and loved. Most of them were doubtless home-made, but they could be purchased in milliners' shops and general stores in Virginia towns[110] or ordered from London when the family's household supplies were purchased.[111]

Toy makers and merchants often called these dolls "babies," but they were like colonial children in that they were dressed as adults; the baby doll modern children play with was a development of the nineteenth century. Colonial children of course wanted their dolls dressed in the height of fashion.[112] When little Betty Davis of Spotsylvania County was less than two years old, her father paid fifteen shillings for an "English doll with red silk dress for Betty."[113] Another little girl named Elizabeth—Betsy Braxton—spent part of her time dressing her doll when she was visiting her Aunt Anne Blair in Williamsburg, and she demanded silk for the sacque and coat.[114]

Little Patcy Custis, at the age of four, had a doll that cost ten shillings. A year later her stepfather, George Washington, added to her collection of toys a neatly dressed wax doll costing three-and-a-half shillings, and the fashionably dressed doll purchased the following year was worth a guinea. She probably had a dollhouse, too, because Wash-

15. *L'Enfance. (Childhood.)*
*Hand-colored line engraving*
*from a painting by Pierre*
*Mercier. Engraved by Simon*
*François Ravenet.*

16. *Le Jeu de L'Oye. (The Game of the Goose.) Engraved by the son of P. L. Surugue after a painting by J. B. Simeon.*
(Courtesy, New York City Public Library)

ington bought doll furniture for her from a toy maker in London.[115]

Washington was more indulgent than most parents; he had just become a stepfather, he was a rich man, and Patcy was often ill during her short lifetime. The average planter's child could not expect to own more than one imported doll, and the one was a great luxury. Then, as now, little girls loved the dolls that they could play with and their favorites were worn out; the old dolls we see in museums survived because they were too fine to use every day. Imported ones of moderate price had cloth or leather bodies, stuffed, and wooden or wax heads and hands, real hair, and painted features. The eyes might have been made of glass, fitted into the wood or wax of the head. More expensive hand-carved dolls, particularly if they were made in Germany, had wooden bodies expertly jointed at shoulders, elbows, hips, and knees.[116]

Homemade dolls were doubtless fashioned from any material a mother's ingenuity might direct. Rag and corn-shuck specimens have survived, and wooden heads were surely whittled out by fathers and craftsmen accustomed to working with the most plentiful raw material in the New World.

The other favorite toy of little girls—the tea set—was available in Williamsburg shops. Sarah Pitt and Mary Dickinson, milliners, advertised them, and in one instance specified pewter as the material from which they were made.[117] Patcy Custis had a Tunbridge tea set that cost one shilling fourpence.

Little boys, too, had formal toys. Patcy's elder brother, John Parke Custis, owned an unusual collection that included a Prussian dragoon, a man smoking, a grocer's shop, a stable with six horses, and a coach-and-six in a box.[118] None of these were mechanical toys in the modern sense. Less fortunate boys played with marbles, tops, balls, toy

*17. Mama Giving Toys. Mezzotint by Edward Fisher from a painting by Charles D. J. Eisen.*

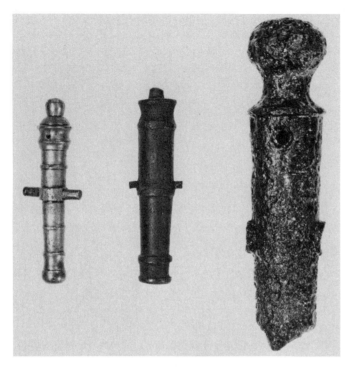

*Brass and Iron Cannon Barrels.*

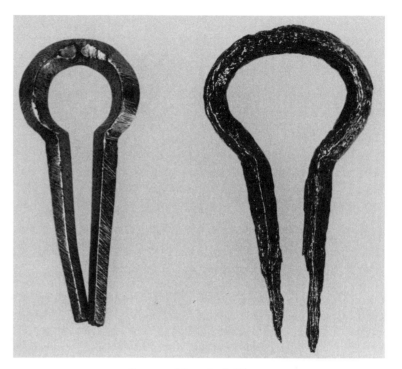

*Brass and Iron Jew's Harps.*

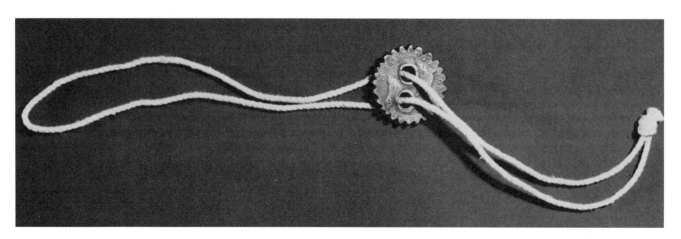

*Whirligig Made from a Hungarian Coin of 1763.*

19. *Toy Tea Table with Tea Service, Doll, and Lead-Glazed Earthenware Cat.*

20. *Marbles Found at the Site of the Nicholas-Tyler House in Williamsburg.*

22. *The Infants' Wooden Horse. Engraving by John Faber from a painting by Philip Mercier.*

21. *Youthful Amusement. Colored engraving by Charles Spooner from a painting by Philip Mercier.*

*23. Ivory Bilbo-Catcher.*

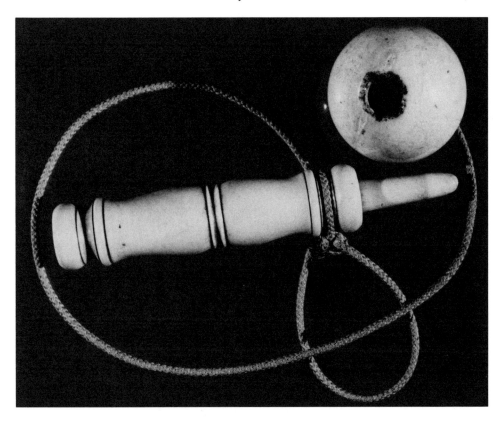

*24. Ivory Top.*

*25. Wooden Tops Recovered from a Well
     at the John Custis Site in Williamsburg.*

43

fiddles, toy watches, toy soldiers, and other "curious" toys that Virginia merchants carried on their shelves.[119] One of these, a bilbo-catcher (from the French *bilboquet*), was a cup and ball or ball and stick joined with a string. Holding the conical cup or stick in his hand, the player tossed the ball into the air and caught it again—either in the cup, on the point of the cone, or on the stick.[120] For babies, a combination rattle and teething ring was provided; this was called a "coral and bells."[121]

## GAMES FOR CHILDREN

In tidewater Virginia, where the weather is warm half the year, children could play out of doors a great deal of the time. Eighteenth-century prints[122] show a number of informal ball games in progress with no more than half a dozen children playing: stool-ball, cricket, fives, tip-cat, base-ball. (The first three of these are described in the chapter on sports that follows. In tip-cat there was a pitcher, a catcher, and a batter-in-the-ring. In base-ball, three upright posts in a triangular arrangement seem to have been used as markers for the players, who struck the ball outside the triangle and then ran between bases.)

Hopscotch, leapfrog, blindman's buff, hide and seek, prisoner's base, rolling the hoop, flying kites—all these games are easily identified in the prints. Ring games, counting games, and singing and kissing games were played then too.

Indoor amusements for children often took the form of paying forfeits. Lucinda Lee mentioned playing grind the bottle and hide the thimble when adults joined in the parlor games.[123] At Nomini Hall they played button to get forfeits for redemption, and kissing the ladies was an important part of the payment that even Fithian frankly enjoyed.[124] The Carter boys, aged sixteen and eighteen, had outgrown children's games; they preferred hunting, fishing, and horseback riding. Betsy, Fanny, and Nancy—aged ten to thirteen—liked to imitate their elders. They knitted with straw needles, tied strings to chairs and pretended to spin, and sometimes—with more realism in playing house—they spit on the floor and then scrubbed away with stick brushes and "with great vigor." Fanny and Harriot once carried their imitation a bit further: "by stuffing rags and other Lumber under their Gowns just below their Apron-Strings, [they] were prodigiously charmed at their resemblance to Pregnant Women!" In their favorite game of checks, which they played with peach stones, Nancy was household champion.[125]

Little Sally Fairfax, too, played checks well; she won ten shillings from Mr. William Payne at the game.[126] Apparently "checks" was a colonialism; it probably referred to the ancient game of checkstones, but there are other possibilities. Americans were calling draughts "checkers" before the Revolution. In eighteenth-century England the pebbles used in the various forms of merrils were sometimes called "chequers," and on the later American frontier poker chips were called "checks," as in the colloquialism "to hand in one's checks." The Virginia children, therefore, may have been playing Nine-men's Morris or Fox and Geese.[127]

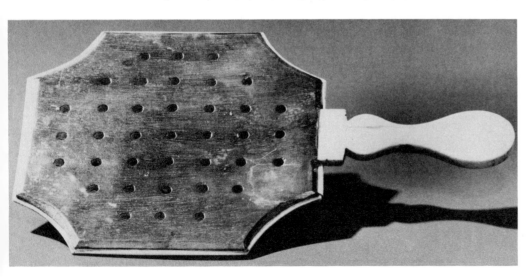

26. *Fox and Geese Board.*

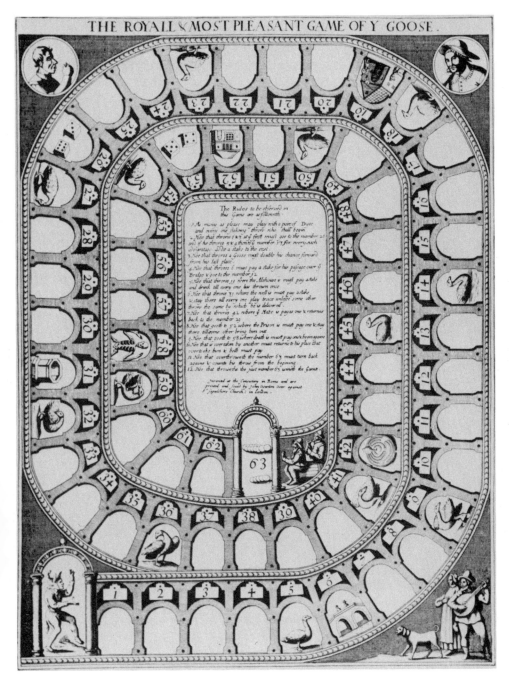

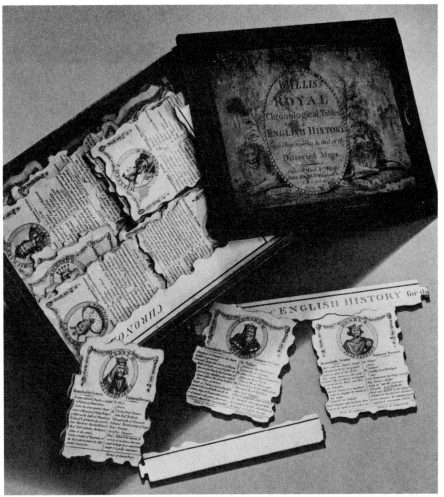

28. *Puzzle, "Royal Chronological Table of English History for the Instruction of Youths." Published by John Wallis, London, 1788.*

27. *The Royall & Most Pleasant Game of the Goose.*

29. *The Humorous Diversion of the Country Play at Blindman's Buff. Line engraving, London, 1753.*

30. *Buffet the Bear. Engraving by Bartalozzi from a painting by W. Hamilton.*

## PETS

Since most Virginia children lived in the country, they were surrounded with dogs and cats and little farm animals suitable for pets. William Byrd once gave Drury Stith's son "a little cat to carry to his sister" after a brief visit.[128] Robert Wormeley Carter entered in his almanac diary an important event in April 1780: "This morning our old cat Corrytang died. She was given to my Son George, when he just began to talk. He was 17 last Decr. so that the Cat must have been near 17 years old. He was a favorite cat of my Fathers and I have taken great care of him on that account, tho' very troublesome."[129] And little Sally Fairfax indignantly recorded a servant's cruelty to a pet cat.[130]

Wild animals and birds were plentiful everywhere, and squirrels and deer were easily tamed. Thomas Jones attempted to cage and tame a fawn, squirrels, and birds to send to his young stepson who was visiting his grandfather in England.[131] The son of the Reverend Mr. Dunlop of King and Queen County was carrying a pet squirrel in his pocket during a summer thunderstorm; the squirrel was killed by lightning, but the boy escaped injury.[132] When William Byrd visited Spotswood's Castle at Germanna, he found Mrs. Spotswood and her sister playing with tame deer that ran in and out of the house like big dogs.[133]

Cardinals and mockingbirds were especially valued as pets, and they were often sent to England as gifts or for sale. The numerous bird cages—sometimes more than a dozen—that appear in inventories evidently were not all used as chicken coops. Mrs. Frances Baylor of Newmarket, writing the family news to her son in England, reported in 1770: "We caught a great many redd and Mock'g Birds but by one accident or other lost them all."[134] When the Swiss traveler Francis Louis Michel was in Virginia in 1702, he observed that the most valuable birds were mockingbirds, which were already being sent to England for sale at two

31. *Children's Games. Detail from printed fabric, ca. 1790.*

guineas or more.[135] Pet birds included some that were not native to Virginia—parrots, for example. George Pottie of Louisa County ordered a parrot cage from John Norton in an invoice dated November 2, 1772.[136] Another order that Norton presumably filled was for "a very Small Organ for teaching Birds"; this request was made by John Minzies on behalf of Lord Dunmore.[137]

Altogether, the children of colonial Virginia amused themselves as readily as their elders—and as spontaneously—when lessons and chores were done.

32. *Miss Kitty Dressing. Black and white mezzotint engraving from a painting by Richard Wright. Engraved by Thomas Watson.*

33. *Anne Byrd with a Pet Dog. Painting attributed to Charles Bridges.*

# III. SPORTS AND OUTDOOR GAMES

## HORSEBACK RIDING

Virginians of both sexes and all ages and classes were at home in the saddle, and their horses were "their pleasure and their pride."[1] It was fortunate that they enjoyed horseback riding because they did a great deal of it. Most roads were only paths through the woods, plantations were far apart, and for any trip that could not be made by water a horse was ridden.[2] Like American cowboys of a later period, they valued their horses in proportion to their need of them.[3]

The Swiss who visited Virginia in 1702, Francis Louis Michel, noted that nearly everyone owned riding horses, which, like the English breed, were very light footed and were always ridden "in a gallop, as if a deer was running."[4] This "planter's pace" was already proverbial when the Reverend John Clayton defined it in 1688 as "a good sharp hand-Gallop."[5]

Other visitors commented on the reluctance of Virginians to walk even a short distance. Hugh Jones, for example, declared:

> They are such Lovers of Riding, that almost every ordinary Person keeps a Horse; and I have known some spend the Morning ranging several Miles in the Woods to find and catch their Horses only to ride two or three Miles to Church, to the Court-House, or to a Horse-Race, where they generally appoint to meet upon Business; and are more certain of finding those that they want to speak or deal with, than at their Home.[6]

Twenty years later Edward Kimber made the identical observation. "They are all great Horsemen and have so much Value for the Saddle, that rather than Walk to Church five Miles, they'll go eight to catch their Horses, and ride

there; so that you would think their Churches look'd like the Outskirts of a County Horse Fair."[7]

At the end of the colonial period the English horse lover J. F. D. Smyth found the same curious personal characteristic. "The Virginians, of all ranks and denominations," he wrote, "are excessively fond of horses. . . ; even the most indigent person has his saddle-horse, which he rides to every place, and on every occasion; for in this country nobody walks on foot the smallest distance, except when hunting: indeed a man will frequently go five miles to catch a horse, to ride only one mile upon afterwards."[8]

William Byrd declared that the Indians, too, were amused at this trait in men "who can't Stir to Next Neighbour without a Horse." They felt that "2 Legs are too much for such lazy people, who cannot visit their next neighbour without six."[9]

Virginia horses, the finest in the country,[10] were hardy, strong, fleet, and pleasant to ride because they paced naturally.[11] Not everyone, of course, admired their gait. The young Irishman Isaac Weld was especially critical of American horsemanship. After attending a race in Petersburg, he decided that

> The horses in common use in Virginia are all of a light description, chiefly adapted for the saddle; some of them are handsome, but they are for the most part spoiled by the false gaits which are taught. The Virginians are wretched horsemen, as indeed are all the Americans I ever met with, excepting some few in the neighbourhood of New York. They sit with their toes just under the horse's nose, their stirrups being left extremely long, and the saddle put about three or four inches forward on the mane. As for the management of the reins, it is what they have no conception of. A trot is odious to them, and they express the utmost astonishment at a person who can like that uneasy gait, as they

*34. Bridling, Sadling, Breaking & Training. Line engraving by T. Smith.*

call it. The favorite gaits which all their horses are taught, are a pace and a *wrack*. In the first, the animal moves his two feet on one side at the same time, and gets on with a sort of shuffling motion, being unable to spring from the ground on these two feet as in a trot. We should call this an unnatural gait, as none of our horses would ever move in that manner without a rider; but the Americans insist upon it that it is otherwise, because many of their foals pace as soon as born.

These kind of horses are called "natural pacers," and it is a matter of the utmost difficulty to make them move in any other manner; but it is not one horse in five hundred that would pace without being taught. In the wrack, the horse gallops with his fore feet, and trots with those behind. This is a gait equally devoid of grace with the other, and equally contrary to nature; it is very fatiguing also to the horse: but the Virginian finds it more conducive to his ease than a fair gallop, and this circumstance banishes every other consideration.[12]

On the other hand, the English actor who visited the colony in the same decade, John Bernard, was extravagant in his praise of Virginia riders. Their knowledge of the science, he thought, was "as profound as that of the English nobility."[13]

## RACING

Horse racing as a sport developed from informal, often impromptu, tests of speed and endurance. As soon as a proud owner's boast of his mount's performance was challenged by another horseman and they agreed to settle the argument in action, then match racing had begun. It became a sport when each contestant backed his horse with his purse and spectators made side bets on the outcome of the race. Such wagers were taken seriously. County courts recognized them as contracts and often settled disputes growing out of some irregularity in performance or in payment. For this reason the early history of the sport is recorded in the county records.

Once a wager was made, there was no acceptable excuse for withdrawing it. The race could be canceled only if one of the horses died between the date of the wager and the time set for the contest. These strict rules are illustrated in a breach of contract suit tried in Henrico in August 1690.[14] Gentlemen of the highest dignity and reputation appeared as witnesses, and the case illustrates, too, the high standing of racing in colonial society.

Mr. Robert Napier had agreed to run his white horse against Mr. Littlebury Eppes's sorrel and had covered a wager of £10 that Captain William Soane laid on the sorrel. At the appointed hour of the contest Napier's white horse did not appear at the designated place, the Varina track.

Soane then sued Napier to collect the wager. Captain William Randolph of Turkey Island, founder of the Randolph clan in Virginia, testified before the Henrico Court that the amount of the wager was £10, that both Napier and Soane "put down earnest" to bind it, and that "the said Mr. Napier did leave his horse at Mr. Blair's but a little before the day of running he sent for his horse . . . and did not appear upon the day appointed." Furthermore, he continued, "it was proposed and discours'd at the time of making the race that the horse that did not appear upon the ground at the time appointed should lose the wager or words to that effect."

Another deponent was Benjamin Harrison II of Brandon, who clearly confirmed the terms of the wager and the formal agreement—proposed by Napier—that the man who withdrew his entry lost the wager.

The chief witness for Soane was Harrison's son-in-law, the Reverend James Blair, rector of Varina Parish, recently appointed deputy of the bishop of London, and one of the judges chosen for the race. Commissary Blair testified—without formal oath, simply on his word as a priest—that he was present at the track as Soane's judge and that Napier brought in the white horse earlier in the day but led it away before starting time. The jury decided for the plaintiff: the wager was a legal contract, and Soane collected the stakes even though the race had not been run.[15]

By the middle of the seventeenth century Saturday afternoon—a holiday—had become the popular time for holding these public tests of speed. By the decade of the 1770s there were favorite race tracks in the settled areas of the colony, notably in the level country of the Eastern Shore and in Henrico County. As early as 1674 Northampton people were speaking of the fall races customarily held at Smith's field. In Henrico there were tracks in regular use at Bermuda Hundred, Varina, the Ware, Conecock, and Malvern Hill. Also there was Devil's Field in Surry, and in Rappahannock, the Rappahannock Church Course. In the 1690s the lower Northern Neck peninsula was already establishing its eighteenth-century reputation for fine horses and skilled riders with active tracks at Yeocomico, at Willoughby's Old Field in Richmond County, and at the Coan Race Course in Westmoreland.[16]

The seventeenth-century track was a straight path about a quarter of a mile in length, laid out in an abandoned field near a convenient gathering place—a church, a courthouse, or an ordinary located at a crossroad. The narrow path, ten or twelve feet wide, had an open space at each end large enough for the horses to maneuver into position and to pull up to a quick stop. The finish end of the track was customarily marked by upright stakes or poles where the judges stood.[17]

Only gentlemen entered horses in these races,[18] and the owner usually rode his own horse. Anyone who was interested could attend, however, and large crowds often did,[19] closely packed along the sides of the track. The official starter sounded the signal—a drum beat, a trumpet blast, or a gunshot—and the horses, which had been rearing and circling, jockeying for position in the better part of the path, suddenly took off at full speed. Further jostling was customary in the course of the race, and riders used whip and knee to unseat opponents or drive their mounts off the track. Daring and skillful riders as well as fast horses made the match a sporting event, for the outcome was seldom predictable.

Until the end of the colonial period, the short sprints characteristic of seventeenth-century contests were popular as "quarter racing" in Southside Virginia and in the backcountry.[20] Pioneers took the sport with them into western North Carolina, into Tennessee and Kentucky, and finally into the cattle country of the Southwest, where it still survives, "one of the most picturesque and vivid aspects of turf sport ever seen in this or any country."[21] The Plains Indians borrowed the sport and still hold quarter races; their race paths have been graded and elevated and new racing forms have been added, such as starting from opposite ends of the track or turning and repeating the run,[22] but it is still the quarter racing developed in Virginia in the first century of its history.

English travelers who saw them in the latter part of the eighteenth century were struck with the novelty and color of the sport and the crowds that attended them. Smyth thought the race itself was merely an excursion of speed, but he admired the horses. They performed, he decided, with an astonishing velocity not to be excelled by any horse in England, or perhaps in the whole world.[23] Thomas Anburey complained: "If you happen to be looking another way, the race is terminated before you can turn your head."[24] The young actor, John Bernard, loved the drama of the scene. Quarter racing, he thought, was "the most animated" sport that he "had the fortune to stumble on." The track was in a field near a tavern, a path hedged in for the competitors by a motley multitide of Negroes, Dutchmen, Yankee peddlers, and backwoodsmen. Contestants rode among the crowd, clearing the ground with long whips that they held in their hands.

The horses were a peculiar breed, shaggy as bears but frisky as lambs. When the starting signal sounded, they went off at full speed so that the affair was over before you imagined it had begun. The end of the race was proclaimed by a "tornado of applause from the winner's party," the Negroes in particular "hallooing, jumping, and clapping their hands in a frenzy of delight, more especially if the horses had happened to jostle and one of the riders been thrown off with a broken leg." The fun of the Negroes, the wrangling of the owners and bettors, the slang of the grooms, the diversities of the spectators—all these elements made up a colorful scene that Bernard never forgot.[25]

Mrs. Anne Ritson, the English wife of a Norfolk merchant, was equally impressed with the crowds, which she described in verse:

> A race is a Virginian's pleasure,
> For which they always can find leisure:
> For that, they leave their farm and home,
> From ev'ry quarter they can come;
> With gentle, simple, rich, and poor,
> The race-ground soon is cover'd o'er;
> . . . . . . . . . . . . . . . . . . . . . . . . . . . . . . . . . .
> Males, females, all, both black and white
> Together at this sport unite.[26]

Horse lovers from Bernard's time to our own have been interested in the "peculiar breed" of the quarter horse, whose powerful hind legs gave him remarkable speed for short distances. The late Fairfax Harrison, who made a special study of horse breeding and racing in Virginia,[27] concluded that the first horses brought to the colony were the "high" horses of Queen Elizabeth's age, noted for their easy gaits. Even while they were scarce, they were not pampered. The French traveler Durand of Dauphiné wrote in 1686:

> I do not believe there are better horses in the world, or worse treated. All the care they take of them at the end of a journey is to unsaddle, feed a little Indian corn and so, all covered with sweat, drive them into the woods, where they eat what they can find, even though it is freezing.[28]

Neglect was still the rule in 1783, when Dr. Johann D. Schoepf wrote:

> With the exception of those horses upon which as racers a high value is placed, all the others are let run about in the fields for pasture, without giving them in the hardest winter any protection against the inclemencies of the weather . . . and many of these poor beasts are actually forced to get what little nourishment they can from under ice and snow.[29]

Even this neglect, however, does not explain the average reduction of six inches in size within the first century. Harrison concluded that the small Virginia quarter horse was

> The native product of an unrecorded practice of crossing the English horse with a remote infusion of Andalusian blood, derived from the southern Indians, following Edward Bland's Occaneechi exploration of 1651. This hypothesis would account not only for the sudden increment of Virginia's stock of horses about 1688, but also for the consequent combination of spirit and small size in the individual.[30]

The size and endurance of the Virginia horse increased rapidly after 1730, when the first Arabian, Bulle Rock, was imported. By 1774, when the nonimportation agreements cut off the supply, 50 English stallions known today by name and pedigree were purchased by Virginia breeders; 167 were sent to all the other American colonies combined. All these 217 horses and all modern thoroughbreds were descended from three Arabians imported into England at the turn of the century: the Byerley Turk, the Darley Arabian, and the Godolphin Arabian. Bulle Rock, from the Darley stables in Yorkshire, crossed the Atlantic in James Patton's ship. The Scotch-Irish trader, frontiersman, and land speculator delivered him to a Hanover merchant, Samuel Gist, who bred him successfully to Virginia mares for several years. The stallions that followed Bulle Rock to Virginia were imported by planters who were improving their stock of saddle and harness horses, the best of which were used for racing. Between 1735 and 1765 Secretary John Carter imported six; John Baylor, four; William Byrd III, William Nelson, and John Spotswood, two each.[31]

Fairfax Harrison identified and listed twenty-seven stud farms in pre-Revolutionary Virginia. On the James River there were Carter of Shirley, Harrison of Brandon, Byrd of Westover, Ambler of Jamestown, Ludwell of Green Spring, Cary of Ampthill, Harrison of Berkeley, Randolph of Tuckahoe, Lightfoot of Tedington, Bland of Cawsons, Baird of Hallsfield, and Evans of Surry; on the York, Nelson of Yorktown, Booth of Ware, Burwell of Carter's Creek, Baylor of Newmarket, Braxton of Elsing Green, and Syme of Newcastle; on the Rappahannock, Wormeley of Rosegill, Tayloe of Mount Airy, Morton of Leedstown, Spotswood of Newpost, and Fitzhugh of Chatham; and on the Potomac, Thornton of Stafford, Brent of Richland, McCarty of Pope's Creek, and Lee of Stratford.[32] The list is indeed a roll call of the tidewater aristocracy.

Of the aristocrats among the stallions, five stand out in the eyes of modern authorities on race horses.[33] Nathaniel Harrison's Monkey (1725), of the Byerley strain, was bred by the Earl of Lonsdale and won an 800-guinea sweepstakes at Newmarket and the King's Plate at York before Harrison bought him in 1737. His portrait, painted in watercolor by James Seymour, probably came with him to Virginia—the only known portrait among all the horses imported into America before the Revolution.

Joseph Morton's Traveller (1746), also a Byerley, was imported in about 1748 when Morton was most active in promoting race meetings at Leedstown. He raced several seasons before he was put to stud in 1751.[34] After Morton's death in 1759 he was sold to John Tayloe II. He was especially distinguished as a sire—the best Virginia and Maryland mares were reserved for him, and his sons were eminent on the turf and in stud.

Colonel John Spotswood's chestnut, Jolly Roger (1743), was a Darley-Godolphin. He was bred by the Duke of Kingston, who raced him successfully for three years before he sold him to Spotswood and Bernard Moore in 1751. Jolly Roger stood at Newpost until 1758, then at Rosegill for six years after Ralph Wormeley II bought him. His daughters were more famous than his sons; through them he appears in many modern pedigrees.

Mordecai Booth's Janus (1746), the most perfect horse in colonial America, started a brilliant racing career at the age of four, a career suddenly cut short in 1752 when he was injured. Booth, a shipowner trading with England as well as a planter, saw the horse in 1756 and brought him to Gloucester County, where he recovered from his injury in time to defeat William Byrd's Valiant in May 1757. He stood at Booth's until 1761, when he was sent to the Southside to spend the remaining twenty years of his life traveling all over the area and into North Carolina.[35] His descendants made up a tribe of quarter horses that inherited his remarkably powerful hind quarters and marvelous speed; the Januses became the first family of sprinters in turf history anywhere in the world and fixed the type, apparently forever, for modern quarter horses are readily recognized in appearance and performance as members of the Janus clan.[36]

John Baylor's Fearnought (1755), a grandson of the Godolphin, won three King's Plates in one year of racing as a six-year-old. Baylor imported him in 1764, two years after an injury removed him from active racing; the traditional price Baylor paid for him was £1,000. He stood at Newmarket for eight years, commanding a fee of £8 or £10 at the time when Janus was bringing only £4.[37] Like the fabled Arab chieftain, he had forty famous sons.

By mid-century foreign visitors were commenting on the high quality of Virginia-bred horses. J. F. D. Smyth, who knew and loved good horses, exclaimed: "Indeed nothing can be more elegant and beautiful than the horses bred here, either for the turf, the field, the road, or the coach; and they have always fine long, full, flowing tails." The reason for their excellence, he explained, was that the gentlemen of Virginia spared neither trouble nor expense in importing the best stock and improving the breed by proper and judicious crossing.[38] In the period before the French and Indian War and immediately after, the Rappahannock area produced the best blooded horses. In about 1768 the center shifted to the James River, especially at the mouth of the Appomattox. After 1800 it moved to the upper waters of the Roanoke and into Carolina, Tennessee, and Kentucky. Since the Civil War it has shifted back into the Virginia Piedmont and the Shenandoah Valley.[39]

The decade of the 1730s marks another development in the history of racing in Virginia—the growing popularity of course racing on a mile-long circular track where a field of horses competed for a subscription purse. The new kind of Virginia horse resulting from the introduction of Arabian blood was not a sprinter but a distance racer, ready to perform capably on a longer course. Both the improved horse and the more formal sport were part of the economic prosperity that built mansions along the Virginia rivers and furnished them with imported luxuries.[40] By mid-century the more sophisticated tastes of tidewater planters associated quarter racing with frontier sport; subscription meets had become customary seasonal events in Williamsburg, Yorktown, Gloucester, Leedstown, and Fredericksburg,[41] and, by the end of the colonial period, in almost every town and county seat.[42] Races in Williamsburg were part of the schedule of public entertainments during Publick Times and when the town was crowded with people attending agricultural fairs.[43] In other towns and villages they were the chief attraction at autumn festivities that were the high point of the year's social calendar, as friends gathered in house parties for rounds of balls and feasting and traveling shows, cockfights, and other sports gave variety to everyone's amusements.[44]

In subscription races the purse was made up from both membership and entry fees. Each horse was required to run several heats—usually three—and the winner of two heats won the race and the purse. In each heat the slower horses were eliminated if they were "distanced"—that is, if, when the winner of the heat crossed the finish line, they had not passed the distance post an eighth of a mile behind. Each heat might be four times around the mile course; a horse that ran all three heats therefore covered twelve miles. This was distance racing, and the performance required "bottom" as well as speed. Smyth observed in the early 1770s that "very capital horses are started here, such as would make no despicable figure at Newmarket; nor is their speed, bottom, or blood inferior to their appearance."[45]

Bernard was impressed with the skill of the riders and with the varied appearance of their mounts—a sight to make an Englishman stare.

Imagine [he exclaimed] beside the sleek, proud, well-trained, elegant-limbed English racer, just imported, and pawing the ground with the conscious dignity of an aristocrat, a low, long-backed, shaggy plebeian, undressed and dirty, his legs pillars, and his monstrous head set upon a short, straight neck, poking the earth as if ashamed of his presumption in venturing into such noble company. Judging with a common eye, I gave the republican no chance; indeed, I ventured upon a small bet that this four-legged Caliban, this outrage on all the rules of English stable lore, would imagine that he had a cart at his tail, and not achieve the winning-post before sundown. What, then, was my surprise when, on the signal for starting, away this fellow went, all fire and spirits, not galloping or springing *secundem artem,* but scouring the earth like a demon of pestilence, his nose erect as if he snuffed a distant feed of corn, and his mane and tail floating like a pirate's pennons. His rider, a tall man in red sleeves, whose only solicitude was to keep his seat, gave me an idea of Aeolus, the god of storms, hurrying over the ocean to engulf a fleet. I need scarcely say that, to the shame of all science and propriety, this animal came in first, and without whip or spur. But he crowned his triumph with a real trait of magnanimity. When the noble Briton arched his neck and his usual air of high-breeding, the victor, heedless of the shouts about him, poked his nose again into the ground, as if only anxious to show that humility which ever marks the true hero.[46]

As a usual thing about half a dozen horses started the course, and the going was as rough on mounts and riders as in quarter racing. In England, too, at this time a race was often a running fight among jockeys who whipped and kicked and attempted to unhorse each other by entwining their legs. An English collector of racing folklore and history, John Lawrence, remembered a fellow "who was accustomed to boast of the execution he had formerly done with the but end of his whip, and of the eyes, and teeth he had beat out!"[47]

The newspaper account of a sweepstakes race in Richmond County in 1768 explained that there were eleven subscribers of £10 each, but only four horses started. "Colonel John Tayloe's filly, Small Hopes, got a kick from Mr. Parker's horse, in passing by, soon after starting, whereby she was so lame as to be distanced. Mr. Carter's bridle rein broke at starting, and his colt, after running one mile, took out of the course, and threw his rider." The contest was left to Mr. Parker's horse, the favorite, "who was backed by the knowing ones," and to the victor, Dr. William Flood's chestnut colt.

The next day Colonel Tayloe's five-year-old, Nonpareil, easily won the race despite a "tender-footed start." A genteel and numerous company, with a good ordinary close by the track, made the event a successful social occasion. All "brothers of the bridle and lovers of the turf" were immediately invited to make up a new subscription for the coming year; both the race track and the young housekeeper at the ordinary were encouraged to continue to please and oblige.[48]

Five years later Fithian attended a race at the same track where two horses ran for a purse of £500 "besides small Betts enumerable." Once again the contestants were Colonel Tayloe and Doctor Flood. Tayloe's best horse, Yorick, came in forty rods ahead of Flood's Gift at the end of a five-mile run, both horses lame after carrying 180 pounds that distance. The race started precisely at five minutes after three, and the time for the first mile was two minutes. The assembly on this occasion was "remarkably numerous," Fithian thought, far beyond his expectation and "exceedingly polite in general."[49] Perhaps the young tutor expected to be embarrassed by rowdy behavior among the Virginia gentry, who took their pleasures as seriously as people back home in New Jersey but not so sedately. Other visitors enjoyed "all the bustle and confusion"[50] of the races.

Fithian's comments on weights and racing time point up the rapid formalization of racing customs after the middle of the century. By the decade of the 1770s it was customary to make agreements about the weights horses were to carry, and amateur jockeys began to replace owners as riders. In advertisements for runaway servants Negroes are several times mentioned as skillful and experienced jockeys. The next year Fithian, amazed to hear of a rider who weighed only forty-seven pounds, pondered: "Strange that so little substance in a human Creature can have strength and skill sufficient to manage a Horse in a Match of Importance."[51] The use of stopwatches for precise timing was a development of the nineteenth century.

One of the most famous Virginia contests was run at Anderson's Race Ground in Gloucester County on December 5, 1752. For this race William Byrd III advertised a wager of 500 pistoles on his chestnut horse Tryal "against any that could be brought." Colonel John Tayloe met the challenge with two entries—his bay horse Childers and his bay mare Jenny Cameron. Colonel Francis Thornton entered a grey mare, and Colonel Benjamin Tasker, Jr., brought down from Maryland the best import in his Belair stable—the bay mare Selima, winner of the Annapolis purse the preceding spring. The *Maryland Gazette* reported that the five horses ran one four-mile heat and came in thus:

| | |
|---|---|
| Col. *Tasker*'s Bay Mare *Selima*, | 1st |
| Col. *Byrd*'s Chestnut Horse *Trial*, | 2d |
| Col. *Thornton*'s Grey Mare——, | 3d |
| Col. *Tayloe*'s Bay Mare, *Jenny Cameron* | 4th |
| His Bay Horse *Childers*, | distanced.[52] |

Interpretations of how the purse was subscribed and paid vary considerably. Most modern writers conclude that Byrd put up 2,500 pistoles and lost it all to Tasker, who took the entire purse; to them the event illustrates Byrd's reckless gambling habits. This view of the betting, however popular, does not present Byrd as a gambler, for what would he have gained by winning? It seems more reasonable to suppose that he wagered 500 pistoles against Tasker, 500 against Thornton, and 1,000 against Tayloe, losing only the 500 to Tasker; therefore, Tayloe was the heavy loser.

Whatever the details of the wagers may have been, the purse was one of the largest recorded in the colonial period. The race was significant, too, as an early example of inter-colonial rivalry and of the eminence of the sportsmen and horse breeders who participated in it. The winner, Selima, the first great matriarch in American breeding history, was acclaimed in her lifetime as "the best of the best."[53]

The seven-year-old Selima was a daughter of the great Godolphin Arabian. The Belair estate, with its deer park, hunting hounds, and training track, had been built for Maryland's first sportsman, Governor Samuel Ogle, by his father-in-law, the elder Tasker. After Ogle's death the younger Tasker enlarged the Belair stables and bred a number of famous race horses from Selima and the imported stallion Othello, a Darley Arabian. When Tasker died in 1760, Selima was bought by John Tayloe and remained at Mount Airy until her death six years later.[54]

Another result of the Gloucester race of 1752 was that Virginia sportsmen closed their contests to Maryland-bred horses; thereafter, Maryland breeders sent their best horses and mares across the Potomac to produce Virginia-bred entries for Virginia races. Selima herself is one example. Othello is another; Nathaniel Harrison bought him in 1760 and kept him at Brandon for five years, then sold him to Governor Horatio Sharpe.

On the other hand, there was no restriction on Virginia horses in Maryland competitions. The Annapolis Subscription Plate, which originated as early as 1743, attracted both contestants and spectators from Northern Neck plantations. During the heyday of the Annapolis Races, 1769–1773, George Washington was often present, sometimes as a guest of Governor Sir Robert Eden. In 1773 he saw his friend William Fitzhugh of Chatham win three of the principal events with his grey mare Kitty Fisher and his bay horse Regulus; both winners were offspring of Fearnought. Although Washington loved good horses and attended important races whenever it was convenient—in Alexandria, Fredericksburg, and Williamsburg as well as Annapolis—and usually wagered modest sums on the outcome,[55] he was never one of the contestants.[56]

The most successful racing year in the Virginia colony was the last—1774.[57] Both spring and fall seasons were especially active in Fredericksburg, where the Jockey Club of forty-odd members organized subscription races during the agricultural fairs in May and October. To promote attendance the club awarded premiums for prize bullocks and sheep.[58] At the October fair Robert Wormeley Carter was one of the judges appointed by the club to award the prize "for the largest and fattest Beef brought to market." The committee divided the premium equally between Mr. Selden and Mr. Taliaferro—"Selden's as the fattest wt. 706 Nett; Taliaferro's as the largest wt. 867, nett exceedingly fat."[59]

In addition to the fair contests, two match races in April were sponsored by the Jockey Club. On April 1 the purse of 200 guineas went to Mann Page, whose horse Damon easily defeated Moore Fauntleroy's mare Miss Sprightly. Two weeks later Miss Sprightly again came in second, and the 100-pistole purse was won by Maximilian Robinson's horse Roundhead.[60]

The first day of the May fair Fauntleroy won the subscription purse of £50 when his mare Miss Alsop defeated William Fitzhugh's Kitty Fisher, winner of the Annapolis sweepstakes a month earlier. The second day of the fair Alexander Spotswood's Fearnought won two of the three heats for the entrance money.[61]

The *Virginia Gazette* used modern summary form for the first time in reporting the October Fredericksburg races.[62] The first day's contest, the Jockey Club Plate, was open to members only. William Fitzhugh's Regulus took the 100-guinea purse over five other horses, winning two of the three heats. Alexander Spotswood's bay horse Eclipse ran second in the last two heats and in the race. The favorite, Mann Page's Damon, was distanced in the second heat, and Moore Fauntleroy's mare Shepherdess threw her rider. Bets at the starting were five to four Damon against the field, three to one against any single horse, and even that Regulus would be distanced. Wormeley Carter stayed on for this race and lost £20 betting on Damon.

On Wednesday, the second day, bets were even and eight horses competed for the Give and Take Purse of £50. The winner was John Tayloe's bay mare Single Peeper, a daughter of Yorick. On Thursday the Town Purse of £50 was run for and won by William Fitzhugh's Kitty Fisher, the favorite. Both Mann Page's Damon and Moore Fauntleroy's Shepherdess were distanced in the second heat, and only Mr. Proctor's gelding finished the third heat with Kitty Fisher. On Friday, the last day, the Town and Country Purse of £50 was won by Fitzhugh's chestnut gelding Volunteer, the favorite; only one of his three competitors finished with him in the fourth heat.

The October races, sponsored by the Fredericksburg Jockey Club, were dominated by club members, yet they were not strictly local affairs. Mr. Proctor, whose given name and home plantation were presumably unknown to the reporter, was probably not a local man. Certainly many of the entries competed in other Virginia races that year. Fauntleroy's Miss Alsop, which beat Kitty Fisher at Fredericksburg, was a winner at Port Royal in May and at Portsmouth in September. Fitzhugh, Spotswood, and Tayloe regularly raced their horses all over the Tidewater, in Maryland as well as Virginia.

Newspaper advertisements and reports publicized course races in the larger towns—Williamsburg, Leedstown, Tappahannock, Richmond, Fredericksburg—where purses were large and the organization was semiformal. But most Virginians knew racing only as they saw the sport in the counties. Even at the end of the colonial period, this was largely quarter racing, with two horses competing at a time, although there might be several matches in an afternoon.

William Byrd II recorded a number of these occasions. In the summer of 1720, shortly after his return from England, he attended races in Surry, Prince George, and Charles City counties. On August 6, for example, he went to the race at Captain Drury Stith's, "got there about 11 o'clock and stayed till one before the races begun. Abundance of people were there. After dinner," he reported, "we walked to the field again and saw more races and about 6 o'clock I took leave of the company and returned home."[63]

The following spring he recorded more details about the convivial nature of race day. On May 11 two neighbors, Mr. Harrison (young Ben of Berkeley?) and Mr. Tullitt, called for him before breakfast. At about 7:30 they crossed the river into Surry County. There they overtook Captain Isham Randolph, Tom Bolling, and Mr. Adams and rode with them to Captain Henry Harrison's, where they drank some chocolate and then rode about two miles to the race. Once again "abundance of people" were present. Mr. Simons's white horse beat Captain Harrison's Spaniard, and Byrd won ten shillings. It rained in the afternoon, and so

the company returned to Captain Harrison's at about four o'clock, where they had a good supper, then drank rack punch until eleven, and retired, Byrd and Randolph sharing a bed in the crowded house.[64]

Half a century later, neighborhood racing events were still social affairs. Fithian often gave the Carter children a holiday so that everyone might attend matches close by. On one occasion the children presented a formal petition requesting permission to go to Hickory Hill, the Turberville estate in Westmoreland; Fithian reluctantly granted it, formally stating his attitude as follows:

> This Race happening so soon after the other, which was at the same place, and so much like it seems to promise nothing that can require your attendance, it is therefore my *desire* and *advice* that you stay contented at home. But if your inclination be stronger than either of these, and you still choose to go, you have my consent provided you return by Sun set in the Evening.[65]

Girls and boys chose to go, of course, for races were always great fun.

After the Revolution the sport was resumed in the old style. Robert Hunter attended the Tappahannock races in the spring of 1786 and recorded in his diary:

*Wednesday, May 17.* The races began today. They started five horses at twelve. Mr. Thornton's Slouch won. Mr. and Mrs. Beverley, Lucy, the three younger ones, Mrs. Daniel, Miss McCarty, etc., dined and stayed with us all night. In the evening we went to a ball at Banks', where I danced with Miss Upshaw. The two Braxtons, Wylles, Mr. Lewis, Billy Ritchie, Miss Rhones, etc., were present. . . .

*Thursday, May 18.* In addition to our company of yesterday Colonel Peachey and his niece, who is to be married to Mr. Williams, came today. Two horses only started.

Mr. Thornton's Fayette won against Mr. Fitchou's [Fitzhugh's] colt. This was a race of honor, as no money could be collected from the two-guinea subscribers. Mr. Fitchou dined with us. I declined going to the ball in the evening, being rather unwell. Hadfield and Samuel accompanied the ladies. I stayed at home and played at whist with Colonel Peachey, Mrs. Flood, and Mr. McCall, and retired early to bed.

*Friday, May 19.* All our company left us today. . . . We found ourselves quite happy in each other's society, after all the bustle and confusion of the races.[66]

## BOAT RACES

Occasional boat races on the tidewater rivers provided similar opportunities for social gatherings. Fithian learned from a dinner guest at Nomini Hall, Captain Dobby of the *Susannah,* that there was to be a Rappahannock race on July 30, 1774, a Saturday. Each boat was to have seven oars and row a four-mile course around a ship lying at anchor in the river. The chief attractions were the £50 purse and a great ball in the evening. The weather had been unpleasantly warm for several days, and Fithian decided not to attend. "I believe," he declared, "both the *Rowers* and *dancers,* as well *Ladies* as *Gentlemen* will perspire freely—Or in plain English they will soak in Sweat!" They all accepted Captain Dobby's invitation to dine on board the *Susannah* the following Tuesday and wish him a pleasant passage when he sailed the next day.

When Tuesday came, the Carters joined the Tayloes at Mount Airy for the journey to the ferry landing opposite Tappahannock. There they were met by a long boat from the *Susannah* "well furnished with a large Awning and rowed with four Oars." At about noon Captain Dobby received the party on board with every possible token of welcome and entertained them with great elegance. A large awning stretched from stern to mizzenmast "made great Room, kept off the Sun, and yet was open on each Side to give the Air a free passage." At three dinner was served to more than one hundred ladies and gentlemen, all dining at once, uncrowded. The race began immediately after dinner:

A Boat was anchored down the River at a Mile Distance—Captain *Dobby* and Captain *Benson* steer'd the Boats in the Race—Captain *Benson* had 5 Oarsmen; Captain *Dobby* had 6—It was *Ebb-Tide*—The Betts were small—and chiefly given to the Negroes who rowed—Captain Benson won the first Race—Captain Purchace offered to bett ten Dollars that with the same Boat and same Hands, only having Liberty to put a small Weight in the Stern, he would beat Captain *Benson*—He was taken, and came out best only half the Boats Length—About Sunset we left the Ship, and went all to Hobbs's Hole, where a *Ball* was agreed on—

Twenty-five ladies and forty gentlemen attended the ball, which was so friendly and agreeable that Fithian enjoyed it thoroughly. He met all the ladies and was able to describe each of them after he got home. He even noticed other reactions than his own. "Mr. Ritche's Clerk," for example, "a limber, well dress'd, pretty-handsome Chap," was much taken with Miss Dolly Edmundson, a "Short pretty Stump of a Girl" who danced well and sang a sprightly song to great applause. "The insinuating Rogue waited on her home, in close Hugg too, the Moment he left the Ball-Room." They all got to bed by three, after a day spent in constant violent exercise. "For my part," Fithian concluded soberly the next day, "with Fatigue, Heat, Liquor, Noise, Want of sleep, And the exertion of my Animal spirits, I was almost brought to believe several times that I felt a Fever fixing upon me, attended with every Symptom of the Fall Disorders."[67]

## HUNTING

Hunting and fishing were necessary activities of the very first pioneers, and the abundant game and fish remained important sources of food even after the wilderness was tamed. And not only food. The New World was a paradise for sportsmen, either individuals or groups, and wilderness hazards added to the charms of hunting for those who found it a recreation as well as a necessity. Hunting, in fact, more than any other frontier activity illustrates the point that in a struggle for subsistence there is little time for play and one must find his fun somewhere in his work.

The fact that legal hunting in England was restricted to the landed gentry doubtless influenced the attitude of transplanted Englishmen at Jamestown, where everyone might enjoy the sport but the connotation of privilege associated with landholding persisted. Virginia land patents specifically listed hunting, fishing, and fowling as privileges restricted to the owners of the lands described—in the Northern Neck as well as in areas administered by the governor and Council.[68] From time to time the General Assembly set up penalties for hunting on posted lands similar to those in force in England.[69] At the same time, hunting deer, wolves, and other game in the forests was encouraged; the multiple purpose, stated in 1632, was that "thereby the inhabitants may be trained in the use of theire armes, the Indians kept from our plantations, and the wolves and other vermine destroyed."[70]

When Robert Beverley described life in Virginia at the turn of the century, he explained to his sporting English readers: "They have Hunting, Fishing, and Fowling, with which they entertain themselves an hundred ways."[71] Thirty years later John Clayton, the botanist, declared that "the Gentlemen here that follow the sport place most of their diversion in Shooting Deer."[72] The Virginia deer, Clayton explained, were "very swift of foot, larger and longer legged than the English fallow Deer, and less than the red Deer."[73]

Deer hunting took several forms. Most hunters used dogs to drive them into the open and shot them running. Others used stalking techniques borrowed from the Indians: they felled trees for the deer to browse on and lay in hiding behind the brush pile, or they trained their horses "to walk gently by the Huntsman's side, to cover him from the sight of the Deer."[74] Still others, Beverley continued, "set Stakes, at a certain distance within their Fences, where the Deer have been used to leap over into a Field of Peas, which they love extreamly; these Stakes they so place, as to run into the Body of the Deer, when he Pitches, by which means they Impale him."[75]

Even as Beverley wrote, the reckless destruction of deer had reduced the Virginia herds so greatly that the General Assembly found it necessary to protect them. An act of 1705 set up a closed season from December through September for everyone except frontiersmen who could prove in court that they were providing venison necessary for the subsistence of their families, and even then they could not sell skins.[76] Later restrictive legislation outlawed the use of fire to round up herds in the woods and the killing of them in great numbers in the snow, proscribed the hunting of deer for skins only and leaving the flesh to rot and attract wolves, and protected them from dogs running at large.[77]

By the end of the colonial period wild deer were scarce in the Tidewater, and Virginia planters, like English country gentlemen, were reserving hunting rights for parties of friends. William Lee, for example, explained to Richard Eggleston: "Whenever I find there is sufficient of Deer on my lands to create good and successful sport at a proper season to have hunting at stated periods all my neighbors are welcome to attend and on such occasions I shall always be glad to see you."[78]

There were other conservationists among Virginia

planters who enjoyed hunting as a sport. George Washington in retirement was especially interested in protecting the deer at Mount Vernon, where he kept a tame herd and defended them against neighbors and friends and their dogs. At Belvoir, too, the woods were posted against deer hunters, for Fairfax was of the same opinion in this matter.[79] Washington had special trouble with Chichester neighbors. Just before his death he brusquely informed them: "I shall be obliged to you, or either of you, who may be in the practice of hunting, or driving Deer on my land, for desisting from that practice. My Lands have been Posted, according to Law, many years; and never has, nor while I possess them, will be revoked." Furthermore, he explained, he had posted printed handbills at his mill and other places "to prevent the plea of want of information." He had been at much expense and a good deal of trouble to procure the deer in his woodlands, which he never killed for his own table. He had hoped "that upon the principle of doing as one would be done by, they would not have been injured by my neighbors"; yet neighbors hunted them and sometimes drove them, wounded and maimed, into the river.[80]

Everywhere the hunting of wolves and foxes remained pure sport, unrestricted by game wardens, closed seasons, or private sentiment, for they were pests that ought to be exterminated. Wolves were a special hazard to farmers' sheep, cattle, and swine, and their destruction was encouraged by public bounties; the use of pits, traps, or big dogs was publicly recommended for ruthless extermination.[81] So effective were these measures that the menace of wolves and bears was no longer serious in the Tidewater by 1724, when the Reverend Hugh Jones wrote:

> There is no danger of wild beasts in traveling; for the wolves and bears, which are up the country, never attack any, unless they be first assaulted and hurt; and the wolves of late are much destroyed by virtue of a law,

which allows good rewards for their heads with the ears on, to prevent imposition and cheating the publick, for the ears are cropped when a head is produced.

> The bears are also much destroyed by the out-planters, etc. for the sake of their flesh and skins.[82]

Dogs were generally used in "vermin hunting," but the kind of dog is now a matter of some dispute. When he was in Virginia in 1686, the Reverend John Clayton observed that:

> Every House keeps three or four mungrel Dogs to destroy Vermin, such as Wolves, Foxes, Rackoons, Opossums, etc. But they never Hunt with Hounds, I suppose, because there are so many Branches of Rivers, that they cannot follow them. Neither do they keep Grey-hounds, because they say, that they are subject to break their Necks by running against Trees, and any Cur will serve to run their Hares into a hollow Tree, where after the aforesaid manner they catch them.[83]

Beverley described the sport in 1705 in these terms:

> They have another sort of Hunting, which is very diverting, and that they call Vermine Hunting; It is perform'd a Foot, with small Dogs in the Night, by the Light of the Moon or Stars. Thus in Summertime they find abundance of Raccoons, Opossums, and Foxes in the Corn-Fields, and about their Plantations: but at other times, they must go into the Woods for them. The Method is to go out with three or four Dogs, and as soon as they come to the place, they bid the Dogs seek out, and all the Company follow immediately. Wherever a Dog barks, you may depend upon finding the Game; and this Alarm, draws both Men and Dogs that way. If this Sport be in the Woods, the Game by that time you come near it, is perhaps mounted to the top of an high Tree, and then they detach a nimble Fellow up after it, who must have a scuffle with the Beast, before

he can throw it down to the Dogs; and then the Sport increases, to see the Vermine encounter those little Currs.[84]

A later John Clayton, the Gloucester botanist, in 1739 informed a friend in England that some Virginians "hunt the foxes w'th hounds as you do in England," but did not explain precisely what he meant by "hounds."[85] They were not English foxhounds, bred especially for the sport, and at that time there were no organized packs. Dr. Thomas Walker of Castle Hill in Albemarle is believed to have had the first such pack in Virginia; family tradition dates its use in 1742, when he imported his first English dogs.[86] Toward the close of the colonial period other planters sometimes followed Dr. Walker's example. Thomas Jett in 1770 ordered from London "a pair of the best fox hounds to be got in England."[87] Jett's case was unusual. Most planters did not keep special foxhounds but used the same hunting dogs for all game. Young Robert Hunter, visiting in the Tappahannock neighborhood in 1785, was vastly impressed with a Mr. Waring, who was distinguished for keeping "a most noble pack of foxhounds of the English breed"[88] because Hunter's host, Mr. McCall, had only pointers. Indeed, Virginia-bred hounds were still in general use at the end of the nineteenth century, when fox hunting was revived in the Piedmont, and the dispute about their inferiority to the English breed was still going on.[89]

The modern formalized ritual of the fox hunt as a rich man's sport—high hat, pink coat, special horses and hounds, an imported red fox carried along in a bag—was introduced into Virginia within the last century;[90] as a matter of fact, the existence of hunt clubs of any kind cannot be established much earlier than 1850.[91] Fox hunters in Beverley's time followed their hunting dogs on foot because their quarry, the native grey fox, led them through woodlands too dense for horseback riding. For this reason, all wild animals living in the forest were hunted in this way; "little currs" were used for smaller "vermin" and hares, which were very numerous.[92] "Great Dogs" were trained to go against wolves, bears, panthers, wildcats, and other large beasts of prey.[93]

Englishmen found that Virginia afforded extraordinary opportunities for enjoying their "genteelest and best sport,"[94] bird hunting. Most writers were amazed by the wonderful variety of native fowls. John Clayton, the botanist, described them with English analogies as follows:

> Then for fowls, wild Turkey's very numerous, Partridges (the size and colour like y'r Quails), wild Geese, Swans, Brants, Cormorants, Teal, Duck and Mallard, Black ducks and another sort we call Summer Ducks, Plover 2 or 3 sorts, Soris (a delicious eating bird in Shape and way of living like y'r Water Rails), Heath Fowls (called here improperly Pheasants) 2 sorts, wild Pidgeons in prodigious great flocks, Fieldfares, Woodcocks (but what is very strange they come here only in summer) Snipes, Herons, Bitterns, Eagles, Larks 2 sorts one of w'ch are here all the year round, are as big as Quails, the other are seen only in winter and are much like your lark.[95]

All these were killed in the English manner—with nets[96] and traps as well as dogs—or in imitation of Indian hunting methods. The Reverend Andrew Burnaby was especially impressed with the sorus hunting he saw here in 1760. "The manner of taking these birds is remarkable," he thought.

> The sorus is not known to be in Virginia, except for about six weeks from the latter end of September: at that time they are found in the marches in prodigious numbers, feeding upon the wild oats. At first they are exceed-

ingly lean, but in a short time grow so fat, as to be unable to fly: in this state they lie upon the reeds, and the Indians go out in canoes and knock them on the head with their paddles. They are rather bigger than a lark, and are delicious eating. During the time of their continuing in season, you meet with them at the tables of most of the planters, breakfast, dinner, and supper.[97]

The chase on horseback probably developed first in the lower Piedmont, where Beverley and his neighbors hunted wolves without the extra hazard of tidewater rivers and creeks. For another kind of sport which the young people took great delight in, it was always necessary to go astride; this was wild horse hunting, which was done sometimes with dogs and sometimes without. The wild horses, foaled "in the Woods of the Uplands," were as shy as any savage creature. Having no mark on them, they belonged to the first who captured them. "However," Beverley observed, "the Captor commonly purchases these Horses very dear, by spoiling better in the pursuit; in which case, he has little to make himself amends, besides the pleasure of the Chace. And very often this is all he has for it, for the wild Horses are so swift, that 'tis difficult to catch them; and when they are taken, tis odds but their Grease is melted, or else being old, they are so sullen, that they can't be tam'd."[98]

When wolves were no longer a menace in the settled areas, they were replaced by foxes as prey suitable for hunting in the saddle. By this time enough land had been cleared to enable riders to gallop headlong after the hounds.[99] Now the English red fox could be followed; he was a long distance runner capable of covering fifteen miles without stopping. But the native grey fox, who ran at a jogging trot for three or four miles and then craftily doubled back on his trail, remained the favorite of Virginia sportsmen until the Civil War.[100]

Today George Washington is the most famous colonial Virginia fox hunter. In the winter of 1768 he was at home at Mount Vernon and had the leisure for the favorite sport in the Northern Neck peninsula. On New Year's Day he went fox hunting with Captain Posey, Robert Alexander, and Mr. Colvill, but caught nothing. The next week Bryan Fairfax joined the group and they went out two days; again they caught nothing, although they started one fox and ran him four hours until night fell and ended the day's chase. At the end of the month Washington and Mr. Alexander spent nearly a week at Toulston, Bryan Fairfax's estate near Alexandria, "in order to Fox hunt it" on special invitation from their host, who warned his guests that his hounds were not anything to brag about.[101] In four days of hunting they caught nothing; once the hounds started a fox at about ten, then lost him after a five-hour run. Another day they ran off after a deer.

The group had better luck in February. On February 12 Washington reported: "Fox hunting with Colo. Fairfax, Captn. McCarty, Mr. Chichester, Posey, Ellzey, and Manley, who dind here, with Mrs. Fairfax and Miss Nicholas—catchd two foxes." The next day the same hunters caught two more foxes, and the company went home without dining at Mount Vernon. Four other days that month Washington went out with Captain Posey; they caught only one fox, although several were started.[102] In other years when he was at home he continued to enjoy the sport.

On the Eastern Shore, too, fox hunting was popular, for the country is level, streams are small, and the land was cleared early. Lewis Beebe, a New England doctor and minister, described the sport there as he saw it in 1799:

> From about the first of Octor. this amusement begins, and continues till March or April. A party of 10, and to 20, or 30, with double the number of hounds, begins early in the morning, they are all well mounted.

They pass thro' groves, Leap fences, cross fields, and steadily pursue, in full chase wherever the hounds lead. At length the fox either boroughs out of their way, or they take him. If they happen to be near, when the hounds seize him, they take him alive, and put him into a bag and keep him for a chase the next day, They then retire in triumph, having obtained a conquest to a place appointed where an Elegant supper is prepared. After feasting themselves, and feeding their prisoner, they retire to their own houses. The next morning they all meet at a place appointed, to give their prisoner another chance for his life. They confine their hounds, and let him out of the bag—away goes Reynard at liberty—after he has escaped half a mile—hounds and all are again in full pursuit, nor will they slack their course thro' the day, unless he is taken. This exercise they pursue day after day, for months together. This diversion is attended by old men, as well as young—but chiefly by married people. I have seen old men, whose heads were white with age, as eager in the chase as a boy of 16. It is perfectly bewitching. The hounds indeed make delightful musick—when they happen to pass near fields, where horses are in pasture, upon hearing the hounds, they immediately begin to caper, Leap the fence and pursue the Chase—frequent instances have occurred, where in leaping the fence, or passing over gullies, or in the woods, the rider has been thrown from his horse, and his brains dashed out, or otherwise killed suddenly. This however never stops the chase—one or two are left to take care of the dead body, and the others pursue.[103]

Cleared land in the Virginia peninsula was good fox hunting country. Among those who enjoyed it were Rochambeau and Von Closen, two of the officers in the French army stationed in Williamsburg after Yorktown. Von Closen wrote in his journal:

M. de Rochambeau, who liked hunting very much, amused himself during the whole winter riding through the woods, followed by twenty or so enthusiasts. We ran down more than 30 foxes. The dog packs belonging to the Gentlemen of the neighborhood are wonderful. It is only a pity that the species of foxes is not as strong as that in Europe; ordinarily, after an hour of hunting, they are tracked down, sometimes even in less time and rarely in more. The country around Williamsburg favors this kind of hunting. There are many clear woods and little thickets, across which one can always follow the hounds, and although there are several *creecks* and swamps, the fords are not dangerous and are always marked.[104]

One visitor, John Bernard, enjoyed hunting in Virginia but found it "a far different thing from its English original." He described the custom in these words:

A party of horsemen meet at an appointed spot and hour, to turn up or turn out a deer or a fox, and pursue him to a standstill. Here a local peculiarity—the abundance of game—upsets all system. The practice seemed to be for the company to enter the wood, beat up the quarters of anything, from a stag to a snake, and take their chance for a chase. If the game went off well, and it was possible to follow it through the thickets and morasses, ten to one that at every hundred yards up sprung so many rivals that horses and hunters were puzzled which to select, and every buck, if he chose, could have a deer to himself—an arrangement that I was told proved generally satisfactory, since it enabled the worst rider, when all was over, to talk about as many difficulties surmounted as the best.[105]

Bernard himself had been the worst rider and chief adventurer in a group hunting near Richmond. Separated from the other riders during the chase and lost in a "Tartarean wood," he suddenly came face to face with a growling beast displaying a fine set of teeth. He was never able to describe the animal later because his "survey was so concentrated on the construction of his jaws" that he "neglected to note his other features." But, he concluded, "I think the most fervid natural philosopher would have concurred in my query—not, Is this beast a wolf or a panther?—but, Has he dined?" The hapless horseman apologized for his intrusion and escaped, to encounter further hazards—thickets, bramble, bogs, hedges, and ditches. Still lost, he heard the baying hounds, his horse carried him to the spot where they had cornered their prey, and he had the honor of being *"the first in at the death."*[106]

The guns used in hunting were fowling pieces, which were household necessities everywhere. Most of them were ordered from England, but they could be purchased in Williamsburg from the gunsmith Spotswood brought over—John Brush—or James Geddy and his sons. Rifles and muskets did not come into common use until the 1770s, and Charles Dick's gun factory at Fredericksburg did not begin operations until 1775.

While the English borrowed some of the Indian hunting methods, they did not adopt their bows and arrows. However, shooting matches were not always target practice with guns and pistols.[107] Byrd several times mentioned "shooting in the bow" or "shooting with arrows," sometimes at a target for small stakes, sometimes at birds and squirrels, but always as a diversion either at Westover or Berkeley.[108] They may have been using crossbows, which were not unknown in Virginia, for James Geddy once advertised the loss of a steel one with a broken spring, which he presumably was mending when it was stolen.[109] Like so many of Byrd's amusements, archery may or may not have been an unusual recreation in Virginia; it had fallen into disfavor in England, and no other reference to the sport in the colony has been found.

## FISHING

Fishing was almost as popular as hunting, for food and for sport. Beverley described the abundance of fish and variety of fishing methods:

The Indian Invention of Weirs in Fishing, is mightily improved by the English besides which, they make use of Seins, Trolls, Casting-Netts, Setting-Netts, Hand-fishing, and Angling, and in each find abundance of Diversion. I have set in the shade, at the Heads of Rivers Angling, and spent as much time in taking the Fish off the Hook, as in waiting for their taking it. Like those of the Euxine Sea, they also Fish with Spilyards, which is a long Line staked out in the River, and hung with a great many Hooks on short strings, fasten'd to the main Line, about three or four Foot asunder. The only difference is, our Line is supported by Stakes, and theirs is buoyed up with Gourds.[110]

Indians in Beverley's time had a special technique for catching sturgeon. Clapping a noose over the tail of the big fish and holding firmly to the other end of the rope, the fisherman followed his prize—swimming, wading, diving—until he brought it ashore.[111] Chastellux found Virginia Negroes using a similar but less sporting method of sturgeon fishing nearly a century later. "As I was walking by the riverside," he wrote:

I saw two negroes carrying an immense sturgeon, and on my asking them how they had taken it, they told me that at this season, they were so common as to be taken easily in a sean (a sort of fishing-net), and that fifteen or twenty were found sometimes in the net; but that there was a much more simple method of taking them, which they had just been using. This species of monsters, which are so active in the evening as to be perpetually leaping to a great height above the surface of the water, usually sleep profoundly at mid-day. Two or three negroes then proceed in a little boat, furnished with a long cord, at the end of which is a sharp iron crook, which they hold suspended like a log line. As soon as they find this line stopped by some obstacle, they draw it forcibly towards them, so as to strike the hook into the sturgeon, which they either drag out of the water, or which, after some struggling, and losing all its blood, floats at length upon the surface, and is easily taken.[112]

Sturgeon was plentiful in Chesapeake rivers until mid-nineteenth century, when it began to disappear because the value of its roe—American caviar—brought on its ruthless destruction.

Advertisements for fishing equipment were not so frequent as one would expect; perhaps it was part of most merchants' regular stock of goods. On the other hand, one gets a vivid impression of the amount of fishing being done in colonial Virginia from extant orders for equipment. In the Norton Papers, for example, there is evidence that Virginia merchants often ordered Kirby's best hooks by the gross, assorted from perch to trout, and trout lines by the dozen. Among individuals, John Clayton's annual order for hooks usually ended with a request for two dozen trout hooks, two dozen perch hooks, a dozen sheepshead hooks, and trout lines.[113]

## COCKING

In the opinion of visitors, colonial Virginia sporting tastes placed cockfighting immediately after hunting and horse racing. Historically, the sports seem to have developed here in that order. In England the ancient sport of cocking enjoyed especial éclat under the personal examples of the first two Stuarts, who were devotees, and most towns had cockpits patronized by the gentry until race tracks gradually replaced them in the eighteenth and nineteenth centuries. But in America cockfighting was never adopted as first choice of the sporting gentry; in the seventeenth century—its heyday in England—it was forbidden in Puritan New England and ignored elsewhere.

Early Virginia laws against gaming did not include cocking. Dice and cards were forbidden in 1619, and in 1728 table games, tennis, and bowls were added to the earlier list. Not until May 1740 did the General Assembly consider gambling at horse races and cockfights sufficiently widespread to include them in their proscription of "excessive and deceitful Gaming" practices.[114] By this time horse racing was an old and honored pastime in Virginia. Perhaps there were early unrecorded cockmatches, too, where wagers were collected on the spot without disputes leading to suits in the county courts. In 1724 Hugh Jones mentioned it as an already popular sport when he wrote: "The common planters leading easy lives don't much admire labour, or any manly exercise, except horse-racing, nor diversion, except cock-fighting, in which some greatly delight."[115] He had no further word about cocks, in contrast to his detailed observations on horses. Significantly, too, Beverley made no mention of cockfighting.

It seems reasonable to conclude that horse racing came into popularity first, in point of time, because horses were imported quite early and quickly became necessities in the Virginia way of life. Game cocks, on the other hand, served no utilitarian purpose and were imported for fighting only because roosters used in chicken raising would not have been expendable even if they had been satisfactory fighters. The loser in a match race between horses could run again, and even if he was injured, he could be put to stud. But the loser in a cock match was usually dead.

Public opinion against cruelty to animals was as rare in Virginia as in England, where bearbaiting, bullbaiting, cockthrowing, and gooseriding were popular events in religious festivals as well as ordinary village get-togethers.[116] A letter to the editor published in the *Virginia Gazette*, January 2, 1751, denounced the "growing evil" of cockfighting in the colony because it was against divine law and led to habitual drinking and gaming. The author invited comment from other subscribers, but no one accepted the invitation, probably because the prohibitionist's point of view was unusual.

The next month the *Virginia Gazette* carried instead the first extant announcement of a cockfight, one to be held in Williamsburg at the George and Dragon[117] on Tuesday, February 19.[118] John Blair noted that it was "a fine warm sunny day for the cock fight" but neglected to mention the outcome of the match or indicate whether he attended.[119] A decade earlier William Byrd had paid a visit to the Carter family at Shirley and learned that Secretary John Carter had "gone to the cockfight."[120] Unfortunately, the extant parts of the diary contain no further reference to the sport; Byrd evidently was indifferent to it here and in England.

Other recorded matches at mid-century took place in Yorktown, Tappahannock, and New Kent Court House. George Washington attended the first of these in company with Colonel Robert Lewis in January 1752 when "a Great Main of cocks" was fought between gentlemen of Gloucester and York counties. The prize money was 5 pistoles for each battle and 100 pistoles "the odd."[121] The fact that Washington and Lewis left "before it was decided" suggests that this was not a battle royal, where all contestants are put into the ring at once and left there until all except one have been killed, but rather that it was a series of battles between pairs of cocks with a 5-pistole prize for each winner. After the series was over, a majority of victories in individual matches earned the main prize of 100 pistoles. In this way an entire afternoon might be taken up in a cockfight between two local teams of cockers. Another conclusion suggested by their early departure is that these two onlookers were not much interested in the sport; certainly Washington was not, for his diaries contain no other mention of it.

The Tappahannock match was advertised for April 7, 1752, at Seayre's Ordinary for a prize of 60 pistoles. The names of contestants and outcomes of the match were not recorded.[122] The fight at New Kent Court House on Tuesday, May 20, 1755, was between Gloucester and New Kent teams for 10 pistoles a battle and 100 pistoles the main. In the eighteen battles of the match New Kent won ten, Gloucester seven, and one was a drawn battle. The main purse of 100 pistoles therefore went to New Kent. The reporter of the event remarked that "Some James River Cocks that fell on the New-Kent Side, distinguished themselves in a very extraordinary Manner" and left his readers to wonder just how the champions behaved.[123]

The next advertisement announced a match between Brunswick and Sussex gentlemen on Easter Monday, April 4, 1768, at Sussex Court House. Each group was to fight thirty cocks for £5 a battle and £50 the odd. Ladies were encouraged to attend the event with the promise of a ball in the evening.[124] The following month, on May 3, a main between Colonel Edward Carter and Colonel Anthony Thornton was fought in Chesterfield County at Stephen Pankey's house at Lucy Springs.[125] Robert Wormeley Carter traveled all the way from Sabine Hall to attend this one. After spending the preceding night at Anthony Winston's house in Hanover, Carter reached Rocky Ridge for breakfast and then went on the five miles to Pankey's. While the diarist gave no details of the match, it seems to have been an all-day affair, for sixty-one cocks fought and Carter lost

£21.16.3[126]—a larger sum than he was accustomed to wager on cards or horses.

Another match at Sussex Court House was announced for Easter Monday two years later, April 16, 1770. The Sussex gentlemen were opposed this time by a Charles City team, and again the ladies were promised a ball in the evening.[127] The Charles City gentlemen scheduled another match three weeks later at King William Court House, where they were joined by James City gentlemen to oppose a combination of King William and Caroline County cockers. Twenty-one cocks were to compete for the customary £5 the battle and £50 the main.[128] On Whitsun Tuesday, June 5, another match of thirty cocks to a side was to be fought at Goochland Court House.[129]

The next year two other Southside teams—Lunenburg and Dinwiddie gentlemen—advertised a match at Lunenburg Court House on September 16, when "good entertainment" was guaranteed "for all Gentlemen" that were "disposed to come."[130]

In succeeding years two matches were fought at Gloucester Court House—one on Whitsun Monday 1772[131] and the other on Easter Thursday 1773.[132] A great match in Williamsburg between the upland and lowland gentlemen advertised for Tuesday, May 25, 1773, lasted two days and the uplanders won by one battle only.[133]

In 1774 the Charles City gentlemen were still advertising their cock matches. On Whitsun Monday, May 23, two Charles City teams made up of gentlemen from the upper and lower ends of the county competed for a £15 main prize at Mr. Hardyman Dancy's ordinary. The ladies were again enticed by the promise of a ball in the evening.[134]

By this time sporting gentlemen in the Northern Neck like Wormeley Carter were having cockfights of their own. Carter attended one at Tappahannock early in April, probably during the Easter holidays.[135] On Easter Monday Fithian noted that the Nomini Hall Negroes were enjoying a two-day holiday "at Cock Fights through the County." He himself had been urged by Mr. Taylor [Tayloe?], Mr. Randolph, and others "to attend a Cock-Fight, where 25 Cocks are to fight, and large Sums are betted, so large at one as twenty five Pounds," but the tutor chose rather to stay at home and read Plato.[136]

It was not necessary to leave Nomini Hall to see a cockfight. One Sunday morning before breakfast Fithian "saw a Ring of Negroes at the Stable, fighting Cocks."[137] All the Carters loved horseback riding and regularly attended races, and young Ben preferred "the company of a Horse" to that of any other friend; but of all Fithian's charges, only Carter's nephew Harry Willis had tastes so depraved as to prefer cockfighting to other sports. Indeed, Harry's habits illustrated to his tutor all the evils associated with the sport; "Harry's Genius," he decided, "seems towards Cocks, and low Betts, much in company with the waiting Boys, and, against my strongest Remonstrances and frequent severe corrections, he will curse, at times, horribly, and swear fearfully!"[138]

In the summer of 1777 when Ebenezer Hazard was traveling through Virginia as surveyor-general for the Post Office, he spent a hot day in Surry County and dined at Nelson's ordinary, where great bets were being laid on a cock match between Isle of Wight and Surry. "Horse-Racing and Cock-fighting," he observed, "seem to be the principal Objects of Attention between Williamsburgh and Smithfield at present."[139]

Five years later Baron Von Closen described Virginia cockfights as "something to see once out of curiosity, but the spectacle is a little too cruel for you to enjoy; you see these poor things knocked about, pricked, blinded, and finally killed with their steel spurs." A military man, he was especially interested in the weapons used in these battles. "I will bring back with me some of these spurs," he decided, "to satisfy the curiosity of those who would like to see a cock-fight. Those in North America are pointed like the aal of shoemakers; those of Spain are like pen knives with a double edge." Some of the cocks were very expensive. "I have seen some very dextrous ones," he continued, "who played with this instrument with the greatest daring and skill; thus they often win a reputation for fifty miles or more."[140]

Another of Rochambeau's officers, the Marquis de Chastellux, once stopped at Willis's ordinary, a little house in the middle of the woods, and found a great deal of company assembled there.

As soon as I alighted [he wrote],

I enquired what might be the reason for this numerous assembly, and was informed it was a cock-match. This diversion is much in fashion in Virginia, where the English customs are more prevalent than in the rest of America. When the principal promoters of this diversion, propose to [match] their champions, they take great care to announce it to the public; and although there are neither posts, nor regular conveyances, this important news spreads with such facility, that the planters for thirty or forty miles round, attend, some with cocks, but all with money for betting, which is sometimes very considerable.

Whilst our horses were feeding, we had an opportunity of seeing a battle. The preparation took up a great deal of time. . . . The stakes were very considerable; the money of the parties was deposited in the hands of one of the principal persons, and I felt a secret pleasure in observing that it was chiefly French. I know not which is the most astonishing, the insipidity of such diversion, or the stupid interest with which it animates the parties. . . . Whilst the interested parties animated the cocks to battle, a child of fifteen, who was near me, kept leaping for joy, and crying, Oh! it is a *charming diversion*.[141]

A visiting New Englander has left the best description of a Virginia cockfight in progress. While Elkanah Watson was living on his Chowan plantation in North Carolina, in 1787, he explored the surrounding country. "In one of these excursions," he recorded,

I accompanied a prominent planter at his urgent solicitation, to attend a cock-fight in Hampton [Southampton] County, Virginia, a distance of twenty miles. We reached the ground about ten o'clock the next morning. The roads, as we approached the scene, were alive with carriages, horses, and pedestrians, black and white, hastening to the point of attraction. Several houses formed a spacious square, in the center of which was arranged a large cock pit; surrounded by many genteel people, promiscuously mingled with the vulgar and debased. Exceedingly beautiful cocks were produced, armed with long, steel-pointed gaffs, which were firmly attached to their natural spurs.

The moment the birds were dropped, bets ran high. The little heroes appeared trained to the business, and were not the least disconcerted by the crowd or shouting. They stepped about with great apparent pride and dignity; advancing nearer and nearer, they flew upon each other at the same instant with a rude shock, the cruel and fatal gafts being driven into their bodies, and, at times, directly through their heads. Frequently one, or both, were struck dead at the first blow, but they often fought after being repeatedly pierced, as long as they were able to crawl, and in the agonies of death would often make abortive efforts to raise their heads and strike their antagonists. I soon sickened at this barbarous sport, and retired under the shade of a wide-spread willow.[142]

The young Frenchman, César de Saussure, traveling through rural England in 1728, saw cockfighting for the first time and, like young Watson in Virginia, wrote down his impressions:

The stage on which they fight is round and small. One of the cocks is released, and struts about proudly for a few seconds. He is then caught up, and his enemy appears. When the bets are made, one of the cocks is placed on either end of the stage; they are armed with silver spurs, and immediately rush at each other and fight furiously. It is surprising to see the ardour, the strength, and courage of these little animals, for they rarely give up till one of them is dead. . . . The noise is terrible, and it is impossible to hear yourself speak unless you shout. . . . Cocks will sometimes fight a whole hour before one or the other is victorious.[143]

We have no description of the Virginia cockpit. In London it was a circular stage about twenty feet in diameter, surrounded by a barrier to keep the birds in the ring. Spectators leaned on this barrier.[144] The platform floor was customarily covered with matting: the rules of the sport permitted the trainer or "feeder" to touch his fighting bird if its feet became entangled in the matting. At Virginia taverns probably a spot of bare ground, packed down to a level surface, was all that was required, for it was an outdoor sport here.[145] Country folk in England, too, were more informal than the townspeople who patronized indoor cockpits. A village cocker often entered a tavern carrying his cock in a bag and offered to pit it against anyone present. Competitors then shook their bags and dropped the birds on the floor and the match was on; hence the cocking terms "shake-bag" and "turn-poke."[146] These sportsmen could not always afford to buy steel or silver spurs, and village champions doubtless fought with natural spurs sharpened with the penknives used to trim beaks and wing feathers.[147]

In contrast to the number of records left by Virginia horse breeders, no details of the breeding and training of cocks have survived. If an owner wanted to study the subject scientifically, expert advice was readily available in printed treatises. The classic book on preparing cocks for battle, Gervase Markham's *The Pleasure of Princes* (1614), may have been found in at least two Virginia libraries. The list of books in Robert Beverley's collection, prepared in 1734, included *Markham's Works.* The library that "King" Carter inherited from his father and elder brother included several Markham titles: an earlier work on horses called *Markham's Masterpiece* (1610), and a group of separate treatises on raising cattle, horses, and fowls, collected under the title *Way to Get Wealth.*[148] Lacking the Markham books, the owner might find the classic training method explained in Cotton's *Compleat Gamester.* Cotton was enthusiastic about this noble pastime "so full of delight and pleasure . . . and . . . in so great an estimation among the gentry." In twelve closely packed pages he gave directions for choosing, breeding, feeding, dosing, training, matching, and fighting cocks.[149]

Readers of the *Virginia Gazette* knew something of the gentry's love of the sport at home in England, for results of important mains, regularly reported in the *Racing Calendar,* and incidental news of colorful matches were sometimes reprinted for Virginia readers. For example, in the issue of July 2, 1772, Purdie and Dixon related the following anecdote:

The late Sir John Astley, Member of Salop, was a remarkable Cocker. About forty Years ago he fought a single Battle for a Thousand Guineas, during which his Cock received a Blow which staggered, and was supposed by every One present to have done for him; but the Feeder immediately handled the Cock, and set him against his Antagonist, whom with one Blow he killed, after which Nichols, the Feeder, took up the Conqueror and kissed his Rump. Sir John preserved him as long as he lived, and when he died erected a Monument to him, on which, in Bass Relief, is to be seen Nichols, the Feeder, kissing his Rump, on whom also he settled an Annuity of fifty Pounds a Year. The Monument is of Marble, at his Seat in the Country, and cost about five Hundred Pounds.[150]

## WRESTLING AND BOXING

Wrestling, next to cocking, was standard recreation in the backcountry and among the lower classes; it offered opportunity for testing individual stamina and courage—the first qualities of a frontiersman—and appealed to the sporting instincts of onlookers, who usually placed bets on the contestants.[151] The "English Gentleman" who translated Chastellux's *Travels* went over some of the same ground and barely escaped becoming involved in a gouging match, which he described in a footnote to the Frenchman's book, and then observed:

> The indolence and dissipation of the middling and lower classes of white inhabitants of Virginia, are such as to give pain to every reflecting mind. Horse-racing, cock-fighting, and boxing-matches,[152] are standing amusements, for which they neglect all business; and in the latter of which they conduct themselves with a barbarity worthy of their savage neighbours.[153]

While Lieutenant Thomas Anburey was a prisoner of war in the vicinity of Charlottesville, he traveled about the area and witnessed a similar scene.

> An English boxing match [he thought] though a disgrace to a polished nation, is humanity itself, compared with the Virginian mode of fighting; for, previous to the combatants falling too, they enter into an agreement, whether all advantages are allowable, which are biting, gouging, and (if I may so term it) Abelarding each other. If these three preliminaries are agreed upon,

they instantly fall to, and after some little struggling, seize upon their adversaries with their teeth. What is very remarkable, and shews what coolness there must be in these disputes, and that they are not wholly the effect of anger is, that whatever terms are specified, if only one or two out of the three conditions, let the conflict be ever so severe, they never infringe on any other.[154]

On a visit to Richmond Anburey saw a victim of the sport, which he later described in vivid detail:

> As I was walking with some officers, I was shewn a gentleman of the town, a Mr. Fauchee, a surgeon and apothecary who had the misfortune to have one of his eyes gouged out, it was happily in time replaced, and there were hopes that he would recover the use of it. I shall relate the way the accident happened, to shew the ferociousness of the lower class in this country; this gentleman was at play in the billiard-room, where there were a number of gentleman, and several of our officers: a low fellow, who pretends to gentility came in, and in the course of play, some words arose, in which he first wantonly abused, and afterward would insist on fighting Mr. Fauchee, desiring at the same time, to know upon what terms he would fight, as the lower sort have various modes; Mr. Fauchee declined any, saying, that he was totally ignorant as to boxing, but the other calling himself a gentleman, he would meet him in a gentleman-like manner; he had scarcely uttered these words, before the other flew at him, and in an instant turned his eye out of the socket, and while it hung upon his cheek, the fellow was barbarous enough to endeavour to pluck it entirely out, but was prevented. You can easily imagine what the officers who were present, must have felt.
>
> This most barbarous custom, which a savage would blush at being accused of, is peculiar to the lower class of people in this province; at one time it was so prevalent, that the Governor and Assembly were obliged to pass a law which made it criminal, and that law is now in force,

but the rabble are such a lawless set, especially those in the back woods, that they are little restrained by any laws the State can pass, and in the back settlement, this savage custom prevails. I have seen a fellow, reckoned a great adept in gouging, who constantly kept the nails of both his thumbs and second fingers very long and pointed; nay, to prevent their breaking or splitting, in the execution of his diabolical intentions, he hardened them every evening in a candle. . . . What a pity it is, that a country where the superior class are of such an hospitable and friendly disposition, should be rendered almost unsafe to live in by the barbarity of the people.[155]

The statutes to which he referred were an act of 1748 to prevent malicious maiming and wounding and its 1772 revision. The earlier law made it a felony to cut out a tongue, put out an eye, slit or bite a nose or lip, or cut off or disable a limb, and the amendment added to the list wounding "by gouging, plucking or putting out an eye, biting, kicking or stomping upon" one of His Majesty's subjects. The stated purpose of this legislation was to protect peaceable and quiet citizens from the "disorderly and quarrelsome persons" who "frequently molest, disturb, or ill treat" them.[156]

Not all spectators wanted to avoid entanglement in these rough and ready disputes. An extreme example was a clergyman, the Reverend Thomas Becket, who was finally discharged from his parish in Culpeper County for scandalous behavior. Governor Gooch explained his conduct in a letter to the bishop of London. "Mr. Becket," he wrote, "is a man of strong Constitution, loves drink perhaps too well, and living in the Northern Neck where drinking and boxing is too much in fashion has been tempted to quarrel; for being unpolished, he is bold and hardy in his temper, and has not yet learnt to turn the other Cheek."[157]

For the gentry boxing was a polite accomplishment like dancing and fencing. When Fithian was coaching his friend and successor at Nomini Hall on the proper behavior of a tutor who hoped to get on with Virginia aristocrats, he explained: "Any young Gentleman travelling through the Colony, as I said before, is presum'd to be acquainted with Dancing, Boxing, playing the Fiddle, and Small-Sword, and Cards."[158] In England the first professional rules were drawn up in 1743 by the champion, Jack Broughton, but they were not generally followed there in the counties.[159] Amateurs had to wait another century for John Graham Chambers to formulate the Marquis of Queensbury rules of 1867. Colonial boxing as a recreation, as distinguished from the professional sport we know today, was a rough and tumble exercise similar to the catch-as-catch-can wrestling of the day, and gentlemen, like contestants for prizes at county fairs, agreed on the rules for each bout according to their individual tastes.

## FENCING

The art of fencing could be learned in Virginia, where a number of competent teachers were available. At mid-century the Chevalier de Peyroney offered to open fencing, dancing, and French classes in Williamsburg as soon as a reasonable number of scholars enrolled.[160] In 1779 two other young men recently arrived from France were in town trying to organize fencing and dancing classes—John K'Dore and Jean Cadou.[161] (Perhaps only one young Frenchman advertised twice in four months' time.) Whether classes were ever established is not known. Perhaps either K'Dore or Cadou was associated with a fencing school recommended for students at the College of William and Mary in 1780.[162] However that might be, the gentry were not indifferent to the art as a social ornament. Charles Carter of Cleve, for example, wanted his sons to stay on at their school in England "to learn the languages, Mathematicks, Phylosophy, dancing and fencing."[163]

Under ordinary circumstances there was no practical use for the art in Virginia. The most famous swordsman here was Daniel Parke—exceptional in so many ways—a "sparkish gentlemen," according to Commissary Blair, who, "knowing something of the art of fencing was as ready to give a challenge, especially before company, as the greatest Hector in Williamsburg."[164] His son-in-law, William Byrd, fenced well enough to best Mr. W—l—s once in a friendly contest at Green Spring,[165] but he did not practice fencing as a favorite diversion, for he made no other note of it in his diaries. This was the sort of thing Fithian meant when he spoke of small-sword *play.*

## CUDGELING

The dueling contests at Virginia fairs were cudgeling matches patterned after the traditional village sport in England. When Thomas Hughes wrote *Tom Brown's School Days* (first edition, 1857), he explained how the "noble old game" was played in his youth:

The weapon is a good stout ash-stick with a large basket handle, heavier and somewhat shorter than a common single-stick. The players are called "old gamesters,"—why, I can't tell you,—and their object is simply to break one another's heads: for, the moment that blood runs an inch anywhere above the eyebrow, the old gamester to whom it belongs is beaten and has to stop. A very slight blow with the sticks will fetch blood, so that it is by no means a punishing pastime, if the men don't play on purpose, and savagely, at the body and arms of their adversaries. The old gamester going into action only takes off his hat and coat, and arms himself with a stick: he then loops the fingers of his left hand in a handkerchief or strap which he fastens round his left leg, measuring the length, so that when he draws it tight with his left elbow in the air, that elbow shall just reach as high as his crown. Thus you see, so long as he chooses to keep his left elbow up, regardless of cuts, he has a perfect guard for the left side of his head. Then he advances his right hand above and in front of his head, holding his stick across so that its point projects an inch or two over his left elbow, and thus his whole head is completely guarded, and he faces his man armed in like manner, and they stand some three feet apart, often nearer, and feint, and strike, and return at one another's heads, until one cries "hold," or blood flows; in the first case they are allowed a minute's time, and go on again; in the latter, another pair of gamesters are called on. If good men are playing, the quickness of the returns is marvelous; you hear the rattle like that a boy makes drawing his stick along palings, only heavier, and the closeness of the men in action to one another gives it a strange interest, and makes a spell at back-swording a very noble sight.[166]

## BOWLING

Another popular outdoor sport—bowling—was enjoyed in England by both men and women of all classes. Ordinary people used public alleys and greens maintained by towns and taverns, and the well-to-do had private bowling greens on their estates.[167] While Byrd was Virginia's agent in London he often bowled at Britwell, the Earl of Orrery's estate near Windsor, and at Petersham, the Duke of Argyll's country seat, which was equipped with an alley for ninepins as well as a bowling green.[168]

In the colony, too, both forms of the sport were enjoyed. Traditionally the Dutch brought ninepins to New York and the English brought bowls to Jamestown, where they played in the streets.[169] But ninepins also was played here, and it was already a popular sport on the Eastern Shore in the 1630s. William Ward, aged twenty-eight or

35.  *A Game of Ninepins or Skittles. Artist unknown.*

thereabouts, got into trouble in 1636 when he went off to John Dennis's house and spent the entire day playing at ninepins instead of looking after Lady Dale's cattle, which strayed into Henry Charelton's cornfield and ate the corn. Ward seems to have been a lazy and unreliable fellow, much given to gossip and loafing. Another time he turned out the cows and then fell asleep, "lazing all the day"; again the cattle trespassed on the long-suffering neighbor, Henry Charelton.[170]

A later game of ninepins at a private home on the Eastern Shore led to a quarrel that had to be settled in court. Joseph Godwin bet his opponent that he would tip seven pins, tipped only five of them, then refused to pay the wager, and an inconclusive fight ensued.[171]

Seventeenth-century Virginia taverns as well as homes sometimes had bowling facilities.[172] Thomas Cocke's tavern at Varina, Henrico County, was the scene of a disorderly game that became a court case in 1681. Robert Sharpe and Richard Rabone (or Rayborne) agreed to play ninepins for a stake of 400 pounds of tobacco on the first four games won at "thirty-one up" and asked young Thomas Cocke, Jr., to keep score. He refused, because Rabone had been drinking, and "went about other businesse." A middle-aged bystander, John Steward, reluctantly served as scorekeeper and later described the match in his testimony before the court.

At his first go, Rabone was sober enough to score seven pins and to win the first game with an exact total of thirty-one. Rabone had almost won the second game when one John Huddlesoe began to quarrel with him and said he had not got the game fairly by so many pins, whereupon Rabone threatened to stop playing if Huddlesoe did not "lett his gaming alone" and Sharpe replied that he would sue Rabone for the tobacco if he did not play out his game. Steward went away while the quarrel was still in progress.

Young Cocke returned to the scene of the game in time to hear the quarrel end with an agreement that the score was three games for Sharpe and two for Rabone. Then "they went to play againe and the other first two games Richd. Rabone wonne running." But the wager was not settled, and Rabone sued Sharpe to collect it. The jury found for the plaintiff, who had won four games out of seven.[173]

Without a careful study of all the county records, it is impossible to determine how many colonial Virginians owned bowling equipment. Philip Alexander Bruce declared that bowls were "frequently" mentioned in the inventories he examined, yet he cited only the set in William Parker's store in Lower Norfolk.[174] In the York County records Elizabeth Brooke's inventory, made December 14, 1716, included "1 Sett Nine pins, bowl and frame" valued at five shillings,[175] and another woman, Mary Hunter, innkeeper at Yorktown, had ninepins, cards, and a gaming table.[176] Robert Ballard's listing included two lignum vitae bowls, but they followed a parcel of china and preceded a parcel of flint glass, and on the same line with them appeared "6 china cups" with which they were valued at 8/6. All these articles seem to have been in a corner cupboard in one of the front rooms of the house; kitchen equipment and bedroom furnishings appear later in the inventory.[177] *Virginia Gazette* advertisements never included playing bowls or ninepins or skittles, and none appear in lists printed in the *Virginia Magazine of History and Biography, William and Mary Quarterly, Tyler's Quarterly,* or the *Lower Norfolk Antiquary.*

In addition to the rarity of available examples of taverns equipped with bowling facilities, there is a peculiar silence about the game in travelers' accounts of visits to the colony. And yet ninepins was popular enough for Daniel Fisher to find games in progress at two of the ordinaries he passed the first day of his trip from Williamsburg to Philadelphia.

At ten in the morning "a number of Planters" were playing at Ashley's, an hour's ride beyond Chiswell's ordinary; at three in the afternoon, just after he crossed the Pamunkey River into King William County, he saw "a great Number of People at Nine Pins" at Mills ordinary.[178] These games were probably being played in an outdoor alley similar to the one at the Raleigh Tavern in the nineteenth century, where students often bowled and little boys in the neighborhood set up the pins.[179]

Eighteenth-century bowling greens, too, are difficult to locate precisely. Williamsburg had one by 1720. William Levingston built a playhouse, dwelling house, kitchen, and bowling green on Palace green sometime after 1716.[180] In the spring of 1721 William Byrd noted in his diary that the green was in general use. On April 26 after dinner he "walked to the bowling green" and "gave the woman a pistole to encourage the green," then went on to Colonel Ludwell's town house and spent the evening. Again on May 3 and 4, he and several other councillors walked by the bowling green, and on May 5, he lost five shillings there and then "returned to court and finished the business."[181]

When Hugh Jones's description of the town was published in 1724, his readers learned that "Not far from hence [the Magazine] is a large area for a market place; near which is a play house and good bowling green."[182] By 1745 the green had disappeared; at that time "the lots and land whereon the Bowling Green formerly was" were sold to the city of Williamsburg for use as a hustings court.[183]

That same spring, after his return from England, Byrd laid out a bowling green at Westover. On March 16, 1721, he "began to turf the bowling green"; on March 24, he "walked about the garden" to see his "people lay the turf"; and by May 10 it was ready for use in a game with the Reverend Peter Fontaine.[184] Guests at Westover were still bowling on pleasant summer afternoons twenty years later.

In the last volume of Byrd's extant diary he recorded ten games in August 1739 when he played with neighbors, business agents, and his eleven-year-old son, William. The following summer there were thirty-two pleasant evenings when guests bowled with him, and in the last summer of the diary, 1741, almost every July afternoon had its bowling game.[185]

East of the mansion house at Nomini Hall there was a bowling green, but no one seems to have used it while Fithian was teaching there. His description of the grounds included this sentence: "The area of the Triangle made by the Wash-House, Stable, & School-House is perfectly levil, and designed for a bowling-Green, laid out in rectangular Walks which are paved with Brick, & covered over with burnt Oyster-Shells."[186] The spacious grounds of other colonial Virginia mansion houses probably had bowling greens, but we have no detailed descriptions of them to support the assumption.

The game of bowls as played in the seventeenth and eighteenth centuries had simple rules. The small round ball of white earthenware, called the jack, was first rolled onto the green to serve as a target. Players then rolled their bowls in turn, trying to place them close to the jack. In the play there was opportunity for both skill and judgment. The bowls were not perfectly balanced spheres, but rather spheroids slightly flattened like the earth at its poles and "biased" or loaded on one side with lead so that they could not be rolled in a straight line without considerable practice. An opponent's bowl resting close to the jack might be knocked out of the way or the jack itself might be moved with a skillful angle shot.[187] Few greens were perfectly level and—as in modern golf—familiarity with the course was an advantage in play.

Ninepins or skittles was played in an alley, either indoors or out. The pins, originally made of bone, were arranged in a single row in the earliest play; later they were set up on a square frame in three rows. Players stood at an agreed distance from the pins and cast the bowl at them; those knocked over or tipped as the ball went into the frame were reckoned as "fair pins" and scored one each for the bowler. When the bowl was thrown with enough force to bounce back from the far edge of the frame, the pins knocked over on its return roll were reckoned "foul pins" and not counted. Skittles, properly scored, required an exact total of thirty-one points. As Joseph Strutt explained the scoring, "Less [than 31] loses, or at least gives the antagonist a chance of winning the game; and more requires the player to go again for nine, which must also be brought exactly, to secure himself."[188]

Cotton's *Compleat Gamester* furnished practical advice rather than rules, which were too simple and generally well known to be worth detailing.

> In bowling [he advised] there is a great art in chusing out his ground, and preventing the windings, hanging, and many turning advantages of the same, whether it be in open wide places . . . or in close bowling-alleys. Where note that in bowling the chusing of the bowl is the greatest cunning. Flat bowls are best for close alleys; round byassed bowls for open grounds of advantage, and bowls round as a ball for green swarths that are plain and level.
>
> There is no advising by writing how to bowl, practice must be your best tutor, which must advise you the risings, fallings and all the several advantages that are to be had in divers greens, and bowling-alleys; all that I can say, have a care you are not in the first place rookt out of your money, and in the next place you go not to these places of pleasure unseasonably, that is when your more weighty business and concern require your being at home, or some where else.[189]

This healthful recreation, Cotton thought, would be much more commendable were it not for the "swarms of rooks" that infested public greens, places where three things were thrown away "beside the bowls, viz: time, money, and curses, and the last ten for one." The scene he described was "a school of wrangling," with onlookers loudly shouting "the bowl is gone 'a mile, a mile,' etc., when it comes short of the jack by six yards and on the contrary crying 'short, short,' when he hath overbowled as far." While losers "fret, rail, swear, and cavel at every thing, others rejoyce and laugh, as if that was the sole design of their creation." To point his usual moral, he concluded:

> It is the emblem of the world, or the worlds ambition, where most are short, over, wide, or wrong byassed, and some few justle in to the mistress, Fortune! And here it is as in the court, where the nearest are the most slighted, and all bowls aim at the other.[190]

Because the game was so widely known, bowling terms have been part of the English idiom since Shakespeare's time. The early seventeenth-century poet and wit, William Strode, canon of Christ Church, Oxford, pointed a moral similar to Cotton's and illustrated the idioms of the game in a bit of occasional verse that he called "A Parallel betwixt Bowling and Preferment":

> Preferment, like a game at boules,
> To feede our hope hath divers play:
> Heere quick it runns, there soft it roules;
> The betters make and shew the way
> On upper ground, so great allies
> Doe many *cast* on their desire;
> Some up are thrust and forc'd to rise,
> When those are stopt that would aspire.

Some whose heate and zeal exceed,
   Thrive well by *rubbs* that curb their haste,
And some that languish in their speed
   Are cherished by some favour's blaste;
Some rest in other's *cutting out*
   The same by whom themselves are made;
Some fetch a *compass* farr about,
   And secretly the marke invade.

Some get by *knocks,* and so advance
   Their fortune by a boysterous aime:
And some, who have the sweetest chance,
   Their en'mies *hit,* and win the game.
The fairest *casts* are those that owe
   No thanks to fortune's giddy sway;
Such honest men good *bowlers* are
   Whose own true *bias cutts* the way.[191]

# QUOITS

A similar outdoor game was quoits and its homespun variant, pitching horseshoes. Since before the time of Edward III it had been popular in England among the working classes, with whom it seems always to have been associated there. The quoit was the ancient discus with a hole in the middle, and it varied in size and weight to suit the strength of the players. Rules of play, as drawn up by Joseph Strutt, were as follows:

> To play at this game, an iron pin, called a hob, is driven into the ground, within a few inches of the top; and at the distance of eighteen, twenty, or more yards, for the distance is optional, a second pin of iron is also made fast in a similar manner; two or more persons, as four, six, eight, or more at pleasure, who divided into two equal parties are to contend for the victory, stand at one of the iron marks and throw an equal number of quoits to the other, and the nearest of them to the hob

are reckoned towards the game. But the determination is discriminatingly made: for instance, if a quoit belonging to A lies nearer to the hob, and a quoit belonging to B is second, A can claim but one towards the game, though all his other quoits lie nearer to the mark than all the other quoits of B; because one quoit of B being the second nearest to the hob, cuts out, as it is called, all behind it: if no such quoit had interfered, then A would have reckoned all his as one each. Having cast all their quoits, the candidates walk to the opposite side, and determine the state of the play, then taking their stand there, throw their quoits back again and continue to do so alternately as long as the game remains undecided.

Formerly in the country, the rustics not having the round perforated quoits to play with, used horse-shoes, and in many places the quoit itself, to this day [1801] is called a shoe.[192]

The most famous quoits player in colonial Virginia was young John Marshall. His casting technique was later described in colorful detail by George Wythe Munford in *The Two Parsons:*

> With his lone arms hanging loosely by his side, a quoit in each hand, leaning slightly to the right, he carried his right hand and right foot to the rear; then, as he gave the quoit the impetus of his full strength, brought his leg up, throwing the force of the body upon it, struck the meg near the ground, driving it in at the bottom, so as to incline its head forward, his quoit being forced back two or three inches by the recoil. Without changing his position, he shifted the remaining quoit to his right hand, and fixing the impression of the meg on the optic nerve by his keen look, again threw striking his first quoit and gliding his last directly over the head of the meg. There arose a shout of exulting merriment.[193]

On court day at the county seat pitching quoits was a popular recreation between sessions of the court or in the

*36. Playing at Coits. Engraving by John Boydell.*

idle intervals when lawyers and their clients were waiting for their cases to come up. No doubt John Marshall perfected his game on occasions such as this. Two other young lawyers, John Mercer and Thomas Jefferson, kept detailed accounts of expenditures when they were practicing in the counties, and these accounts have survived to tell us that they wagered small sums on their pitching skill. In Mercer's ledger for the period 1726 to 1731, the account with Enoch Innis shows 1/3 "won at Quoits and running with you" in 1728. Other entries record winnings and losses "at pitching," whether quoits or coins or stones is not shown, but the game was probably quoits or horseshoes because sometimes there were four adult players in the game—as on April 2, 1726, when Mercer and Battaley won 2/6 from Quarles and Steward.[194]

On three occasions in 1769 young Jefferson lost small sums playing "at pitchers" with Mr. John Madison and Thomas Bowyer in Staunton while he was attending the

Augusta Court.[195] Bowyer operated a tavern on the courthouse lot and on at least one occasion Jefferson stopped there.[196] John Madison, the father of Bishop James Madison, was for many years clerk of the Augusta Court.[197] Family tradition has it that Madison acted as Jefferson's guide on his visit to Staunton. When the two entered a loft where a group of men were playing cards by torchlight, Madison quietly laid a trail of powder across the floor behind the players and out the door then, waiting outside until one of them invoked the devil's participation in the game, Madison set fire to the powder and he and Jefferson watched the gamesters rush headlong out of the loft.[198] On court days in the backcountry horseplay was as common as horseshoe pitching.

# CRICKET

Before he laid out the bowling green at Westover, Byrd often played cricket with energetic friends. His diary for the years 1709 and 1710 records games at Green Spring, Shirley, and Berkeley as well as Westover.[199] In the early spring of 1710 there was a round of strenuous games with neighbors on both sides of the James River. On February 1 he rode with Isham Randolph to Shirley, where they found Colonel Hill just leaving to go to court with Benjamin Harrison. Randolph and Byrd stayed on to win a game of cricket against the Reverend Charles Anderson and Colonel Littlebury Eppes (now twenty years older than when he was involved in the Soane-Napier horse race dispute, but still active). In another game at Shirley on February 20 Byrd sprained his backside but continued to play in spite of the fact that he could not run and on leaving had to get on his horse by a chair. Two days later he had recovered sufficiently to play again with Colonel Hill, Mr. Anderson, and Colonel William Randolph, who were spending the

afternoon at Westover. The next two days it rained and snowed, but on the twenty-fifth cricket was resumed and one of the guests sprained his thigh.

The series of games continued through March. Colonel Hill was the host on the fourth and Byrd on the tenth. Benjamin Harrison had not been able to come to Westover because he had the gout, but he felt able to play at Berkeley on the fifteenth, although he soon tired. An "abundance of company" assembled at Shirley on March 22, and they played four to a side, among them Harrison, "who looked exceedingly red a great while after." The next day Harrison was ill, but after breakfast, which included a dram of cherry brandy, the others played until rain drove them indoors for dinner and an afternoon of dancing.

Until Harrison's death eighteen days later, his friends and relations gathered at Berkeley and Westover to inquire about the sick man, sit up with him, and offer other services to the household. Sometimes the group at Westover passed the waiting time at games. On March 27, Byrd recorded,

About 10 o'clock Dr. Blair, Mr. James Burwell and Major and Captain Harrison came to see us. After I had given them a glass of sack we played at cricket and after that at billiards till dinner. . . . In the afternoon we played at billiards. John Bolling and young Woodson came. Then we played at shooting with arrows till about 4 o'clock when we went all to Mr. Harrison's, whom we found better. Here we went to cricket again till dark; then we returned home.

And on the twenty-eighth:

About 10 o'clock Major Harrison, Hal Harrison, James Burwell, and Mr. Doyley came to play at cricket. Isham Randolph, Mr. Doyley, and I played with them three for a crown. We won one game, they won two. Then we played at billiards till dinner, before which

*37. Trap Ball, Played at the Black Prince, Newington Butts. Artist unknown.*

Colonel Ludwell came on his way to Mr. Harrison's. They all dined with us and I ate boiled pork. Soon after dinner the company went away and I took a nap. Then we walked to Mr. Harrison's, whom we found better. We played a game at cricket again. . . . This was my birthday, on which I am 36 years old, and I bless God for granting me so many years. I wish I had spent them better.

A modern cricketer would not recognize the informal sport these Virginia planters were enjoying. But he would feel no closer identity with an early eighteenth-century cricketer in England, for not until the Hambledon rules were drawn up in 1774 can one see the British national game beginning to develop.[200] Before that time the wicket was two "stumps" or posts about a foot high with a "popping hole" space between; that is, the stumps were placed about a foot apart and the striker had to run to the popping hole and put the end of his bat into it before the wicketkeeper could pop the ball in.[201] The bat was "similar to an old-fashioned dinner knife, curved at the back, and sweeping in the form of a volute at the front and end—an instrument for hitting, not blocking.[202] Since there were no set positions for members of a team, any number could play.

Earlier forms of the game continued to be popular with boys after adults had gone over to cricket. The equipment and play for trap ball are shown in the accompanying print. Stool ball was described by Strutt in 1801:

consists simply in setting a stool upon the ground, and one of the players takes his place before it, while his antagonist, standing at a distance, tosses a ball with the intention of striking the stool, and this it is the business of the former to prevent by beating it away with the hand, reckoning one to the game for every stroke of the ball; if, on the contrary, it should be missed by the hand and touch the stool, the players change places; the con-

queror at this game is he who strikes the ball most times before it touches the stool. I believe the same also happens if the person who threw the ball can catch and retain it when driven back, before it reaches the ground.[203]

A citizen of Norfolk complained in the pages of the *Herald* that young men and boys sometimes played cricket and bandy in the streets of the town, to the peril of innocent passers-by. (Bandy players used sticks resembling large cricket bats or giant-sized curved billiard sticks to drive the ball along the ground in a game similar to hockey.) Turning to sarcasm he declared:

The national, manly, and innocent game of bandy ought not to be suppressed by the officers of the police in the borough. The loss of an eye now and then by the force of a ball helps the [medical] faculty a little, as the sickly season is over; and the panes of glass that are broken put a few dollars in the pockets of the glazier. All trades must live and the practice of bandy, it is hoped, will be tolerated.[204]

Mrs. Anne Ritson, another resident of Norfolk at the turn of the century, mentioned a public playground on the edge of town, the Wigwam Skittle Ground:

It's there in winter young men go,
To pitch the bar, or quoits to throw;
Cricket and bowls they often play,
Wasting many an hour away.[205]

## FIVES

Another ball game colonial Virginians played was fives or hand tennis—what we call handball today. In 1758 John Bowyer, a younger brother of Jefferson's friend Thomas, disturbed the Augusta Court by playing at fives and was fined five shillings for the offense.[206] Students at the College of William and Mary sometimes played hand tennis. One of them, David Yancey, explained to a friend that he was too busy studying to enjoy much recreation, "but sometimes," he wrote, "we go out and take a game of fives against the old House. If a person comes here for improvement, he must study hard, but if pleasure be his object, it is a fine place for spending money as ever I saw."[207] Fives was already popular with students at Eton, where the favorite playing wall was the space between the buttresses on the north side of the college chapel.[208] Walls of church towers were generally preferred all over England, and the north side of the churchyard was the usual choice of playground because customarily there were no graves on that side.[209] Perhaps the north wall of the Wren Building, the nearest approach to a church tower on the college grounds, was the students' choice here.

The name "fives," in Strutt's opinion, may have come from the custom of having five competitors on each side; this is a guess. Another conjecture is that "fives" was a slang term for the human hand; however, this use is assigned a later date by the editors of the *Oxford English Dictionary.* Hand tennis in France was called *le jeu de paume,* but there is no evidence of British borrowing of the French term. In a word, the origin of the name and of the game is uncertain. Before the end of the eighteenth century a batlike racquet was sometimes used instead of the hand, and then the game was called "bat-fives." Eighteenth-century tennis was a more formal game with intricate rules played on an indoor court; the equipment was expensive, and only the wealthy played it in France and England. There is no evidence that anyone in colonial Virginia played tennis; however, tennis balls were to be found in the colony. The inventory of Thomas Bennet of York County, for example, included a parcel of tennis balls that were valued with ten churns at 6/10.[210] These balls were probably used in playing fives rather than formal tennis.

## BADMINTON

Early badminton, called shuttlecock, was a fashionable pastime in seventeenth-century England,[211] but in colonial America only children seem to have played it. There is no direct evidence of its popularity in Virginia, either in personal papers or in travel literature. The racquet in this game was called a battledore, a name given also to a child's hornbook of similar shape. For this reason it is difficult to use the testimony of merchants' accounts and customers' orders to estimate the popularity of the game. In the business papers examined for this study of Virginia amusements only one example of battledores and shuttlecocks together has been found, and this lone example was a Maryland order. The London merchant John Gibson explained to Mrs. Ross of Annapolis: "You sent for shuttlecocks and no Battledores; whether you intended to omit them I could not guess, but as they are used together I sent them so, with variety, I hope tis not wrong."[212] Gibson's invoice for this order included a box of toys at 7 shillings with the battledores and shuttlecocks at 6 shillings.[213] Perhaps some of the Virginians who ordered battledores were sent shuttlecocks as well, but no example has been found and the possibility is weakened by the circumstance that battledores appear in the lists with books rather than toys.

## SKATING

Another outdoor sport requiring special equipment was ice skating. Although this is a pastime usually associated with more northern localities, Virginia winters were colder two hundred years ago than they are today, and ponds and creeks often had enough ice to support a man when the tidewater rivers were not frozen over. Fluted and plain skates, with or without leather, could be purchased at Sarah Pitt's shop in Williamsburg, and in Norfolk skates could be found at Balfour and Barraud's.[214] Other merchants doubt-

38. *The Pleasures of Skaiting or, A View in Winter. Colored mezzotint from a painting by John Collet.*

less stocked them without special advertisement. Or they could be ordered from England along with other supplies; for example, John Hatley Norton billed Robert Gosling for one pair in 1766.[215]

Travelers seldom commented on skating—perhaps because they usually visited Virginia in warm weather. But Fithian spent the winter, and when millponds in the Northern Neck froze over, he joined neighborhood groups who "diverted" themselves "on the Ice," either with skates or without them.[216] Byrd's friends, too, played on the ice at Westover and experienced some of the hazards of the sport in this climate. On an unusually cold day in December 1709 he entertained a group of house guests with billiards and reading in the morning and more billiards after dinner until they lost one of the balls. Then they walked about the plantation and "took a slide on the ice." The following morning they took a walk and "slid on skates, notwithstanding there was a thaw." In the evening they "took another walk and gave Mr. Isham Randolph two bits to venture on the ice. He ventured and the ice broke with him and took him up to the mid-leg." Then they went home and played a little whist, but everyone was sleepy and went to bed early.[217]

## SWIMMING

Another informal water sport suitable for one person or many was swimming. Again, Byrd recorded the pastime for posterity. During a hot spell in July 1710 he enjoyed almost daily swimming in the river, where guests sometimes joined him. More than twenty years later, when he visited his lands south of the James River, he still enjoyed swimming. On that occasion he wrote:

To help restore Our Vigour, several of us plung'd into the River, notwithstanding it was a frosty morning. One of our Indians went in along with us, and taught us their way of Swimming. They strike not out both hands together, but alternately one after another whereby they are able to swimm both farther and faster than we do.[218]

Was this early form of the crawl stroke generally used by American Indians? If so, one wonders how many colonists learned it from them. The best known American enthusiast—Benjamin Franklin—wrote about the art and utility of swimming and furnished practical suggestions about overcoming a fear of the water and learning to float but had nothing to say about swimming strokes. His own characteristic improvements were mechanical ones—paddles for hands and feet and a kite to furnish motive power. He acknowledged indebtedness to the European authority, Melchisédech Thévenot's *De l'Art de Nager* (Paris, 1695), but made no mention of contact with Indian swimmers.[219]

It seems reasonable to conclude that the eighteenth-century man went swimming for the pleasure of being in the water, and the whole art of the sport consisted in staying afloat. Indians were more proficient than the colonists because they used the art in warfare[220] and taught their skill to the white man only in unusual circumstances, as on the journey to Byrd's Eden.

"The Black Swan" could never be considered an average planter; yet his attitude toward outdoor exercise and diversion was typical of his time and the rural society in which he lived. His diaries—unique in their detail of day-to-day routine—furnish the most vivid picture we have of spontaneous, informal enjoyment of outdoor life in the mild climate of tidewater Virginia.

# IV. PUBLICK TIMES AND PUBLIC OCCASIONS IN WILLIAMSBURG

Jefferson estimated Williamsburg's normal population to be 1,800, and the Frenchman who was here in the spring of 1765, distressed by crowds wherever he went, thought there were 5 or 6,000 people in town. There is little real disparity in these estimates, for Williamsburg in Publick Times was quite different from Williamsburg during the remainder of the year. With his customary insight, Rutherfoord Goodwin has described this difference:

> It was not in normal Seasons of the Year, when Men went about their usual daily Tasks and the City was concerned only with its casual Offices as Capital and County Seat, that *Williamsburg* enjoyed its true Prominence and Power. It was during the Publick Times (usually in the *Spring* and *Fall*) when the Assemblies were held or the Courts sat . . . that the City became the true Metropolis: For then . . . the Taverns, Inns, Publick Houses, Ordinaries, private Dwellings, and nearby Plantations were filled to overflowing; then all Men of publick Office or Prominence, and even most Persons of private Wealth or Consequence thronged to *Williamsburg,* as did those who lived by their Wits and the Influence to be sought there. So that there was no publick Commotion to be seen in all *Virginia* . . . which could compare with *Williamsburg* at Publick Times; for as *Virginians* lived apart, so they came together, and the Isolation of a Half-year was lost in a Fortnight or more of Society, Merriment, Commerce, and Politicks, so long as the Assembly stood convened.
>
> And of such great Moment were these Publick Times, that most Events that could be so adjusted were set to fall within them: So that the Fairs, which were held in *April* and *December,* often coincided with such Occasions; . . . the Season in the Theatre reached its Height at such Times; Race Meetings for the best Horses were held upon the Mile Course near the City; . . . the Craftsmen then displayed their finest Works, and the Merchants advanced the latest Fashions out of *London;* Slave Auctions were held; the Prize-winners in Lotteries and Raffles were announced; and the Merchants and Men of Affairs gathered upon *The Exchange* beyond the Capitol, where Debts were paid and contracted and the Money Business of the Country transacted.
>
> The best People of every Section of the Colony stopped in *Williamsburg* and appeared in its Streets at Publick Times; so that even an ill-disposed Traveller . . . wrote of his Amazement at "the prodigious Number of Coaches that croud the deep sandy Streets of this little City." These were the People who were in Attendance at the elegant Balls, Banquets, Lawn Fetes, and Displays of Fireworks given at the Palace; so that Colonel *Spotswood* showed small Concern in reporting that upon an official Occasion he had entertained two Hundred Guests at his House.[1]

## PUBLIC CEREMONIES

Celebration of the king's birthday was a regular annual event in Williamsburg. The first of these ceremonies took place on May 29, 1677, birthday of Charles II and anniversary of his restoration to the throne. Sir William Berkeley had finally departed for England earlier in the month and

Governor Herbert Jeffreys was eager to end the political and personal squabbles following Bacon's Rebellion and promote peace with the Indians. Accordingly, he called a meeting of the chieftains of tidewater Indian tribes at his camp at Middle Plantation to arrange a treaty with them.

As the representative of King Charles II, Governor Jeffreys presided.[2] The two other commissioners appointed under the Great Seal of England, Sir John Berry and Francis Morrison, attended him, together with the British regulars who had remained in the colony after the main body of troops accompanying the commissioners had returned to England. The people of the colony of Virginia were represented by the Council of State.[3] The queen of the Pamunkey and her son, John West, represented Powhatan's old confederacy, and eight subordinate chieftains attended and signed the treaty for their tribes.

It was a colorful and dignified assemblage. The Englishmen doubtless appeared in full uniform, attended by the redcoats in camp with Jeffreys, and members of the Virginia Council wore formal attire. The native Virginia royalty in ceremonial regalia were headed by the queen of the Pamunkey, dressed in a mantle of deerskins bordered with deep fringe and wearing on her head a three-inch circlet of black and white wampum.[4] The ceremony opened with gunfire salutes in formal recognition of King Charles II, whom the Indians publicly acknowledged as their overlord. To symbolize this dependence, the commissioners promised to replace wampum headbands and deerskin mantles with small silver coronets gilded and adorned with "false stones of various colours" and purple robes "of strong cloth."[5] After the customary formalities in Indian negotiations, each chief signed the treaty with his mark.[6]

The next recorded ceremony of this kind was ordered by Governor Francis Nicholson in 1702 to proclaim the accession of Queen Anne. On May 30 he met the Council in formal session at the home of Colonel Matthew Page and notified them of the death of William III two months earlier. The governor and Council then sent orders to commanders of the county militia units to call with all convenient speed general musters at the county courthouses. There the militia officers, justices of the peace, sheriffs, and other officials "joyntly in most solemn manner by Sound of Trumpet and beat of Drumm" were to "proclaime her most sacred Majesty Queen Anne" and "testify their rejoyceing by a triple Discharge of all their musquets and fire armes and other publick acclamations of Joy usuall on the like occasions."[7]

More elaborate ceremonies were planned for the city of Williamsburg. The appointed day was June 18, the date already set for a meeting of the General Assembly. Councillors and burgesses were to be joined by the clergy. Her Majesty's royal College of William and Mary was to be represented by the rector, trustees, governors, president, masters, and scholars—including alumni as well as students then enrolled. Nearby military units were commanded to attend with their best arms and accoutrements, prepared to spend two days and a night in town: York and James City militia (horse, foot, and dragoons), Colonel William Bassett's troop of horse in New Kent, and the horse and dragoons of Charles City, Elizabeth City, and Warwick. At the same time all Indian interpreters in the colony were ordered to send as many young men and boys as could conveniently come to Williamsburg, to appear with their bows and arrows and other arms.

When the great day came, about two thousand troops and forty Indians were in attendance, and another guest was on hand to write down a description of the proceedings—Francis Louis Michel, a Swiss traveler. His account follows:

[As part of the preliminary preparations] inquiry was made whether any one knew how to set off fireworks. Several from the warships volunteered. . . . Three theatres [grandstands] were erected before the college where the fireworks were to be set off. On the appointed day a large number of people appeared with as well as without arms. The celebration began on a Thursday morning. The armed contingents, on foot as well as on horse, were drawn up in line. Two batteries were also mounted and a tent was pitched, where the bishop delivered an oration on the King's death. The armed men were then drawn up before the college in a threefold formation, in such a way that the college building formed one side. Then there were soldiers on both sides and also opposite, making three divisions, so that the cavalry and the dragoons were stationed on the two wings and the infantry in the center. I have already given their number as about 2000. As can be seen from the drawing, the college has three balconies. On the uppermost were the buglers from the warships, on the second, oboes and on the lowest violinists, so that when the ones stopped the others began. Sometimes they all played together. When the proclamation of the King's death was to be made they played very movingly and mournfully. Then the constable appeared with the scepter. It was like the English standards [flags], which were woven with gold, covered with crape. Likewise those who carried them were dressed in mourning. Then followed the Governor in mourning, as also his white horse, whose harness was draped with black. The death of King William was then announced by the Secretary. Afterwards the Governor ordered the rifles reversed under the arms and with mournful music they marched with the clergy to the above named tent, where a touching oration was delivered, which caused many people to shed tears. After considerable marching and counter-marching, the troops were ordered back to their former place [before the college] holding their rifles as is customary. It was now

noon. The musicians began to play a lively tune. Then the constable appeared in a green suit, the scepter no longer draped. The Governor, who had retired, appeared in blue uniform, covered with braid. He had also exchanged his horse. The Secretary then read publicly, while heads were uncovered everywhere, the royal letter and edict, that the second daughter of the departed and late King James had been chosen and crowned Queen, in accordance with royal decree and law, with this added command to render her obedience and dutiful homage. Then everybody shouted three times Hurrah! that is, may she live. They waved their hats in the air, gave three salutes with the cannons as well as with the small arms. After this was done, the arms were stacked. Then the Governor caused most of those present, i.e., the most prominent people, to be entertained right royally, the ordinary persons received each a glass of rum or brandy with sugar.

After the meal was finished, the troops were again drawn up in line as before and marched to the State House which is under construction, at a distance of about three rifle shots, where the new Queen was proclaimed. . . . Finally it began to grow dark. . . . As there were not enough houses to lodge all the people, they had to be content to camp under the open sky.

At night the Governor entertained again as at noon, the various toasts were repeatedly answered by cannons and buglers. A master [of ceremonies], who was stationed on one of the bridges, was considered the most expert and boasted of his skill. But the result showed that he did not succeed in gaining much honor. In order to preserve his reputation he acted as if the fire had fallen unintentionally into the fireworks, for he blew up everything at once in a great blaze and smoke. As there were all kinds of fireworks, many and large rockets, he like others had to run and he had his clothes burnt. Many regretted the accident, but others saw clearly, that it had been set on fire intentionally, in order that his false boasts and clumsiness might not come to light. When the proper time had come, the Governor mounted his horse to superintend the rest of the fireworks himself. The college was full of the leading people, to see them, as also a large number of people outside; for such a performance had never been seen nor held there before, the windows were set with a double row of candles, the musicians played as best they could, the buglers were especially good. When it was to begin the Governor asked if they were ready. They answered: yes. Then he commanded them to set off the fireworks. This was done with a reversed rocket, which was to pass along a string to an arbor, where prominent ladies were seated, but it got stuck half way and exploded. Two stars were to be made to revolve through the fireworks, but they succeeded no better than with the rockets. In short, nothing was successful, the rockets also refused to fly up, but fell down archlike, so that it was not worth while seeing. Most of the people, however, had never seen such things and praised them highly. The one who had set his part on fire carried off the highest praise, because they thought he had done something extraordinary. The fireworks were very expensive, but there was not much diversion for one who had seen much more than these.

[The next morning] the troops were again drawn up in line. They rendered the oath of allegiance and the Governor ordered some military drills. After much marching and skirmishing noon came, when the dinner, as on the preceding day, began with much pomp and sumptuousness. After it was over, the Governor showed his liberality by arranging a rifle match. When the soldiers had finished, no one was allowed to shoot except those born in the country and some Indians. The prizes consisted of rifles, swords, saddles, bridles, boots, money and other things. When most of the shooting was done, two Indians were brought in, who shot with rifles and bows so as to surprize us and put us to shame.

The Governor, when he was sitting at the table in the evening, with the other gentlemen, had the young [Indian] queen come in, who was wearing nice clothes of a French pattern. But they were not put on right. One thing was too large, another too small, hence it did not fit. She was covered all over with her ornaments, consisting of large and small pieces, of all kinds of colors. Her crown was like those of the others, but it was much more beautiful, set with stones more artistically. She was a nice person, but timid and shy, like the others. When she entered the hall, the gentlemen took off their hats, she, the queen, bowed also. When the Indian king himself is present, the Governor gives him the right hand. Then they began to play, but the queen danced so wonderfully, yea barbarously, that everyone was astonished and laughed. It has no similarity to dancing. They make such wonderful movements with body, eyes and mouth, as if they were with the evil one. At one time they rave as if they were angry, then they bite their arms or other parts with their teeth, or they are entirely quiet. In short, it is impossible to describe this mad and ludicrous dance.[8]

A decade later, when Queen Anne died, the Capitol in Williamsburg had been completed and King George I was proclaimed "in the most Solemn manner," first in the General Court room, then in the marketplace of the city and at the College of William and Mary. On this occasion, October 19, 1714, the principal gentlemen of the colony were assembled in the capital for the meeting of the General Court, and they assisted the governor in the ceremonies. The night's festivities concluded with Spotswood's entertainment for all the gentlemen in town, when "his Maj't's health was drank with the firing of Guns and all suitable demonstrations of Joy for his Maj't's happy and peaceful accession to the Throne, whose undoubted and rightful Title the people of this Colony do unanimously acknowledge."[9] Whether there were fireworks and military maneuvers this year we do not know; no Michel was present to describe them. The customary announcements were made in the counties, funeral sermons in commemoration of Queen Anne were ordered in all the churches, and the common prayer for the royal family was properly altered.[10]

The next proclamation of a new monarch coincided with the arrival of a new governor in Williamsburg. Spotswood had been succeeded by Hugh Drysdale, who died in the summer of 1726, and Robert Carter of Corotoman as president of the Council occupied the governor's chair while the colony awaited the arrival of a new executive. After several delays Governor William Gooch "arrived into James River" on September 7, 1727, and "King" Carter went out to meet him. Carter's cryptic diary set forth the ceremonies:

*September 9.* I got to town at night. Let the Governor know I was come.

*10.* Waited on him. Went to church and dind with him. Sat till sunsett. Very civilly entertaind.

*11.* Governors commission opened in the General Court. From thence went into Council. Governor and Council took the oaths as usual. Mr. Randolph as Clerk [during illness of Robertson] and Atturney General. Proclamations for continuing in all offices, Commissarys commission read, ordered to be recorded in Secretarys Office. Orders to proclaim the King and through the countrie.[11]

Then we went and proclaimd the King at the Capitol, in the Market Place, on the Colledg green. Pack the Herald on horseback, Governor and myself in first coach. The guns fired 3 times. Invited to dinner at the Pallace. After drank all the roial healths. Guns fired at every health. 3 tables. Rack punch at each table. Governor drank all the healths at the table. We took our leaves at 12 clock.

*12.* Met in Council. Addresst the King on his accession. Vidal pardond. I left the papers relating to him to the clerk. The Governor dined with me, a very handsom

dinner we had. Governor went at sunsett. A great bowl Rack Punch.

*13.* Came out of town with Colonel Page, Mr. Grimes, my son Robert.[12]

The pardoning of John Vidal, a convicted pirate, had been recommended by the Council "in respect of his Majesty's Succession to the Throne, and the arrival of the Governor" as an act of mercy "very fit to begin his administration."[13] Already Carter had reluctantly agreed to reprieve the pirate because so many worthy gentlemen had interceded for him. "However," he explained to William Robertson, "I have very little compassion for persons convicted of his crime; and let what mincing so ever be made use of in his favour, it appeard very plainly to me from the testimony against him as well as the rest that his heart was fully prepared for perpetrateing the blackest of all vilianys, altho the designe was laid with the greatest improbability of success. But that was no foundation of merit in the contrivors; however, charity should cover a multitude of sins and may wee all meet with mercy in the day of our distress."[14]

Vidal's gratitude for the reprieve was expressed in a letter written in the Public Gaol on August 31. Many misfortunes in the tenderness of his youth had almost bereaved him of his senses, he decided, for he had "never intended to go a pirating." He planned to spend the "longer time of repentance" before his execution, now scheduled for October 6, in making preparations for answering before the great tribunal of heaven. "What a comfortable thing it is for a Dying man," he concluded, gratefully, "to have a little time to make his peace with God."[15]

Thus Governor Gooch's administration got off to a good start, but his introduction was "attended with a great charge" to His Excellency. For entertaining "the town and all the neighbours around us" on September 11 he spent fifty guineas of his own money.[16] The guests had hardly gotten home before it was time to return to Williamsburg to celebrate His Majesty's birthday, October 30. Back in the spring it had seemed very likely that the governor would not arrive before the birthday, and Carter had made preparations for the event. Since his chronic gout had become so acute that he was unable to get about, he instructed his son John—secretary of the colony—to act in his place[17] and asked Robertson to make all the arrangements. "I resolve to have the birthday kept with as much show as it was by Colonel Drysdale," he informed Robertson.

> In order to this herewith I Send a Letter to the Secretary which you are to Send away by Express Desireing him to Personate my room and if he Should decline it, I must rely upon You and Mr. Hickman to do your utmost and I will by you request the Town Gentlemen, Mr. Atturney, Major Holloway and Major Blair to be Assisting in the Government and direct the Affair. The Governours house to be Sure is the fittest Place. You may very well conclude when I laid in that wine at Town I had this day in my thoughts in Case a Governour should not Arrive. Whatever Sorts of drink Colonel Drysdale and I would have the Same and in all respects keep pace with him. My Salary is as large and I thank God I have as little reason to be sparing of it. I speak more particularly in the Enclosed paper.

> [Enclosure] The Necessarys requisite for the Birth Night in all respects Equall the last birth night.

> The Governours house to be Illuminated, Mr. Clayton also and likewise the Capitol if it was so before. I beleive the Colledge and all the houses in Town will be also Illuminated, bonnfires to be made as before.
> All the Loyall healths to be drink. The Guns to be fired and the Batterys to fire. The flaggs to be hoisted as was orderd by Colonel Drysdale.

> The Gentlemen and Ladys that will come to be Invited, Cold Treats to be provided, a Ball to be had for the Ladys, the Gentlemen of the Council and their familys particularly to be Invited. Mr. Grimes's family I shall invite. Whatever I have omitted to be Supplyd, the Charge an Account to be kept of and paid of[f]. Mr. Grimes I Expect will let me have the money.

> My wine you may be free with. I beleive one of the Pipes will Sufficiently answer the Occasion. Other Liquors etc you must provide as well as you can.

> [Post script] All Imaginable care must be taken to prevent disorders and disasters.[18]

Fortunately for Carter, Gooch arrived in time to spare him the expense and trouble of the birthnight celebration. Governor Gooch, in turn, complained to his brother that it cost him "near 100 guineas," but he did it "very magnificently." Then in January came the birthday of Frederick Louis, Prince of Wales, and this celebration cost the new governor twenty guineas. Small wonder that he found his income inadequate to the "constant great expense of House keeping" at the Palace.[19]

By this time a routine procedure had been set for all three of these ceremonies: proclamation of a new monarch, arrival of a new governor, celebration of royal birthdays. Only one other king was to be proclaimed in Virginia— George III, on February 12, 1761. Governor Francis Fauquier declared his dissatisfaction with this celebration, although he had done the best he could. Because of the inclement weather only four councillors were able to attend, but the routine was followed with the customary solemnity and in the presence of all the gentlemen Fauquier could "collect," the college scholars and masters, the corporation of the city of Williamsburg, and the local militia. The usual procedure was followed in the counties also.[20]

When a new governor took office, the official ceremony was held in the Capitol building and the general public had no share in the affair. Since the resident governor was usually a lieutenant, two commissions were read in the General Court—Orkney's or Albermarle's, Loudoun's or Amherst's, as the case might be, as well as the new arrival's. Back in the Council chamber other royal appointees took new oaths of office and had their appointments formally renewed. Then there was an elegant dinner in the governor's honor, attended by all the officials and principal gentlemen of the colony who were in town at the time. All the loyal healths were drunk with appropriate discharge of cannon and small arms, and often in the evening there was a ball, which the ladies too might enjoy.[21]

Lord Botetourt's arrival in October 1768 was attended with more elaborate ceremonies, for he was the governor rather than his lieutenant and all ranks of people in Virginia "vied with each other in testifying their gratitude and joy that a Nobleman of such distinguished merits and abilities" had been appointed "to preside over, and live among, them." A sixty-gun man-of-war, the *Rippon,* brought him into Hampton Roads on October 25, and he landed near Hampton at Little England the following morning. There he was greeted with a cannon salute and entertained with an elegant repast. At sunset he arrived in Williamsburg and was met at the gate of the Capitol by the Council, speaker, attorney general, treasurer, and other gentlemen of distinction, who conducted him to the Council chamber for the customary reading of his commission and administering of oaths of allegiance. Then the Council went out into a city brilliantly illuminated in his honor and supped with him at the Raleigh Tavern. At ten o'clock he went into residence at the Palace.[22]

Three years later the successor to the beloved Governor Botetourt was received with equal enthusiasm. Lord Dun-

more arrived in Yorktown on Tuesday night, September 24, 1771, after traveling from Philadelphia down the Eastern Shore and across Chesapeake Bay.[23] William Nelson, president of the Council, John Page of Rosewell, and Thomas Nelson, secretary of the colony, met him in Yorktown and accompanied him to Williamsburg. The swearing-in ceremony took place at the Palace, where the principal gentlemen in the city called to pay their respects and stayed to dinner. In the evening there were "illuminations etc" but no ball—probably because Lady Dunmore had not yet arrived.[24]

When the governor's family joined him in the spring of 1774, they were welcomed with a general illumination, an elegant set of fireworks, "repeated acclamations," and special addresses of congratulation by the president and professors of the College of William and Mary and by the mayor, aldermen, and common council of the city of Williamsburg. The *Virginia Gazette* reported the festivities in grand style and added two poems to Lady Dunmore celebrating her arrival "While Cannon roar" and "Bonfires blaze, And Joy 'round every Heart exulting plays." The House of Burgesses finished off the welcome with an elegant ball.[25]

The king's birthday was celebrated with great regularity, usually in the manner specified by "King" Carter in 1727. The colors were displayed at the Capitol and salvos were fired from the cannon at the Palace, at the forts, and on board the king's ships in Virginia waters at the time. In the evening the Capitol, the Palace, the College, and "most of the Gentlemen's and other Houses of Note" were illuminated and bonfires were sometimes set in public squares in the city. At the governor's dinner the drinking of all the loyal healths consumed a great deal of time, a variety of choice wines and liquors, and a large store of gunpowder. The populace was sometimes treated to "plenty of liquor" and drank the same healths outside the Palace or at one of the taverns.[26] The day's festivities closed with the governor's ball for all the ladies and gentlemen in town.[27]

Things were a bit different in 1718. That year Governor Spotswood's squabbles with the Council were reconciled, he thought, just before March 28, the birthday of George I. He discovered the error of this thinking when "the Chief Engines of Faction"—Philip Ludwell and Commissary Blair—and six other councillors ignored the public entertainment at the Palace and "the Play w'ch was Acted on that occasion" and "got together all the Turbulent and disaffected Burg's's, had an Entertainment of their own in the Burg's House and invited all the Mobb to a Bonfire, where they were plentifully Supplied with Liquors to Drink the same healths without, as their M[aste]rs did within, . . . without taking any [more] Notice of the Gov'r, than if there had been none upon the place."[28]

This was not the only time when the resident governor called in theatrical talent to help honor the king on his natal day. In 1752 "several beautiful Fireworks were exhibited in Palace Street, by Mr. Hallam, Manager of the Theatre in this city," whose company had performed *Othello* the preceding evening before a special audience that included the emperor of the Cherokee nation, his empress, their son the young prince, and attending Cherokee warriors. Governor Dinwiddie's Indian guests had been greatly surprised at "the fighting with naked Swords on the Stage, which occasioned the Empress to order some about her to go and prevent their killing one another."[29]

Outside the capital city, too, Virginians recognized the king's birthday as a suitable occasion for expressing their loyalty to the crown. The Virginia and North Carolina commissioners and their party surveying the boundary line between the two colonies in 1728 celebrated October 30 with conventional fervor. William Byrd described the proceedings:

This being his Majesty's Birth-Day, we drank all the Loyal Healths in excellent Water, not for the sake of the drink, (like many of our fellow subjects) but purely for the Sake of the Toast. And because all Public Mirth shou'd be a little noisy, we fir'd several volleys of Canes, instead of Guns, which gave a loud report.

We threw them into the Fire, where the Air enclosed betwixt the Joints of the Canes, being expanded by the violent Heat, burst its narrow Bounds with a considerable explosion![30]

The formalities marking His Majesty's birthday were used for other special occasions. In 1746, for example, when the news of the victory at Culloden reached Williamsburg, all ranks of Virginians joined the other loyal subjects of the House of Hanover in expressions of universal joy. The ball and supper were held in the Capitol instead of the Palace because Governor Gooch was ill. After dancing for some time, the numerous company withdrew to supper:

A very handsome Collation [was] spread on three Tables, in three different rooms, consisting of near 100 Dishes, after the most delicate Taste. There was also provided a great Variety of the choicest and best Liquors, in which the Healths of the King, the Prince and Princess of Wales, the Duke, and the rest of the Royal Family, the Governor, Success to His Majesty's Arms, Prosperity to this Colony, and many other Loyal Healths were cheerfully drank, and a Round of Cannon, which were reserv'd to the Capitol for this Purpose, was discharg'd at each Health, to the Number of 18 or 20 Rounds, which lasted 'til near 2 o'Clock. The whole Affair was conducted with great Decency and good Order, and an unaffected Cheerfulness appeared in the Countenances of the Company. All the Houses in the City were illuminated, and a very large Bonfire was made in the Market-Place, 3 Hogsheads of Punch given to the Populace; and the whole concluded with the greatest Demonstrations of Joy and Loyalty.[31]

During the Revolutionary years colonial victories over Parliament and the king's armies were marked with similar demonstrations of joy and loyalty to the American cause. The repeal of the Stamp Act was celebrated on Friday, June 13, 1766, with a general illumination, a ball, and elegant entertainment at the Capitol, where Governor Fauquier joined the large company in town for the regular summer session of the Oyer and Terminer Court; "with much mirth and decorum" they all drank the "loyal and patriotick toasts," signalizing the conciliation of differences between the colonies and the mother country.[32] Burgoyne's surrender was honored with a general illumination,[33] described by John Page of Rosewell, who was in town at the time:

> We have had a Feu de Joye from our troops, ringing of bells and a grand illumination, and tho' it is now past 10 at night the people are shouting and firing in Platoons about the streets. . . . I have been obliged to go down into the streets and prevent a riot and to prevail on my neighbor [Walter] Lenox [wigmaker] to cease firing, who drunk as a lord has been endeavoring to imitate a Cannon.[34]

The capitulation at Yorktown was the occasion for special rejoicing in Williamsburg as well as the rest of the country. Baron Von Closen, Rochambeau's aide, recorded the celebration from the point of view of the French allies:

> On the 15th [of November] the Te Deum was sung for the capture of Yorck. The Congress ordered public celebrations to be held on that day throughout the country. The garrison presented arms and fired three volleys from their muskets, followed by *Long Live the* [French] *King!* and artillery salvos. M. de Rochambeau gave a large dinner for the leading residents of Williamsburg, and a ball to which all the Ladies were invited; everyone very pleased with it.[35]

And not victories alone. When the speaker and gentlemen of the House of Burgesses entertained Lord Botetourt in December 1769 with a ball at the Capitol, colonial resistance to the Townshend Acts was publicized by a hundred Virginia ladies who attended the ball wearing homespun dresses—"a lively and striking instance of their acquiescence and concurrence in whatever may be the true and essential interest of their country" and an "example of public virtue and private economy, so amiably united."[36] Lord Botetourt tactfully returned the complimentary courtesy of the burgesses a fortnight later with a ball and elegant entertainment at the Palace.[37]

## PUBLIC EXECUTIONS

One of the spectacles that regularly attracted large crowds in England and in many of the American colonies was public executions, where the condemned sometimes harangued the spectators from the foot of the gibbet. In London about once every six weeks there was a procession of condemned criminals being carried to Tyburn for execution, "attended with the Compassion of the meek and tender-hearted, and with the Applause, Admiration, and Envy of all the bold and hardened." These hanging days were recognized holidays for London journeymen until public executions were abolished in 1783. Doctor Johnson spoke for his fellow townsmen when he protested against the "innovation" of private hangings: "The publick was gratified by a procession; the criminal was supported by it. Why is all this to be swept away?"[38]

Newspapers in some of the British colonies—notably South Carolina, Pennsylvania, Maryland, and New York—carried detailed accounts of executions there that suggest crowds in attendance. But in no extant issue of the *Virginia Gazette* is there comment beyond a brief statement of the criminal's attitude—whether he confessed or denied his guilt and whether he seemed penitent or composed or resigned to his unhappy fate. When the *Maryland Gazette* printed stories of Williamsburg executions, there were more details. The case of Lowe Jackson is an unusual example because it created unusual interest. His crime was counterfeiting. He had been taken prisoner in Charleston and brought to Williamsburg for trial at the cost of £100 from the public treasury. After he was condemned by the General Court, his friends and attorney had moved for a retrial, then for an appeal to the king for pardon. The Council had split on the question of granting the appeal, but the acting governor, Lewis Burwell, supported Jackson and granted a reprieve until His Majesty's good judgment could be received. The new governor, Dinwiddie, on special royal command investigated Jackson's trial and upheld the decision of the General Court. Jackson accordingly was hanged in April 1753, two years after he was condemned.[39] The *Maryland Gazette* reported in May:

> Williamsburg. April 13. This Day Lowe Jackson, pursuant to his Sentence, was executed at the Gallows near this City. He was drawn on a Sledge from the Prison to the Place of Execution, where he addressed himself to the Spectators, in a very moving and pathetic Speech on the fatal Consequences attending an early Habit of Vice, which had been the Means of bringing him to that shameful and untimely End. He appeared with a Composure of Mind, not frequently attending Men in his unhappy Circumstances, and died in a very penitent Manner. His body being put into a Coffin, with this inscription *Mercy! triumph over Justice*, was delivered to his Friends, and is to be interr'd in the County of Nansemond, where he was born.[40]

No doubt many Williamsburg people accompanied the sledge to the gibbet on Capitol Landing Road and heard the young man's moving and pathetic speech.

The record of Lowe Jackson's case is unique. Since we do not have the minutes of either the General Court or the Court of Oyer and Terminer, we are dependent upon the *Virginia Gazette* for records of criminal trials and executions, and these newspaper reports are too spotty for statistical analysis.[41] It was customary to publish a list of condemned criminals immediately after the court rose; then in about a month a list of executions followed, but there was no regularity in either kind of reporting. Sometimes the actions of sessions of the General Court were given; at other times, of the Oyer and Terminer; never all four courts in any one year. For the period 1736 through 1778 (from the first issue of the *Gazette* until the courts changed their place of meeting to Richmond) only twenty-two years are represented, and there is no evidence to suggest whether these years might be considered typical. The extant lists supply the names of 113 criminals who received the death sentence: 23 murderers, 23 horse thieves, 22 robbers and burglars, 4 counterfeiters, and 41 other felons. Executions of 27 of these persons were later reported, and in addition 23 others whose names do not occur in the first lists (the condemned). The relative incidence of crimes in this list is somewhat different: 18 murderers were hanged, 7 horse thieves, 10 robbers and burglars, all 4 condemned counterfeiters, and 11 felons.[42]

In short, we know the names of 136 persons who received the death sentence in twenty-two more or less haphazardly chosen years of the century. Presumably nearly all of them were executed, for those granted reprieve, pardon, or benefit of clergy were so reported;[43] but the number of them hanged at one time was never large enough to make much of a public spectacle. The greatest number of recorded executions in one day was seven; this report, typical in tone and illustrative of the public attitude, follows in full:

This Day [November 23, 1739] 7 of the 9 Malefactors, who receiv'd Sentence of Death, at the last General Court, were carried from the Public Prison, to the usual Place of Execution, and were hang'd, viz.

*Constantine Matthews,* for Robbing the Store of his Master, Col. *Woodford,* of *Caroline* County.

*Charles Quin,* an Overseer, and *David White,* an Accessory, from *Essex* County, for the Murder of a Negro, belonging to Col. *Braxton,* by Whipping him to Death, in a most cruel and barbarous Manner.

*Joseph Lightburn,* from *Prince William* County, for Robbery on the Highway, and for Horse stealing.

*Nathaniel Morgan,* from *Prince George* County, for Horse-stealing.

John Cobidge, a Servant, from *Essex* County, for the Murder of a Negro Woman, by killing her with an Axe, without any provocation. And,

*Elizabeth Maze,* from *Lancaster* County, for the Murder of her Bastard Child.

The other Two, that receiv'd Sentence, *viz. Sarah Matts,* an Accessory with *Constantine Matthews,* in Robbing Col. *Woodford,* and *William Barbesore,* for being concern'd with another (who dy'd in Prison before Tryal) in Robbing the Store of the Hon. *Philip Lightfoot,* Esq., in *York,* were (upon Intercessions in their Favour) pardon'd by His Honour the Governor.

We hear that Intercessions have also been made to the Governor, in Behalf of some of the other Criminals; but their crimes being either of a high Nature, or the Criminals old Offenders; and his Honour's Clemency having been often abus'd by hardened Wretches who had receiv'd the Benefit of his great Lenity, and instead of making a good Use of it, had return'd to, and repeated their wicked Courses, it is no Wonder his Honour has ordered Justice to be executed on these unhappy deluded Wretches, as Examples to others; tho' so much against his merciful Disposition.[44]

The unmistakable conclusion is that attending executions was not the public entertainment in Williamsburg that it was in London and in other colonial capitals that were also cities. There were not enough idle journeymen and people of similar tastes here to make up a crowd that would enjoy leisurely or smug attendance at the gruesome sort of spectacles that attracted the idly curious (and *unemployed*) city proletariat. Moreover, executions were scheduled to take place after the court had adjourned, and the crowds that assembled for Publick Times had by then dispersed. It is significant that no traveler mentioned the Williamsburg gallows and only one visitor saw a gibbet in Virginia. In 1777 Elkanah Watson was riding through the woods between Leesburg and Fredericksburg under a bright October moon. His carriage was guided by his servant Tom, who rode in advance. Suddenly Tom came galloping back towards them, badly frightened by something he had seen moving among the trees and seeming to float in the air—a Negro hanging in chains, executed for the murder of his master.[45]

## THEATER

After the middle of the century theatrical performances were frequently scheduled to coincide with Publick Times, and admission charges were low enough to attract all classes—usually 7/6 for box seats, 5/- in the pit, and 3/- in the gallery.[46] The Murray-Kean Company of Comedians opened the 1751 season in October with a performance of *Richard III,* and for the next twenty years the Waller Street theater back of the Capitol offered a varied theatrical fare to please every taste. On opening night Shakespeare's tragedy was followed by "a Grand Tragic Dance, compos'd by Monsieur Denoier, call'd the Royal Captive, after the Turkish Manner, as perform'd at His Majesty's Opera House, in the Hay-Market."[47]

For the April 1752 session of the General Court, the company featured a new Farquhar play that had been a hit at Covent Garden two years before[48]—*The Constant Couple, or a Trip to the Jubilee*—with added attractions of singing between the acts, a dance called *The Drunken Peasant,* and as an afterpiece Garrick's farce, *The Lying Valet.*[49]

In mid-summer another troupe, Lewis Hallam's select Company of Comedians, arrived in town fresh from the New Theater in Goodmanfields, London, promising new scenery and new plays so that Virginia ladies and gentlemen might "depend upon being entertain'd in as polite a Manner as at the Theatres in London."[50]

The Hallam Company opened on September 15 with *The Merchant of Venice* and Edward Ravenscroft's *Anatomist, or Sham Doctor* "before a numerous and polite Audience" and the performance was received "with great Applause."[51] The ensuing season lasted nearly a year, with performances three times a week in the fall and spring.[52] If the repertoire included the same plays presented by the company when they went to New York the following summer, then Williamsburg audiences enjoyed the variety Hallam had promised—more Shakespeare and newer favorites like Congreve's *Love for Love,* Farquhar's *The Beaux' Stratagem,* Steele's *The Conscious Lovers,* Addison's *The Drummer,* Cibber's *The Careless Husband,* together with short farces or afterpieces.[53] For the command performance before Governor Dinwiddie and his Cherokee guests Hallam may have chosen *Othello* with special care: in seventeenth-century London, certainly, and perhaps later, American Indians were sometimes called Moors.[54]

When the troupe returned to Williamsburg in the fall of 1760, David Douglass was managing the company,[55] which had recently enjoyed modestly successful seasons in New York, Philadelphia, and Annapolis. Their Virginia audience this season included George Washington, who spent £7.11.3 for play tickets in October while he was attending meetings of the House of Burgesses, and again in March 1761 he purchased tickets for £2.7.6.[56] Douglass was not advertising in the *Virginia Gazette* at this period, and the repertoire for the winter 1760–1761 is unknown.

The record of the next year is equally doubtful for the same reason. Again, Washington's account books are the best evidence that the Douglass Company was serving Williamsburg audiences in the winter of 1762–1763; he purchased tickets on November 1, 1762, and on April 26 and 29 and May 2, 3, and 19, 1763.[57] Douglass went on to Charleston in the summer of 1763 and did not reappear in Virginia until 1770; he was playing the New York-Philadelphia-Charleston circuit, with time out in 1764–1765 to return to England for new actors, new plays, and new scenery.[58]

During Douglass's seven-year absence from Virginia—in 1768—one of his actors, William Verling, organized a troupe of his own, using some of the Douglass group and starring Henrietta Osborne, famous for her male impersonations or "breeches parts." Verling named his troupe the Virginia Company of Comedians. After a short run in Norfolk they came to Williamsburg in time for the spring court and opened on Monday, April 4, 1768, with a new tragedy by the Reverend John Home, *Douglass,* followed by a dance and a comic afterpiece, *The Honest Yorkshireman.*[59] A young lawyer in the first-night audience, Thomas Jefferson, spent 11/6 at the playhouse[60]—7/6 for a box seat, probably, and 4/- for refreshments at the bar in the lobby of the theater.[61] On Wednesday, April 6, the company offered Addison's *The Drummer* and Garrick's *Miss in Her Teens,* and on Friday Otway's *Venice Preserved* with Cibber's ballad opera, *Damon and Phillida.*[62] During the following week Otway's *The Orphan* carried two added attractions—a comic dance, *The Bedlamites,* and a new harlequinade with new scenery, *The Burgomaster Tricked.*[63]

Verling did not advertise again in April, but there is evidence that the theater was open. Jefferson purchased tickets on April 11 and 27 (three of them on the latter date) and spent 5/- at the playhouse on the eighteenth and 10/- on the twenty-ninth.[64] George Washington arrived in town on Monday, May 2, traveling from Eltham with Colonel Burwell Bassett, Colonel Fielding Lewis, and Charles Dick of Fredericksburg. After dining with Mrs. Dawson (widow of the president of the College, William Dawson), he attended the play—presumably as host of a theater party since he had bought three or four tickets the day before.[65] Jefferson, too, was present at this performance.[66] On Thursday, May 5, Washington purchased tickets for 12/6,[67] probably for Friday's performance, which Jefferson also attended.[68]

The program on Wednesday, May 18, was advertised in the *Virginia Gazette:* Farquhar's *The Constant Couple* and *The Miller of Mansfield* as the afterpiece.[69] On Friday the twentieth Edward Moore's tragedy, *The Gamester,* was offered with a new dance called *The Cowkeepers,* performed by three gentlemen of the company, and a new farce, George Colman's *Polly Honeycomb.* On Wednesday, May 25, *Henry IV* was followed by Arthur Murphy's new farce, *The Old Maid,* and on Friday *The Merchant of Venice* was offered with a new two-act farce by the Reverend James Townley, *High Life Below Stairs,* which had been performed four times in Philadelphia the year before.[70] We have no attendance records for these weeks; both Jefferson and Washington were out of town. Jefferson had returned by Monday, May 30, when he bought tickets for 15/- and spent 3/9 for punch at the playhouse.[71]

The last production advertised that season was Gay's *The Beggar's Opera* with a dance, *The Drunken Peasant,* and Ravenscroft's popular farce, *The Anatomist,* on June 3. The music for the opera was conducted by Williamsburg's or-

ganist-jailor, Peter Pelham.[72] Jefferson was probably host at a small theater party that night, for he recorded payment of 20/- for play tickets under date of June 4, a Saturday, when the theater was usually closed, and on other occasions Pelham's music attracted the young violinist.[73]

In mid-summer, after a short engagement in Annapolis, Verling's Virginia Company of Comedians disbanded permanently. For the next two years the Williamsburg theater was dark except when traveling magicians and a puppeteer performed there. On April 14, 1769, Jefferson took a guest to a puppet show[74]—Peter Gardiner's "curious set of Figures, richly dressed, four feet high," which appeared "upon the stage as if alive."[75] The play was a popular folk legend, a sentimental tragedy called *The Babes in the Wood.* Gardiner promised other spectacles on the same bill: "a curious view of Water Works, representing the sea, with all manner of sea monsters sporting on the waves"; indoor fireworks representing "the taking of the Havannah, with ships, forts, and batteries, continually firing"; a "curious Field of Battle, containing the Dutch, French, Prussian, and English forces, which shall regularly march and perform the different exercises to great perfection"; and, finally, a performer would "lay his head on one chair and his feet on another, and suffer a large rock of three hundred weight to be broke on his breast with a sledge hammer." All this for 3/9 in boxes, 2/6 in the pit, or 1/3 in the gallery. Of course, no one would be admitted behind the scenes, for illusionists carefully guarded their trade secrets—so carefully, in fact, that they are still withheld from public knowledge.[76]

Jefferson seems to have enjoyed these spectacles, for he again bought tickets on April 17 and 26.[77] On the twenty-seventh Gardiner substituted a comedy, *Whittington and His Cat,* for *Babes in the Wood* and replaced his strong-man act with sleight-of-hand.[78]

Again in the fall Jefferson saw two sleight-of-hand performances at the playhouse.[79] Whether Gardiner was still in town is not known; perhaps another traveling "legerdemain man" was using the Williamsburg theater during the October court. There is no record of performances while the Assembly was sitting from November 7 through December 21; Washington was in and out of town with his family, commuting from Eltham from November 6 through December 22, and although he made daily entries in his diary and account book for this visit, he recorded no plays or play tickets.

The following summer Douglass brought his enlarged and improved troupe—now called the American Company—to Williamsburg and opened on June 16, 1770, with *The Beggar's Opera*.[80] It was a successful season. Both Jefferson and Washington were in town two months as burgesses[81] and attended the theater regularly in June. Washington bought ten tickets and went to plays on June 16, 18, 19, 20, and 22.[82] It has often been suggested that he admired Nancy Hallam's acting with some of the warmth expressed by his stepson's tutor, the Reverend Jonathan Boucher, who saw her star in the company's production of *Cymbeline* in Annapolis later in the summer and composed a panegyrical ode praising the soft speech, Lydian airs, pellucid eyes, faultless form, and nameless grace that charmed every heart.[83] In Williamsburg, her audience included a more faithful admirer than Washington, however, for the red-haired young bachelor burgess from Albemarle bought tickets on ten occasions between June 16 and June 28—every weekday except the twenty-second and the twenty-sixth.[84] Furthermore, in the fall, when the Douglass Company returned from Annapolis, Jefferson patronized the theater with equal regularity—on October 23, 26, 27, 29, 30, and 31 and November 1, 2, 3, 5, 6, 7, and 8.[85]

Douglass's last two years in Williamsburg were his most successful—or at least the most advertised. The first performances of the 1771 season were described by young Hudson Muse of Northumberland County, who returned home from a visit in Maryland via Williamsburg. His bread-and-butter letter explained his delay in writing it:

*39. Nancy Hallam in the Cave Scene from* Cymbeline.
*Painting by Charles Willson Peale, 1771.*

In a few days after I got to Virginia, I set out to Wmsburg, where I was detained for 11 days, tho' I spent the time very agreeably, at the plays every night, and realy must join Mr. Ennalls and Mr. Bassett in thinking Miss Hallam super fine. But must confess her luster was much sullied by the number of Beauties that appeared at that court. The house was crowded every night, and the gentlemen who have generally attended that place agree there was treble the number of fine Ladyes that was ever seen in town before—for my part I think it would be impossible for a man to have fixed upon a partner for life, the choice was too general to have fixed on one.

About the latter end of this month, I intend down again, and perhaps shall make out such another trip, as the players are to be there again, and its an amusement I am so very fond of.[86]

The players did return and announced for performance on April 26 Steele's comedy, *The Tender Husband,* and *The Honest Yorkshireman.*[87] Presumably others followed. The General Assembly did not meet this year until July 11, but Washington was in town for ten days early in May seeking medical care for Patcy. He attended the theater on May 2 and again on the eighth, when he was host to Colonel Robert Fairfax "and some other Gentlemen."[88]

Toward the end of May the company left Williamsburg for an engagement of several months in Fredericksburg and did not return to the capital city for the July meeting of the General Assembly.[89] They were back for the October court, however, opening on Wednesday the twenty-third with Richard Cumberland's new comedy, *The West Indian,* and George Colman's *The Musical Lady,* a double bill repeated on the twenty-sixth.[90] Later announcements promised *King Lear* for Tuesday, November 12; Garrick's version of Ben Jonson's *Every Man in His Humor* with *Damon and Phillida* as an afterpiece for Saturday the twenty-third; George

Colman's *The Jealous Wife* and Isaac Bickerstaffe's comic opera *The Padlock* for Saturday, December 21; and at a later date, *The Fate of Caesar.*[91] We have no record of the audience for these performances. The Assembly was not in session this fall, but Washington was in Williamsburg from October 29 through November 7 recording land claims from French and Indian war services; thus he missed all the announced performances. During the ten-day visit he spent £4.1 for tickets and went to the theater on October 29, 30, and 31 and November 1; on November 1 there was a double attraction—fireworks in the afternoon and a play in the evening.[92]

In 1772 the General Assembly met from February 10 through April 11.[93] The arrival of Douglass's players was announced early in March with the intelligence that three brand-new comedies were in rehearsal: Richard Cumberland's *The Brothers* and Hugh Kelly's *False Delicacy* and *School for Libertines, or A Word to the Wise.*[94] Jefferson did not occupy his seat in the House of Burgesses that year, but Washington arrived on March 2. He went to his first play of the season on the twelfth and was again at the theater on March 17, 19, 25, and 26, and April 3 and 7.[95] The hit of the season, performed first on the twenty-sixth with Washington in the audience, was favorably reviewed in the *Virginia Gazette:*

Mr. Kelly's new Comedy of *A Word to the Wise* was performed at our Theatre last Thursday, for the first Time, and repeated on Tuesday to a very crowded and splendid Audience. It was received both Nights with the warmest Marks of Approbation; the *Sentiments* with which this excellent Piece is replete were greatly, and deservedly, applauded; and the Audience, while they did Justice to the Merit of the Author, did no less Honour to their own refined Taste. If the comick Writers would pursue Mr. Kelly's Plan, and present us only with moral

Plays, the Stage would become (what it ought to be) a School of Politeness and Virtue.[96]

Later productions included Kelly's *False Delicacy* on April 14; on the twenty-first Cibber's *The Provoked Husband, or A Journey to London* and a musical afterpiece, *Thomas and Sally, or The Sailor's Return* by Bickerstaffe and Arne; on the twenty-eighth an Arthur Murphy comedy recently added to the repertoire, *School for Wives, or The Way to Keep Him,* with Mrs. Cibber's translation of a French dramatic afterpiece, *The Oracle;* some time in May a new comedy of Cumberland's then "acting at the Theatres Royal in Drury Lane and Edinburgh"—*The Fashionable Lover.*[97] A young Yorktown merchant, William Reynolds, received a copy of the play from his London friend George F. Norton (brother of John Hatley Norton of Yorktown) and in his thank-you letter dated May 23, 1772, Reynolds wrote: "I am much obliged to you for the *Fashble Lover* which I have had an opportunity of seeing represented on our Williamsburg Stage but dont think it by any means equal to *his* West Indian."[98]

At the end of the April court the Douglass troupe closed the Williamsburg theater for the year [99] and for the colonial period except for Gardiner's return engagement in November. The illusionist advertised only once in the *Gazette,* announcing his program for Monday, November 23: the same four-foot puppets in another folk legend, *Bateman and His Ghost;* waterworks, fireworks;[100] a perspective theater called *Cupid's Paradise;* and the same strong-man trick performed in 1769 except that the stone weighed only 200 pounds this time. French horns and trumpets furnished music between the acts.[101] Although the Assembly was not sitting, Washington was in town with his family until November 20. He left too early to see *Bateman and His Ghost* on the twenty-third; yet he attended a show of Gardiner's, for on the sixteenth he spent 11/6 for "cost of seeing Puppit Shew" and 7/6 for "cost of seeing Wax work."[102] An exhibition of wax figures may have been a separate part of Gardiner's repertoire, but this is not a likely guess, for he did not advertise it in Maryland, either, and waxworks were not an item in an illusionist's stock in trade. It was more probably another exhibit entirely, one that was not advertised.[103]

## EXHIBITIONS AND LECTURES

The most elaborate exhibit advertised for display in Williamsburg was a mechanical one, the celebrated MICRO-COSM, or World in Miniature, built by Henry Bridges of London after twenty-two years of "close study and application," and approved by the Royal Society. It was brought to the theater of the capital city of Virginia in October 1755 after a successful showing in Norfolk, where Mr. Bridges had been warmly commended for his generosity in giving the proceeds from a special benefit night to a fund offered as bounties to persons who would enlist in George Washington's expedition to the Ohio.[104] The Microcosm was built in the form of a Roman temple, a most beautiful composition of architecture, sculpture, and painting. Inside, seven scenes with appropriate sound accompaniment were presented. In the first, the universe was represented with particular emphasis on recent astronomical predictions—Newton's comet, due early in 1758; the transit of Venus over the sun in June 1761; and an eclipse of the sun forecast for April 1, 1764. In the second scene the nine muses played in concert, and in the third Orpheus charmed wild beasts by playing on his lyre and beating exact time to each tune. Then all the branches of the carpenter's trade were "most naturally represented," and warbling birds flew about in a delightful grove. The sixth scene presented a fine landscape with ships sailing on the sea, coaches and carts passing up and down a steep hill (their wheels turning round as if actually on the road), swans swimming in a river and bending their necks gracefully backward and forward, and bird dogs sporting with ducks. The last scene showed the whole machine in motion, when twelve hundred wheels and pinnions were moving at once to the accompaniment of several fine pieces of music on the organ and other instruments playing singly and in concert "in a very elegant Manner."[105] The Microcosm could be seen at six o'clock on Monday, Wednesday, and Friday evenings at a cost of five shillings. Private showings could be arranged, and a season ticket at 15/- entitled its owner to see the machine inside and out as often as he pleased and with company.[106]

Another traveling exhibitor exploited in Williamsburg the layman's interest in science. This was one William Johnson, who offered for the entertainment of the public a "Course of Experiments in that curious and entertaining branch of Natural Philosophy called Electricity" with accompanying lectures on the nature and properties of the electrical fire.[107] The program was scheduled for a Thursday and Friday in mid-October 1766–fourteen years after Franklin's kite experiment had proved that lightning and electricity were one and the same.

Electrical experiments had been the rage in Europe for several decades among professional entertainers and medical quacks as well as serious scientists. On one occasion in France the Abbé Nollet put on a dramatic demonstration for Louis XV and his court: 700 monks were lined up, hand in hand, and an electrical charge was passed from one end of the line to the other; "at the moment of discharge the holy men leaped into the air with simultaneous precision, to the roaring delight of the royal spectators."[108] Johnson could not command so many assistants in Williamsburg, but he had a wealth of precedents from which to choose entertaining experiments with audience participation.

Three months later William Verling entertained in the Great Room of the Raleigh Tavern[109] with a humorous lecture that was being admired and applauded by English-speaking audiences everywhere. This was George Alexander Stevens's celebrated *Lecture on Heads,* which would be published in London the following year. It had been delivered in Charleston in the spring of 1766 by David Douglass, who had doubtless pirated it from Stevens; Verling had been with Douglass in Charleston and he, in turn, had stolen the piece for use in Williamsburg after he left the Douglass Company.[110] It was a full evening's entertainment, for the lecturer ranged widely over the field and from it. Some of the by-ways explored were an oration in praise of the law, the genealogy of genius, a dissertation on sneezing, women of the town, Methodists, Red Riding Hood, face painting exploded, the young wife and old maid contrasted, laughing and crying philosophy.[111]

In late April 1773 a more serious lecturer came to Williamsburg for a stay of six weeks—"Doctor Graham, Oculist and Aurist, at Philadelphia."[112] The learned doctor, an Englishman who had studied medicine at Edinburgh, offered to see patients afflicted with disorders of the eye and ear, to cure deafness and speech defects as well as diseases, and to give public lectures on the structure and diseases of these delicately curious and most important organs. His consultation schedule was so crowded that he had to see charity patients between five and seven in the morning.[113]

Thomas Jefferson was among those who paid 5/9 to hear the lecture but he recorded no comment on it.[114] A number of miraculous cures were reported in testimonials printed in the *Gazette* from time to time during the doctor's stay in town. On June 3, for example, it was announced that

Last Tuesday Mrs. COBB of this City, aged sixty six, who for several Years had been totally blind with a

Cataract in each Eye, was couched by Doctor GRA-HAM, Oculist and Aurist, and in less than five Minutes was restored to the Blessing of Sight in both Eyes.[115]

In October 1772 Joseph Faulks, a trick rider, "gave great Satisfaction to the Spectators" when he performed his "EXPLOITS in HORSEMANSHIP," riding one, two, and three horses in many different attitudes.[116] He took his act to Gloucester Court House in December and was again performing there on Easter Monday eighteen months later. Between riding exhibitions he seems to have made a precarious living from stud fees provided by one of his horses, Young Bajazet, who was advertised at Joseph Harwood's plantation in King and Queen County.[117] Faulks must have found his Virginia audience of expert horsemen more critical than most; Young Bajazet was offered for sale on June 13, 1774, in front of the Raleigh Tavern by one Cuthbert Hubbard, "in whose Possession he was left by Joseph Faulks,"[118] who had disappeared from Gloucester, from Virginia, and from the historical record.

The appearance of itinerant acrobats was not unusual in colonial Virginia. When Durand of Dauphiné visited William Fitzhugh's plantation in 1686, the company was entertained by three fiddlers, a jester, acrobat, and tightrope dancer.[119] There arrived in Williamsburg in April 1738 a man and wife and two children who performed "the Agility of Body, by various sorts of Postures, Tumbling, and Sword Dancing, to greater Perfection" than had been "known in these Parts for many Years, if ever."[120] Nearly forty years later Robert Wormeley Carter spent 3/6 in Williamsburg "at the Wire dancers."[121] This group has not been identified.

Williamsburg fairs, scheduled to run for three days semi-annually in April and December, may have attracted acrobatic performers. These were agricultural fairs rather than public entertainments, yet to encourage attendance prizes were offered in contests that included cudgeling, wrestling, manual exercises, footracing, chasing the greased pig, dancing, fiddling, and singing—in addition to the regular bounties for the best livestock and poultry.[122] Unusual animals seem to have been displayed from time to time as special exhibits. Jefferson paid -/7½ for seeing an elk on April 11, 1768; exactly a year later he viewed a hog weighing more than 1,050 pounds; on October 17, 1769, he saw a tiger at the cost of 1/3, and ten days later he paid 1/3 for seeing a great hog.[123] At all these times theatrical performances were running in the Williamsburg theater and Jefferson was buying tickets for them; the animals, therefore, were doubtless separate exhibits and those seen in October could not have been connected with a fair.

## AMATEUR THEATRICALS

When there was no professional play to be seen in the Williamsburg theater, less formal performances were open to the public from time to time. These were spontaneous productions of amateurs in the community, and the record of them is appropriately incidental. In September 1736, for example, college students presented two of Addison's plays—*Cato* and *The Drummer*—and a group of townspeople in one busy week performed in Mrs. Centlivre's *The Busy Body* and two of Farquhar's hit plays—*The Beaux' Stratagem* and *The Recruiting Officer*.[124] There was much public interest in these productions, for some of the best people were in the cast, notably Governor Gooch's son and sister-in-law. Enthusiastic comments crossed the Atlantic[125] and occupied first place in the pages of the *Virginia Gazette*.[126] Fifteen years later *Cato* was still a popular vehicle for another generation of college students, and John Blair privately reviewed one of their rehearsals:

This evening Mr. Pr[esto]n to prevent the young gentlemen at ye college from playing at a rehearsal in ye dormity., how they could act Cato privately among themselves, did himself, they say, act the Drun[ke]n Peasant; but his tearing down the curtains is to me very surprising.[127]

# CONCERTS

Concerts, too, were largely amateur except when regular theatrical programs included music, for the capital city was a small town most of the year and could support professional musicians only as music teachers. Peter Pelham was exceptional, and even he could not make a living from his music alone. (His salary as public organist at Bruton was £25 a year; as jailor the colony paid him £40.) Another supplement to his income was explained by Ebenezer Hazard, surveyor-general for the Post Office, who was in town in the summer of 1777. He wrote in his diary:

June 4th. There is to be a musical Entertainment and Ball at the Capitol this Evening for the Benefit of Mr. Pelham, the Organist of the Church.

June 5th. The Entertainment last Night was very fine, the Music excellent, the Assembly large and polite, and the Ladies made a brilliant Appearance. A Mr. Blagrave (a Clergyman), his Lady, and a Mrs. Neal [a music teacher who gave guitar lessons at her home on Palace Street] performed the vocal Parts; they sang well, especially Mr. Blagrave. His Lady played excellently on the Harpsichord. After the Entertainment was over, the Company went up Stairs to dance. I think a Mrs. Cuthbert (formerly Mrs. Blair, a Daughter of Dr. Eustis of New York) made the best Appearance as a Dancer.[128]

Pelham's church concerts were famous. John Blair's daughter Anne informed her sister: "They are Building a steeple to our Church, the Door's for that reason is open every day; and scarce an Evening . . . but we are entertain'd with the performances of Felton's, Handel's, Vi-Vally's, etc. etc. etc. etc."[129] Alexander Macaulay, a merchant who visited Williamsburg in 1783, facetiously described the buildings of the old capital with what he considered elegant classical allusion. About Bruton he wrote, "Theres the Church fam'd for its noble Organ of one hundred tones, touch'd by the modern Orpheus—the inimitable Pelham."[130]

A decade later, when the organist was an old man, his concerts were cited as evidence of cultural interests still to be found in the little town after the capital had been moved to Richmond. St. George Tucker, seriously annoyed with the Reverend Jedediah Morse's scornful picture of Williamsburg as a cultural desert, replied in an open letter:

There is however one amusement to which the inhabitants of Williamsburg are not a little addicted, and as it is not very common elsewhere, I shall take the liberty to mention it—Among the Edifices which have hitherto withstood the shock of desolation, there is one, which the reader who relies upon the justice and candour of the author of the American Universal Geography, would probably not expect to hear of, namely, a church dedicated to the service of Almighty God: in this church there is a well toned Organ; and among the ancient inhabitants of the place, who neither migrated to more prosperous places in the union, nor yet set out for 'that undiscovered country from whose bourne no traveller returns,' is the organist; whose skill in his profession still secures him a small subscription from his fellow villagers, as well as a competent number of pupils for his support. A week rarely passes in which a number of the inhabitants do not assemble for the purpose of passing an hour or two at church, while the ancient organist, or some of his pupils perform upon this instrument; and often is the passenger invited into the place, in a fine evening, by hearing 'The pealing anthem swell the note of praise.'[131]

Admission to Pelham's concerts was sometimes by ticket only. Jefferson recorded two occasions when he paid to hear Pelham play: May 5, 1769, and June 2, 1778. Other paid concerts attended by Jefferson and Washington may have been held in Bruton Church. Jefferson's accounts date his attendance on April 30, May 5, and June 20, 1768; May 11, 1769; and May 7, 1777.[132] Washington recorded the purchase of concert tickets on April 27, 1757; May 2, 1765; April 10, 1767; and April 6, 1772.[133]

The music Washington heard on May 2, 1765, was played on the armonica—the musical glasses invented in the eighteenth century and still popular in the nineteenth, when the instrument was called a harmonium.[134] Councillor Robert Carter of Nomini Hall owned the only known armonica in Williamsburg. He had ordered it from London a year earlier, explaining to a London merchant just what it was he wanted:

Mr. Pelham of this Place is just returned from New York, he heard on that Journey Mr. B. Franklin of Phila: perform upon the Armonica: The Instrument pleased Pelham amazingly and by his advice I now apply to you, to send me an Armonica as played on by Miss Davies at the great Room in Spring Gardens, being the musical Glases with out Water: Formed into a complete Instrument, capable off Thorough-bass, and never out of tune. Charles James of Purpoole-lane, near Gray's Inn London is the only maker of the Armonica in England.

Let the Glasses be clear crystal and not stained, for what ever distinction of colour may be thought necessary to facilitate the performance, may be made here. The greatest accuracy imaginable must be observed in tuning the Instrument and directions procured for grinding the Glasses, they, must be packed with great care for if a Glass should be broke the Instrument will be rendered useless until the accident could be repaired in London. The Case of [or?] Frame in which the Instrument is fixed to be made of black walnut.[135]

Franklin not only played the instrument; he invented the improved model Carter described. The Philadelphian had seen a very clumsy set of musical glasses in England several years earlier and had been delighted with the soft tones the musician produced by passing a wet finger around the rims of separate glasses that stood upright on a sort of table. His inventive genius immediately went to work on the problem of how to do it an easier way. Boring a hole in the bottom of each glass, he strung them according to size on a spindle, which he turned with a foot pedal like a spinning wheel. The spindle carrying the glasses was suspended in a little trough that held enough water to keep the rims of the glasses damp. The musician could then play the armonica comfortably seated in front of it, working the pedal with his foot and touching several glasses at once if he wanted to play chords instead of single notes.[136]

By the time Fithian came to Nomini Hall Carter had learned to play his armonica as well as the harpsichord, piano, guitar, violin, German flute, and organ. The tutor praised his employer's good instruments, his musical ear, and his "vastly delicate Taste." One evening in December 1773 Fithian wrote, "Mr. Carter spent in playing on the Harmonica. . . . The music is charming! He play'd, Water parted from the Sea," a song from Arne's new opera, *Artaxerxes*. Fithian thought it "the most captivating Instrument" he had ever heard because the sounds very much resembled the human voice.[137]

Perhaps Carter had mastered his new instrument well enough and quickly enough to play it in public concert less than a year after he ordered it. More probably, Pelham was the performer when Washington paid 3/9 "to hear the Armonica," for Carter would have been unlikely to charge admission.

No doubt there were many unrecorded concerts in Williamsburg like the one advertised in Fredericksburg in

December 1766 "for the Entertainment of all Gentlemen and Ladies" who would subscribe 7/6 for tickets. Several of "the best hands in Virginia" made up an orchestra of three violins, one tenor, one bass, two flutes, one hautboy, one horn, one harpsichord. The music began at six in the evening and was followed by "a genteel Supper, and Liquor suitable for such an Occasion." After supper subscribers were promised a ball that would last "as long as the Ladies stay."[138]

Informal concerts in Williamsburg homes, like those in plantation houses, were often spontaneous affairs for the entertainment of musical guests.[139] John Blair's family, for example, loved music. In 1751, the year of his extant almanac diary, he mentioned five evenings spent in this way in private houses and two at the College.[140] Not everyone, of course, enjoyed his near neighbors' music. As one would expect, Colonel Landon Carter had something to say about this annoyance. Reviewing the day's conversation at Mount Airy, he wrote in his diary on August 21, 1771:

> No news of any sort, only the last rains in July destroyed the crops full as much as the fresh had done, and that Ld. Dunmore's dogs had raised the price of beef in the market of Wmsburgh, and I do suppose they must make a goodly addition to the present modes of concerts, for I hear from every house a constant tuting may be listened to, from one instrument or another, whilst the vocal dogs will no doubt compleat the howl.[141]

## BALLS AND ASSEMBLIES

The amusement that attracted most ladies to Williamsburg during Publick Times was dancing—not only the elegant Palace entertainment that marked the close of every patriotic celebration, but also the less exclusive assemblies in taverns, impromptu dances following concerts, and pri-

vate balls in town houses and nearby plantation homes. When William Byrd was young he loved to dance and attended balls of all kinds when he was in town on public and private business. In the spring and fall of 1709 he was one of the merry company who danced at the home of Colonel David Bray and at Philip Ludwell's country house, Green Spring.[142] One night at Colonel Bray's he did not join in the dancing but "got some kisses among" the "abundance" of ladies present and so enjoyed the evening.

The queen's birthnight ball in 1711 followed an elegant supper at Governor Spotswood's house. About seven o'clock, in spite of the rain, the company went in coaches to the Capitol, where the governor opened the ball with a French dance; Mrs. Byrd was his partner, while Byrd danced with Mrs. Russell.[143] Then they danced country dances for an hour and "the company was carried into another room where was a very fine collation of sweetmeats." At about two o'clock everyone went home, and "because the drive was dirty the Governor carried the ladies into their coaches"—a final bit of the gallantry that characterized his behavior all evening. His servants, too, had behaved well. The next day Byrd learned why: Spotswood had made a bargain with them "that if they would forbear to drink upon the Queen's birthday, they might be drunk this day. They observed their contract and did their business very well and got very drunk today."[144]

In the fall of 1711 dancing was part of wedding festivities that Byrd enjoyed in the homes of Colonel Bray and Mungo Ingles.[145] Then, too, there was an impromptu affair arranged by Dr. William Cocke on November 2. After a long session of the General Court, Governor Spotswood invited a group to dinner, where, Byrd explained, "The table was so full that the Doctor and Mrs. Graeme and I had a little table to ourselves and were more merry than the rest of the company. . . . In the meantime the Doctor secured two fiddlers and candles were sent to the capitol and then the company followed and we had a ball and danced till about 12 o'clock at night."[146]

Again in 1720 Byrd recorded dancing as one of his amusements when he attended Council meetings. In the spring there were two days of dancing and feasting at a christening in the home of Major Robert Mumford, his lawyer and business agent.[147] That fall was an especially active social season. The dancing masters Stagg and De-Graffenreidt gave assemblies at the Capitol. Stagg's cost Byrd a guinea, and at DeGraffenreidt's he danced four dances and ate plumcake.[148] Governor Spotswood sponsored assemblies regularly once a week during the season, either on Thursdays or Fridays, where the dancing stopped at ten o'clock and a supper was served. After supper dancing was resumed until two o'clock, or else the ladies retired and some of the men played cards.[149] One of the social rules for such occasions was illustrated by the behavior of "King" Carter's daughter Anne, who was then about twenty-one years old. At one of the governor's assemblies Byrd asked her to dance a minuet, "but she pretended she was tired and yet danced soon after with Mr. Armistead, without any meaning but only for want of knowing the world."[150]

In later years Byrd seldom danced, although he sometimes attended balls. For the king's birthnight in 1740 Commissary Blair "entertained well" with a ball and refreshments at the Capitol. As president of the Council Blair was acting in Gooch's place, and Byrd "ventured" to the Capitol but left at ten o'clock after eating three jellies.[151]

Innkeepers and dancing masters customarily arranged spring and fall assemblies, primarily for their guests and students, but anyone could attend who wished to purchase a ticket. These assemblies were advertised in the *Virginia Gazette* often enough to suggest some degree of regularity in their scheduling, yet the advertising itself was irregular.

In the 1730s the widows of DeGraffenreidt and Stagg, who were teaching dancing, held both balls and assemblies and advertised them without making clear the distinction between them. Assemblies were always in the Capitol and tickets usually cost half a pistole; balls were sometimes given in Mrs. DeGraffenreidt's home, where for the admission charge of five shillings she furnished music, candles, and liquors or a "collation." Mrs. Stagg sometimes included a raffle as an added attraction at her assemblies.[152] In 1745 and 1746 Byrd's friend William Dering advertised assemblies at the Capitol every other night during spring and fall court.[153] Another dancing master, Richard Coventon, proposed to have a ball for his scholars at the courthouse on Thursday, October 31, 1751, and such ladies and gentlemen who were pleased to favor him with their company were invited to purchase tickets at half a pistole each.[154] That year tavern keepers, too, were advertising assemblies: Mrs. Anne Shields at the courthouse, Henry Wetherburn at his tavern, and Alexander Finnie in the Apollo Room at the Raleigh Tavern. The entrance fee was half a pistole and the entertainment was promised once a week while the General Court sat.[155]

In English towns, assemblies connoted a ball and a feast for subscribers only, rather than by general admission ticket; sometimes they were held in special assembly halls built by the members and supplied with rooms other than ballrooms, like private clubs.[156] In Virginia they seem to have been less exclusive, but refreshments of some kind were usually served. Subscription balls in the Capitol were sponsored by the House of Burgesses or the Council. Washington as a burgess paid £1 subscription to the Burgesses' Ball on several occasions and sometimes bought additional tickets, but when he attended the Council's Ball at the Capitol, he went as a guest and paid no fees.[157]

## RACES

On the eve of the Revolution J. F. D. Smyth reported:

There are races at Williamsburg twice a year; that is, every spring and fall, or autumn. Adjoining to the town is a very excellent course, for either two, three or four mile heats. Their purses are generally raised by subscription, and are gained by the horse that wins two four-mile heats out of three; they amount to an hundred pounds each for the first day's running, and fifty pounds each every day after; the races commonly continuing for a week. There are also matches and sweepstakes very often, for considerable sums.[158]

These races were first advertised in the fall of 1737, to take place every Saturday until October "at the Race Ground near this City."[159] Since the race track was then well known, it had been in use for some time—how long we do not know. An early reference to it is in Byrd's diary. On October 17, 1710, he noted: "About 9 o'clock we went to court where we sat till 12 and then adjourned to see the horse race and I lost 35 shillings."[160] He made no other mention of Williamsburg races until 1740, when he again attended or put up wagers on April 22, May 1, and October 30.[161] An important part of the Williamsburg fair of December 1739 was a horse race around the mile track each of the three days of the fair. First, second, and third prizes, furnished from the contributions of sponsors, were awarded each day: saddles, bridles, and whips, with a silver soup ladle substituted for the saddle on the second day.[162]

There were no further newspaper reports until the 1760s. The Williamsburg Purse was now regularly £100, and winners for the years 1766–1769 were as follows: Colonel John Tayloe's Traveller, spring, 1766; Tayloe's Hero, fall, 1766; Tayloe's Bellair, spring, 1767; William Byrd III's Valiant Tryall, fall, 1767; Captain Littlebury Hardyman's Partner, spring, 1768; Colonel Lewis Burwell of Gloucester's Remus, fall, 1768; Hardyman's Mark Anthony, spring, 1769.[163] These were subscription races where the purse was made up by patrons of the race who paid additional entry fees if they entered their horses. One of the regular subscribers was George Washington, who contributed £1 each spring and fall from 1759 to 1770;[164] yet he made no mention of attending a Williamsburg race, although he was sometimes in town when they were being held. Only once—in May 1759—did he note a bet on the outcome; that day he lost £4.[165]

The sweepstakes races that Smyth mentioned were announced in the spring of 1767 to be run annually for seven years beginning in October 1768. Each race was a four-mile heat, and the King's Plate rules were followed. Anthony Hay at the Raleigh Tavern collected the subscription money under the arrangement that "any person may enter for any particular Year, paying double Stakes for that Year, and standing afterwards as Subscribers."[166] Smyth's is the only evidence that these sweepstakes were ever run, for they were not reported in the *Virginia Gazette*. Formal racing in Virginia ended in 1774, and not until after the Revolution was there a jockey club organized.

## TAVERN CLUBS

The numerous inns and ordinaries in Williamsburg served as headquarters for everyone whose business brought him to town during Publick Times. Councillors and burgesses, ship captains and merchants, lawyers and clients, planters and frontiersmen could all depend upon finding the other men they wanted to see gathered in one of the taverns. Thus Williamsburg inns performed the chief function of contemporary coffeehouses and clubs in London.

But did the colonial institutions duplicate those in the mother country? During the course of the century Virginians used the labels *coffeehouse* and *club* from time to time, yet so casually that their meaning today is obscure. Students of the Revolutionary movement in Virginia would like to know whether Williamsburg had political clubs analogous to the Junto in Philadelphia or the Kit-Cat in London or the Jacobin in Paris. Social historians would like to know the place of clubs in the Virginia way of life. Yet no study of them has been made because the available bits of information about them only invite speculation. Cautious speculation, however, seems an improvement over timid silence, and there is some evidence.

London at the opening of the eighteenth century had between 2,000 and 3,000 coffeehouses; there, for a penny fee, anyone could spend between-meal hours smoking, drinking, talking, reading newspapers furnished by the house, or playing cards. The accommodations always included tables and chairs, newspapers, cards, tobacco, pipes, tea and coffee, and sometimes also light refreshments and alcoholic beverages. Gradually men of similar interests came to frequent the same coffeehouses—lawyers at one, doctors at another, or writers, gamesters, Whigs, and Tories—and they so dominated the general rooms that the houses were in effect closed to the public. Toward the end of the century there were as many exclusive private clubs as there had been democratic coffeehouses at the beginning; although the name had not always changed, the tone and character of the patronage was different and clubs served business and political interests as well as social ones.[167] Merchants in foreign trade met at Lloyd's; doctors at Batson's; booksellers at the Chapter; writers at the Bedford or George's; politicians at Will's or the Kit-Cat; gamesters at White's. American colonials when they "went home" learned the uses of London coffeehouses and clubs and by the end of the seventeenth century had reproduced their essential features in Boston, Philadelphia, and New York taverns.

In the eighteenth century Virginians, too, had what they called coffeehouses.[168] The first use of the name that has been found in the historical record occurs in William Byrd's diary entry on June 20, 1709: "In the evening I sent for Mr. Clayton from the coffeehouse, to whom I gave a bottle of white wine."[169] By the end of 1712 the diarist himself had visited the coffeehouse more than a hundred times, always in such a matter-of-course manner that he never mentioned its location or named the proprietor; however, the reader of the diary can tell that the coffeehouse was close to the Capitol[170] and that it was operated as a tavern too.[171] The proprietor regularly served coffee, tea, wine, and light refreshments between meals and offered facilities for a number of people to sit down while they talked, smoked, drank, gambled, read letters and newspapers, wrote letters, and set in order business and political papers. In the evening it was an amusement center for gambling at cards and dice, for horseplay and practical jokes, social drinking, and conversation. The high spirits of Byrd's friends among the patrons is suggested in comments like these:

> October 27, 1709. . . . We drank some of Will Robinson's cider till we were very merry and then went to the coffeehouse and pulled poor Colonel Churchill out of bed. I went home about one o'clock in the morning.
>
> November 1, 1709. . . . We were very merry and in that condition went to the coffeehouse and again disturbed Colonel Churchill. About 11 o'clock I went home and said a short prayer.
>
> November 15, 1710. . . . Then [after dinner] we went to the coffeehouse where I wrote a sham letter to Dr. Cocke under the name of Mary F–x. Soon after he came and the letter was delivered to him. Then we played at cards.

*40. The Smokers. Colored engraving, artist unknown.*

November 24, 1710. . . . I directed a letter to Nat Burwell with a lampoon in it and threw it into the capitol and Mr. Simons found it and gave it him, which put the House of Burgesses into a ferment, but I discovered to nobody that I had a hand in it. . . . Then [after dinner] we went to the coffeehouse where I played at cards and I lost my money but was diverted to see some of the burgesses so concerned at the lampoon.

November 26, 1710. . . . In the afternoon we sat and drank a bottle of cider till about 5 o'clock and then adjourned to the coffeehouse [from Marot's where they had dined]. Before we had been there long, in came George Mason [II] very drunk and told me before all the company that it was I that wrote the lampoon and that Will Robinson dropped it. I put it off as well as I could but it was all in vain for he swore it.

On visits to Williamsburg recorded in the next surviving part of the diary (1720–1721) Byrd went to *the club* instead of to *the coffeehouse,* and he dined there when he had no invitation to dinner in a private home. Now he was meeting friends at his lodgings[172] or at the homes of fellow councillors who maintained town houses.

What is the significance of this change from "coffeehouse" to "club"? Is it an accident of language? Byrd used the latter word only once.[173] Does it mean no more than a change in the requirements of his daily routine now that he was a widower with no family so long as his daughters remained in England? His middle-aged friends often brought their families along when they came to Williamsburg, and Byrd could find in taverns few congenial contemporaries to help him while away his evenings. Then, too, his eligibility as a widower made a difference in his social life; the colonial father's concern with his matchmaking responsibilities is reflected in Byrd's card playing habits these years when stakes were never high, his partners were often women, and the games were nearly always one of several sociable amusements in private homes in the evening.

Or does the change of term reflect Byrd's tacit recognition in Williamsburg of a parallel development he had recently learned to accept in London? Here, again, we have only hints about the nature of the club and the identity of the tavern where it met. The context suggests Mrs. Sullivan's, the ordinary operated by Jean Marot's widow on the site of Marot's Ordinary. This building was the English coffeehouse that Daniel Fisher described in 1751. Its location meets the requirements of Byrd's coffeehouse of 1709–1712; yet on November 26, 1710, he had dined at Marot's *and then adjourned to the coffeehouse,* and so Burdett's Ordinary or the Palmer House are better guesses for the earlier period. The importance of Byrd's use of the word *club* suffers, too, from the fact that in the third portion of the diary (1739–1741) he reverted to *coffeehouse*. His longest stay in town at this period was from April 14 to May 6, 1740, only twice during those weeks did he visit the coffeehouse, and then he only stopped in briefly.[174] In short, Byrd's recorded experience with Virginia coffeehouses and clubs suggests only informal social and business functions.

Does later evidence present the same picture? Another diarist, George Washington, mentioned visits to clubs in Williamsburg taverns, and he recorded expenditures there as well. He used club facilities at a number of different taverns whenever he was in town, no matter where he was lodging. At the Raleigh Tavern from 1754 through 1774 he paid club fees to Finnie (1754–1763), Trebell (1763–1766), Hay (1767–1770), and Southall (1771–1774). Mrs. Campbell was paid club expenses from 1762 through 1774—while she operated a "coffeehouse" on the site of Burdett's Ordinary and after she opened her "tavern" back of the Capitol on Waller Street. He used Mrs. Vobe's club facilities from 1763 (when her ordinary was on the site of the present Campbell's Tavern) through 1774 (when she was managing the King's Arms). He patronized Richard Charlton's club in 1767 and 1768; Southall's when he was in the Wetherburn Tavern (before 1771); Robert Anderson's at the same location (after 1771); and once—in 1766—Joseph Pullet's brick tavern on Main Street. Washington used all these tavern clubs for the same purposes that Byrd indicated in the Williamsburg coffeehouse half a century earlier. When the meeting was political, he so labeled it. On May 18, 1769, the day following the organization of Virginia's nonimportation association in the Apollo Room at the Raleigh, he entered in his ledger: "By Anthony Hays Acct. 32/9d. and Club at Do. arising from the Assn. meetg. there 20/."[175] When the word "club" in this entry is read in the context of the two ledgers that record so many similar expenditures over a period of twenty years, it cannot be interpreted to mean a closely knit group of politicians following a party line over a period of years, and no analogy to London's October Club or Friends of the People can be drawn.

Washington's diaries offer one additional detail concerning club arrangements. On March 11, 1773, he "Dined and Spent the Evening in the Club Room at Mrs. Campbell's."[176] In summary, he tells us that his clubs were informal gatherings of friends who dined together, talked, and sometimes played cards in taverns because they did not maintain town houses. Such groups were so common that innkeepers generally served them as a unit and sometimes provided separate or private rooms for them. His club fees were not the same thing as today's club dues: they included his share of the total bill for food and drink at any given dinner as well as the proprietor's charge for the use of the room and other facilities of the tavern; therefore, they varied

according to the number of persons present and the nature of the refreshments.

Other personal accounts that listed club fees include Thomas Jefferson's, John Page's, and Robert Wormeley Carter's. Jefferson's papers are less informative than Washington's because his accounts are not supplemented by diary entries. He paid a regular fee of 7½d. "at Coffee house" quite often in 1768 and 1769 but at no regular intervals; sometimes the entry occurs every day for a week, then not at all for ten days, then is resumed spasmodically for the remainder of that visit. On October 23, 1769, he spent 5/9 at Ayscough's for dinner and *club*;[177] on April 29, 1769, he had paid the same amount there for dinner "etc."[178]—probably for club services then too. He used the word again on May 5, 1773, when he "Pd club in arrack 1/3."[179] The reader immediately notices that Washington's favorite clubs do not appear on Jefferson's list. Jefferson's "Coffee house" may have been Mrs. Vobe's ordinary on Waller Street.[180] Christopher and Anne Ayscough kept a small ordinary where the gunsmith's shop now is. Probably there was no significant difference in the taste of the two burgesses, no basis for a guess that the "young men in a hurry" congregated in taverns back of the Capitol while the old hands walked in the opposite direction when they left the building and gathered in taverns on Duke of Gloucester Street. Jefferson's preference for Ayscough's may reflect only his gustatory tastes: Anne Ayscough had been Governor Fauquier's cook when the young student dined at the Palace, and he may have followed a favorite cuisine to its new location.

Other sources of information about Williamsburg tavern clubs furnish only isolated bits. John Page's almanac diary for 1774 baldly records three payments: on July 7, to dinner and club 5/7½; on August 6, to club 3/; on October 15, club 5¾.[181] Page's only hint concerning the identity of the club is the negative suggestion that it was not connected with the social and intellectual-scientific societies of which he was a member, the F. H. C. and the Society for the Promotion of Useful Knowledge; he paid these dues separately.

Robert Wormeley Carter's almanac diaries—so informative about his gaming habits—rarely record visits to Williamsburg and contain only one reference to clubs there. On April 17, 1766, he paid 10/ for club and dinner at Joseph Pullet's.[182] It will be recalled that Pullet's was one of Washington's clubs; he was there on May 2 of that year.

An additional bit of evidence occurs in one of the miscellaneous papers of Richard King's estate. On May 11, 1725, King was indebted to Thomas Crease for "Your Club in Punch 1/10½,"[183] refreshments served at Crease's ordinary on the site of the present Taliaferro-Cole House. The most interesting element in this entry is the date, 1725. Here was a little-known tavern offering club services nearly thirty years earlier than we have been accustomed to suppose them characteristic accommodations. When we read this entry along with Byrd's use of the word in 1720, our guess about the nature and date of Williamsburg clubs and coffeehouses becomes a tentative conclusion.

When colonial Virginians came to the capital during Publick Times, they lodged in ordinaries if they did not own town houses or stay with friends living nearby. Their choice of lodging places was determined by the same personal considerations that govern a modern visitor's selection of hotel accommodations. Councillors, burgesses, lawyers practicing in the General Court, merchants with a large volume of tidewater business—men who were in town each spring and fall—tended to patronize the same taverns year after year. Innkeepers, engaged in a highly competitive business, catered to the needs of regular customers. The need common to all lodgers was a comfortable and convenient place to meet friends and business associates, and innkeepers filled these requirements as best they could. A large establishment like the Raleigh could accommodate several groups at the same time with separate rooms; while some dined, others gambled or planned the next day's business at the Capitol. In a small ordinary like Ayscough's, friends might dine together often enough to reserve one of the tables in the common room, ordering special dinners in advance and lumping all expenses together into a "club" arrangement that permitted them to spend the evening together, using the accommodations of the house as if they all lodged there.

In their efforts to make a living, innkeepers moved about from place to place with a frequency that bewilders the historian. Furthermore, they sometimes changed the names of their establishments in order to attract more or better patronage. *Coffeehouse* and *club* were attractive labels because they connoted the kind of accommodations one would find in London. But Williamsburg was a town, not a city, and the specialization necessary to duplicate the London institutions was not profitable or desirable so long as their conveniences could be provided along with regular tavern services. A Williamsburg club, then, can best be defined as a colonial adaptation of a British social institution, one of many practical compromises that enabled Virginians to feel that they had built in the wilderness a way of life closely resembling the pattern at home.

# APPENDIX A.  CARD GAMES
## Eighteenth-Century Rules of Play

ALL-FOURS. Cotton's *Compleat Gamester,* pp. 53–55.

*All-Fours* is a game very much play'd in Kent, and very well it may, since from thence it drew its first original; and although the game may be lookt upon as trivial and inconsiderable, yet I have known Kentish gentlemen and others of very considerable note, who have play'd great sums of money at it, yet that adds not much to the worth of the game, for a man may play away an estate at *One and Thirty;* as I knew one lose a considerable sum *at most at three throws.*

This game I conceive is called All-Fours from *Highest, Lowest, Jack,* and *Game,* which is the set as some play it, but you may make from seven to fifteen, or more if you please, but commonly eleven.

There are but two can play at it at a time, and they must lift for dealing, the highest Put-card deals, who delivers to his adversary three cards, and to himself the like, and the like again, and having six apiece, he turns up a card which is Trump; if Jack (and that is any Knave) it is one to the dealer.

If he to whom the cards were dealt after perusal of his game like them not, he hath the liberty of begging one; if the dealer refuse to give him one, then he deals three apiece more, but if he then turns up a card of the same suit, he deals further till he turns up a card of another suit. [In modern Seven Up, he "stands" or "begs" the trump suit. If he "begs" and the dealer refused to agree to dealing three more cards to each hand and turning up another trump, then the dealer must give him one; i.e., the elder hand scores 1 extra point as "gift." Cotton's rule may be interpreted in this manner.]

Here note, that an Ace is four, a King is three, a Queen is two, a Knave one, and a Ten is ten [in counting for the fourth point, Game].

Now you must play down your cards, but to what advantage I cannot here prescribe, it must be according to the cards you have in your hand managed by your judgment to the best advantage.

Having play'd your cards you reckon, if you are highest and lowest of what is Trumps, you reckon two; if you are only highest but one, and the like of Jack and Game; sometimes you are Highest, Lowest, Jack, and Game, and then you must reckon four; the game is he that tells most after the cards are play'd, and therefore a Ten is a very significant card, which crafty gamesters know so well that they will frequently take out of a pack two Tens, and hide them contrary to the knowledg of the other, which is a great advantage to this foul player, if he play of the same suit of these Tens he hath absconded, for it must of necessity secure him from losing the game.

Here note, that he that wins Jack wins one also; and furthermore observe that for advantage reneging is allowable if you have Trumps in your hand to trump it.

There is another sort of All-fours called *Running-All-Fours,* at which they play one and thirty up, and in this game the dealer hath a great advantage, for if he turn up an Ace it is four, a King three, a Queen two, and a Knave one, and these are the same also in play. A Ten is the best card for making up.

[In *Pitch,* a variation of All-Fours, the trump suit is determined by "pitching"; that is, leading a card of that suit. See Albert H. Morehead and Geoffrey Mott-Smith, *Hoyle's Rules of Games* (N. Y., 1946, or later editions) under "Auction Pitch, or Setback" and "Smudge, or Pitch."]

**BASSET,** *a French Game.* Cotton's *Compleat Gamester.*

This game, amongst all those on the cards, is accounted to be the most courtly, being properly, by the understanders of it, thought only fit for Kings and Queens, great Princes, Noblemen, etc. to play at, by reason of such great losses, or advantages, as may possibly be on one side or other, during the time of play.

It is in its nature not much unlike our late *Royal Oak Lottery.* And as that, by the lottery-man's having five figures in two and thirty for himself, must certainly be a considerable profit to him in length of time; so here the dealer that keeps the Bank, having the first and last card at his own disposal, and other considerable privileges in the dealing the cards, has (without doubt) a greater prospect of gaining, than those that play. This was a truth so acknowledg'd in France, that the King made a publick edict, that the privilege of a *Talliere,* or one that keeps the Bank at Basset, should only be allow'd to principal *Cadets,* or sons of great families, supposing that whoever was so befriended, as to be admitted to keep the Bank, must naturally in a very short time, become possessor of a considerable estate.

But all others, for fear of ruining private persons and families, are confin'd politickly to a Twelvepenny Bank tho' here they have the liberty of staking what they please.

### *The Terms of the Game are these.*

| | |
|---|---|
| Talliere, | The Pay, |
| Croupiere, | The Alpiew, |
| Punter, | Sept-et-le-va, |
| The Fasse, | Quinze-et-le-va, |
| The Couch, | Trent-et-le-va |
| The Paroli, | Soissant-et-le-va, etc. |
| The Masse, | |

### *The Explanation of the Terms.*

1. The *Talliere* is he that keeps the Bank, who lays down a sum of money before all those that play, to answer every winning card that shall appear in his course of dealing.

2. The *Croupiere* is one that is assistant to the *Talliere,* and stands by to supervise the losing cards; that when there are a considerable company at play, he may not lose by over-looking any thing that might turn to his profit.

3. The *Punter* is a term for every one of the gamesters that play.

4. The *Fasse* is the first card that is turn'd up by the *Talliere,* belonging to the whole pack, by which he gains half the value of the money that is laid down upon every card of that sort by the punters.

5. The *Couch* is a term for the first money that every punter puts upon each card, every one that plays having a Book of thirteen several cards before him, upon which he may lay his money, more or less, according to his fancy.

6. The *Paroli* is a term explain'd thus, that having won the couch or first stake, and having a mind to go on to get a *Sept-et-le-va,* you crook the corner of your card, letting your money lie without being paid the value of it by the Talliere.

7. The *Masse* is when you have won the couch, or first stake, and will venture more money upon the same card; which is only pursuant to the discretion of the Punter, who knows or ought to know the great advantages the *Talliere* has; and therefore should be subtle enough to make the best of his own game.

8. The *Pay* is when the Punter has won the couch, or first stake, whether a shilling, half-crown, crown, guinea, or whatever he lays down upon his card, and being fearful to make the Paroli, leaves off, for by going the Pay, if the card turns up wrong he loses nothing, having won the couch

before, but if by this adventure Fortune favours him, he wins double the money that he stakes.

9. The *Alpiew* is much the same thing as the Paroli, and like that term us'd when a couch is won, by turning up or crooking the corner of the winning card.

10. *Sept-et-le-va* is the first great chance that shews the advantages of this game: as for example, if the Punter has won the couch, and then makes a Paroli, by crooking the corner of his card, as is said before, and going on to a second chance, his winning Card turns up again, it comes to Sept-et-le-va, which is seven times as much as he laid down upon his card.

11. *Quinze-et-le-va* as next in its turn, is attending the Punter's humour who perhaps is resolv'd to follow his fancy, and still lay his money upon the same card, which is done by crooking the third corner of his card, which coming up by the dealing of the Talliere, makes him win fifteen times as much money as he stak'd.

12. *Trent-et-le-va* succeeds Quinze-et-le-va, and is mark'd by the lucky Punter, by crooking or bending the end of the fourth corner of his winning card, which coming up makes him purchaser of three and thirty times as much money as he laid down.

13. *Soissant-et-le-va* is the highest and greatest chance that can happen in the game, for it pays sixty seven times as much money as is stak'd, and is seldom won by some lucky Punter, who resolves to push the extream of his good fortune to the height. It cannot be won but by the Talliere's dealing the cards over again, which if his winning card turns up, pays him with such a prodigious advantage.

And as I sometimes have seen at the Royal-Oak Lottery (before mention'd) a figure come up, that by some guineas laid on it in full, by the winning eight and twenty times as much has broke the keeper of it; so by the courage and extraordinary luck of some pushing Punter at this game,

some great stake with Soissant-et-le-va may turn up, and by that means break the bank.

But this very rarely happens; the Talliere, like the Lottery-Man, being a great deal more likely to break the gamesters than they him. The sense of this great advantage which the dealer has (several families having been ruin'd by playing at it) has caus'd this game to be modell'd to a Twelvepenny Bank in France.

### *The Order of the Game is thus.*

They sit down round a table, as many as please, the Talliere in the midst of them, with the bank of money before him, and the Punters each having a book of thirteen cards, laying down one or two, three or more as they please, with money upon them, as stakes; then he takes the pack altogether in his hand, and turns them up, the bottom card appearing is call'd the Fasse and pays him half the value of money laid down by the Punters, upon any card of that sort as has been said before.

### *The Manner of the Play is thus.*

After the Fasse is turn'd up, and the Talliere and Croupiere have look'd round the cards on the table, and taken half the advantage of the money laid on them, he proceeds in his deal and the next card appearing, whether King, Queen, Ace, or whatever it be, wins for the Punter, who may receive, if he has laid money on such a sort of card the value, or making Paroli go on to a Sept-et-le-va, as has been said, the card after that wins for the Talliere, who takes money from each Punter's card of that sort, and brings it to his bank.

The Talliere's manner of expression in playing the game is thus: If the winning card be a King, and the next appearing after it be a Ten, then he says (shewing the cards that appear to all the Punters round) King wins, Ten loses, paying the money to such cards as are of the winning sort, and taking the money to supply his bank from those that lose; that done, he goes on with the deal, as, Ace wins, Five loses, Knave wins, Seven loses, and so every other card alternately winning and losing, till all the pack be dealt out but the last card.

The last card turn'd up (as I hinted before) is an advantage to the Talliere; because by the rule of the game, which was contriv'd for his benefit, tho' it be turn'd up, and the Punter may happen to have stak'd upon one of the same sort; yet it is allow'd as one of his dues, in relation to his office, and he pays nothing.

The Punter 'tis certain, who is luckily adventurous and can push on his Couch to a considerable stake, to Sept-et-le-va, Quinze-et-le-va, Trent-et-le-va, etc. if he have the fortune to arrive at that pitch, must in a wonderful manner, multiply his Couch or first stake; but that is so seldom done, considering the frequency of the Punter's losses, in comparison to the bank's advantage, that the dimmest eye may easily see, without a pair of spectacles, how much and considerable the design of this court game is in the favour of the Talliere.

The liberty that is used by our English pushing adventurers at this game, makes it of quite another kind than it is in France; for they (as has been said) are compell'd by the sovereign authority to stint the prodigal humours in Punting, and are only to play at a Twelvepenny Bank, where the losses or gains cannot be ruinous, nor so extravagant as to make a desolation in a family: But here in England, the Punters being oblig'd by no such confinement, have the liberty to stake one, two, three guineas or more upon a card, as I frequently have seen some of the nobility do at court, which, the Couch being Alpiew'd or Paroli'd to Sept-et-le-va, Quinze-et-le-va, Trent-et-le-va, etc. (which does

sometimes happen) must needs redound extremely to the Punter's profit, who by the advantage of the multiplication, must undoubtedly raise his Couch, or stake (if he be so couragious to make it valuable) to a very extraordinary sum: And if he be so befriended by Fortune, to bring it to Soissant-et-le-va, he is very likely to break the bank, by gaining a sum so bulky, that 'tis probable at present the Talliere is not able to pay.

But this (like snow in summer) is a rarity that happens very seldom, 'tho it sometimes has been, and therefore is indeed only a decoy for the Punter to urge him to venture his stake boldly: the Talliere's certain advantage, for all this specious demonstration of the Punter's probability of winning being plainly obvious and unanswerable, as shall further appear.

Suppose Ten, or any other card wins for the Punter, if another Ten comes up just after, in the winning card's place, it does not win for him but for the bank, but if it comes up three or four cards after that, it wins for the Punter: If Ace or any other card wins at first, and afterwards comes up again, in the next winning card's place, it does not go; but by a term they have for that part of the game, is said to *retire* till the next opportunity, because by the rule of the game, it must go for the bank before the Punter.

But then in return of this and subtilly to gain the esteem of all the young adventurers, who are apt to set their mony briskly, if the card happens to come in the next losing place, it does not lose, because it has not gone for the Punter, but also retires without paying the bank, having won a Couch, which the Talliere saves, and should have paid.

To conclude, this game, as the aforesaid Royal-Oak Lottery was formerly, is of so tempting and decoying a nature, by reason of several specious multiplications and advantages, which seemingly it offers to the unwary Punter, that a great many like it so well, that they will in some coffee-houses, and other publick places, play at small games rather than give out, and rather than not play at all, will punt at a Groat, Threepenny, Twopenny Bank, so much the hopes of winning the Quinze-et-le-va, and Trent-et-le-va intoxicates them; but the judicious whose love of gaming does not exceed his governable understanding, will not engage at it; or if he does, will play so warily as not to be drawn by the seeming profitable glosses, since 'tis most certain, that it cannot be upon the square, and that the *Talliere,* if he pays you twenty pound in one night's play, only gives you opportunity in another to lose an hundred.

## FIVE-CARD CRIBBAGE. Cotton's *Compleat Gamester,* pp. 51–53.

At *Cribbidge* there are no cards to be thrown out, but all are made use of; and the number of the set is sixty-one.

It is an advantage to deal, by reason of the Crib, and therefore you must lift for it, and he that hath the least card deals.

There are but two players at this game, the one shuffles and the other cuts, the dealer delivers out the cards one by one, to his antagonist first and himself last, till five apiece be dealt to one another; the rest being set down in view on the table, each looketh on his game, and ordereth his cards for the best advantage.

He that deals makes out the best cards he can for his Crib, and the other the worst, because he will do him as little good as he can, being his Crib; which Crib is four cards, two a piece, which they lay out upon the table, not knowing nor seeing one anothers cards, and then they turn up a card from the parcel that was left of dealing, and each of them may make use of that card to help them on in their game in hand, and when they have play'd out their three cards, and set up with counters their games in their hands,

the crib is the others the next deal, and so they take it by turns.

The value of the cards is thus. Any fifteen upon the cards is two, whether nine and six, ten and five, King and five, seven and eight, etc.

A *Pair* is two, a *Pair-Royal* six, a double *Pair-Royal* twelve, *Sequences of three* is two, *Sequences of four* is four, *of five* five, etc. and so is a *Flush of three,* three; *of four,* four, etc. *Knave Noddy* is one in hand and two to the dealer; that is, if you have a Knave of that suit which is turned up, it is *Knave Noddy.* A pair of Aces, Kings, Queens, Knaves, Tens, etc. is two; Three Aces, Kings, Queens, etc. is a *Pair-Royal;* a double *Pair-Royal* is four Aces, four Kings, four Queens, etc. and is twelve games to him that hath them.

Having lookt on your cards, you count your game after this manner. Suppose you have in your hand a nine and two sixes, after you have laid out two cards for the Crib, that makes you six games, because there is two fifteens and a pair, by adding your nine to the two sixes, and if a six chance to be turn'd up, then you have twelve games in your hand; for though you must not take the turn'd up card into your hand, yet you may make what use you can of it in counting, so that the three sixes makes you six, being a *Pair-Royal,* and the nine added to every six makes three fifteens, which six more added to the former, make twelve, which you must set up with counters or otherwise, that your opponent may know what you are, though you must not see his cards, nor he yours; if you think he plays foul by reckoning too much, you may count them after the hand is play'd.

Thus you have set up your twelve, your opposite it may be hath four, five, and six in his hand; that is two, because of *Sequences of three;* then it is two more because it is four, five and six; again, taking in the counting six that is turn'd up, that is in all four, then there is fifteen and fifteen, four and five is nine, and six is fifteen, and then with the six turn'd up 'tis fifteen more, which makes eight games, this he likewise sets up, keeping his cards undiscovered. Here note, he that deals not sets up three in lieu thereof.

Having thus done, he that dealt not plays first, suppose it a six, if you have a nine play it, that makes fifteen, for which set up two, the next may play a four which makes nineteen, you a six twenty five, and he a five that is thirty, you being not able to come in, having a six in your hand, he sets up one (for it is one and thirty you aim at in playing the cards), because he is most, and two for Sequences four, five, and six, which were his four after the fifteen, your five and his six; and that doth not hinder them from being Sequences, though the six was play'd between the four and the five; but if an Ace, Nine, King, Queen, or the like, had been play'd between, they had been no Sequences, so the two for the Sequences, and the one for thirty being most (as at one and thirty) makes him three, which he must set up to the rest of his game, and in this playing of the cards you may make *Pairs, Sequences, Flush, Fifteens, Pair-Royals,* and double *Pair-Royals,* if you can, though that is rarely seen.

Lastly, you look upon your Crib, that is the two cards apiece laid out at first, which is the dealers; if he find no games in them, nor help by the card that was turn'd up, which he takes into his hand, then he is bilkt, and sometimes it so happens that he is both bilkt in hand and crib. Thus they play and deal by turns till the game of sixty one be up.

Here note, if you get the game before your adversary is forty five (forty four will not do it) you must then say, I have *lurkt* you, and that is a double game for whatever you play'd with six shilling, or a greater summ.

LOO or LANTERLU. Cotton's *Compleat Gamester,* pp. 68–70.

[Cotton's rules describe only the five-card, limited game. Hoyle did not include Loo in his books, probably for the same reason that he omitted Put. By the end of the eighteenth century, the three-card game was the more popular one, and changes had been made in the five-card Loo that was played in Cotton's time. In the rules that follow here, Cotton's are given first; then in brackets, later changes in the five-card game and rules for the three-card game adapted from a nineteenth-century Hoyle and from J. Warren, *Rules for Three Card Loo,* summarized in the *Encyclopedia Britannica,* 14th edition.]

*Lanterloo* is a Game may be plaid several ways, but I shall insist on none but two; the first way is thus.

Lift for dealing, and the best Put-card carries it; as many may play as the cards will permit, to whom must be dealt five apiece, and then turn up Trump. Now if three, four, five, or six play, they may lay out the threes, fours, fives, sixes, and sevens to the intent they may not be quickly Lood; but if they would have the Loos come fast about then play with the whole pack.

Having dealt set up five scores or chalks; and then proceed forwards in your game. He that is eldest hand hath the priviledg of passing by the benefit thereof, that is, he hath the advantage of hearing what every one will say, and at last may play or not play according as he finds his game good or bad. If the eldest saith he passeth, the rest may chuse whether they will play or no.

You may play upon every card what you please, from a penny to a pound. [This seems to mean that the amount of each player's stake in the pool is determined before the cards are dealth and that this amount must be divisible by 5; i.e., each player stakes so much for each trick. The rules of play make no provision for separate bets on each trick while the hand is being played.] Trumps as at Whist are the best cards, all others in like manner take their precedency from the highest to the lowest.

You must not revoke, if you do you pay all on the table. If you play and are *Loo'd* (that is, win never a trick) you must lay down to the stock so much for your five cards as you plaid upon every one of them.

Every deal rub off a score, and for every trick you win set up a score by you till the first scores are out, to remember you how many tricks you have won in the several deals in the game.

All the chalks for the game being rub'd out, tell your own scores, and for so many scores or tricks which you have won, so much as they were valued at in the game so much you must take from the stock; thus must every one do according to the number of tricks he hath won.

Here note, that he who hath five cards of a suit in his hand Loos all the gamesters then playing, be they never so many, and sweeps the board; if there be two Loos he that is eldest hand hath the advantage. [Cotton does not describe the second way mentioned in his first sentence.]

As there is cheating (as they say) in all trades, so more particularly intolerable in gaming; as in this for example. If one of the gamesters have four of a suit and he want a fifth, he may for that fifth make an exchange out of his own pocket if he be skil'd in the cleanly art of conveiance; if that fail, some make use of a friend, who never fails to do him that kind office and favour. There are other cheats to be performed, which I shall omit, since it is not my business to teach you how to cheat, but so to play as not to be cheated.

[Pam was in use before 1712, for Pope's *Rape of the Lock,* III, 62, reads: "Ev'n mighty Pam, that Kings and Queens o'er threw And mow'd down armies in the fights of Lu." Along with the wild card, which takes the Ace of trumps, was introduced the flush as the winning hand. Later rules explain that the leader must play a trump if he has one, and other players must play their highest trump. If the leader plays another suit, others may follow suit or trump, as they wish.

In three-card Loo, there is a "widow" or "miss" of three cards. In the first hand, each player stakes the amount agreed upon and they cut for the deal; subsequently the deal rotates to the left. Using a 52-card pack, dealer deals three cards to each player plus three to the miss, one card at a time. Then he turns up the next card for trumps and places it face up on top of the undealt cards. After the deal, the elder hand looks at his cards and announces that he will play, or pass, or take miss. If he passes, he places his cards face down on the table, and the player on his left has the privilege of choosing the miss or passing or playing. If the elder hand takes the miss, he places his own hand face down on the table and picks up the miss, which he must play. Players to the left of the one who chooses miss have only two choices to make in that hand: they either play or pass.

When play begins, the elder hand places his highest trump in front of him on the table, face up, and the play proceeds as in whist except that each player keeps his own cards in front of him instead of collecting the tricks he has taken. (The game looks more like cribbage as play goes forward.) The player holding the highest trump of course wins the first trick. When he leads in the second trick, he may play either of his two remaining cards (except when he has only one opponent; in this case he must play a trump if he has one). Other players must follow suit or trump if they can; holding neither the suit led nor trump, they may play whatever they wish.

Tricks are counted and the pool is divided so that the winner of each trick receives one-third of the pool. Those who play and win no trick are looed, and they must make up among them the pool for the next hand. Thus if five players originally contributed six counters each, the pool of thirty is divided thus: Player A passed; he receives nothing and contributes nothing to the next pool. Player B took one trick; he receives ten counters. Player C took two tricks; he receives twenty counters. Players D and E were looed; they receive nothing and each contributes fifteen counters to the next pool. If the game is unlimited, then D and E each contributes thirty counters, and the next pool is sixty.

When only one player stands in, the dealer must play. In some rules, he may play the miss either for himself or for the pool. In the latter case, his winnings go into the next pool.]

PIQUET. Cotton's *Compleat Gamester,* pp. 39–43.

Before you begin the game at picket, you must throw out of the pack the deuces, treys, fours, and fives, and play with the rest of the cards, which are in number thirty and six.

The usual set is an hundred, not but that you may make it more or less; the last card deals and the worst is the dealers.

The cards are all valued according to the number of the spots they bear [court cards (King, Queen, and Knave) count ten], the Ace only excepted, which wins all other cards, and goes for eleven.

The dealer shuffles, and the other cuts, delivering what number he pleaseth at a time, so that he exceed not four nor deal under two, leaving twelve on the table between them. [i.e., The dealer (or "younger") deals twelve cards to his opponent, twelve to himself and twelve to the stock or widow—either two, three, or four at a time.]

[Scoring: Blank]    He that is the elder, having lookt over his cards, and finding never a court-card among them, says *I have* a blanck, [later called "declaring a *carte blanche*": In order to score ten for this unusual hand, the player must declare it immediately, laying his cards on the table face up and announcing the number he intends to discard. He then takes the cards back into his hand, and the game proceeds with his discard, as though there were no *carte blanche* held.] and I intend to discard such a number of cards, and that you may see mine, discard you as many as you intend; this done, the eldest shows his cards and reckons ten for the blank, then taking up his cards again he discards those which he judgeth most fit: here note he is always bound to that number which he first propounded. This being done, he takes in as many from the stock as he laid out; and if it should chance to fall out that the other hath a blank too, the youngers blank shall bar the former and hinder his *Picy* and *Repicy,* though the eldest hands blank consists of the biggest cards.

[Discard]    It is no small advantage to the eldest to have the benefit of discarding, because he may take in eight of the twelve in the stock discarding as many of his own for them, not but that if he find it more advantageous he may take in a less number; after this the antagonist may take in what he thinks fit, acquitting his hand of the like number. Here note, that let the game be never so good the gamesters are both obliged to discard one card at least.

[Scoring: Ruff]    After the discarding you must consider the *Ruff,* that is how much you can make of one suit; the eldest speaks first, and if the youngest makes no more the Ruff is good, [The elder announces the number of cards in his longest suit. If the younger has no suit of this length, he replies, "Good"; if he holds a longer suit, he says, "Not Good," and takes over the privilege of counting points for the Ruff score. If his long suit contains the same number of cards as the elder's, he replies, "Equal"; the elder then announces the point value of his Ruff and the Ruff score is made by the suit of the higher point value.] and sets up one for every ten he can produce; as, for example, for thirty reckon three, for forty four, and so onward, withall take notice you are to count as many for thirty-five as for forty, and as much for forty-five as fifty, and so of the rest; but from thirty-five to thirty-nine you must count no more than for thirty-five, and so from thirty to thirty-four count no more than for thirty; and this rule is to be observed in all other higher numbers.

[Scoring: Sequences]     As for *Sequences* and their value after the Ruff is plaid, [i.e., counted] the elder acquaints you with his Sequences (if he have them) and they are *Tierces, Quarts, Quints, Sixiesms, Septiesms, Huictiesms* and *Neufiesms,* as thus; six, seven, and eight; nine, ten, and Knave; Queen, King, and Ace; which last is called a Tierce Major, because it is the highest. A Quart is a sequence of four cards, a Quint of five, a Sisixm [sic] of six, etc. These sequences take their denomination from the highest card in the sequence. It is a Tierce Major or a Tierce of an Ace when there is Queen, King, and Ace, a Tierce of a King when the King is the best Card; a Tierce of a Queen when there is neither King nor Ace, and so till you come to the lowest Tierce, which is a Tierce of an eight. You must reckon for every Tierce three, for a Quart four, but for a Quint fifteen, for a Sixiesm sixteen, and so upward; now what ever you can make of all you must add to your blank, and count the whole together.

Here note that the biggest Tierce, Quart, or other sequence, although there be but one of them makes all the others less sequences useless unto him be they never so many; and he that hath the biggest sequence by vertue thereof reckons all his less sequences, though his adversaries sequences be greater, and otherwise would have drowned them.

Farther observe, that a Quart drowns a Tierce, and a Quint a Quart, and so of the rest, so that he who hath a Sixiesm may reckon his Tierces, Quarts, or Quints, though the other may happen to have Tierce, Quart, etc. of higher value than the others are that hath the Sixiesm; trace the same method in all the other like sequences.

[Scoring: Trios etc.]     After you have manifested your sequences, you come to reckon your three Aces, three Kings, three Queens, three Knaves, or three Tens, as for Nines, Eights, Sevens, and Sixes, they have no place in this account; for every Ternary you count three, and they are in value as it is in sequences; Aces the highest and best, King next, after these Queens, then Knaves, and last of all Tens. The higher drowns the lower here as in the sequences. He that hath three Aces may reckon his three Queens, Knaves, or Tens, if he have them, though the other hath three Kings; and this is done by reason of his higher Ternary. Now he that hath four Aces, four Kings, four Queens, four Knaves, or four Tens, for each reckons fourteen, which is the reason they are called Quatorzes.

[Playing]     Now they begin to play the cards, the elder begins and younger follows in suit as at Whisk, and for every Ace, King, Queen, Knave, or Ten, he reckons one.

A card once play'd must not be recalled, unless he have a card of the same suit in his hand, if the elder hand plays an Ace, King, Queen, or Ten, for every such card he is to reckon one, which he adds to the number of his game before; and if the other be able to play upon it a higher card of the same suit, he wins the trick, and reckons one for his card as well as the other. Whosoever wins the last trick reckons two for it, if he win it with a ten, but if with any card under, he

123

reckons but one; then they tell their cards, and he that hath the most is to reckon ten for them.

[Scoring order]     After this, each person sets up his game with counters, and if the set be not up, deal again. Now a set is won after this manner, admit that each party is so forward in his game that he wants but four or five to be up, if it so happens that any of the two have a blank, he wins the set, because the Blanks are always first reckoned; but if no Blanks, then comes the Ruff, next your Sequences, then your Aces, Kings, Queens, Knaves, and Tens, next what cards are reckoned in play, and last of all the cards you have won.

[*Repicy*]     If any of the gamesters can reckon, either in Blanks, Ruffs, Sequences, Aces, etc. up to thirty in his own hand, without playing a card, and before the other can reckon anything, instead of thirty he shall reckon ninety, and as many as he reckons after above his thirty, adding them to his ninety; [i.e., he wins an additional 60 points if his gross score is 30 or more at this point in the game, before the hand is played] this is known by the name of a *Repicy*.

[*Picy*]     Moreover, he that can make in like manner, what by Blank, Ruff, Sequences, etc. up to the said number, before the other hath play'd a card, or reckoned anything, instead of thirty he reckons sixty, and this is called a *Picy*. [Either *Pique* or *Repique* is made by one player if he has scored 30 before the other has scored at all. *Pique* gives him a bonus of 30 points if his own gross 30 is scored partly in the play. For example, he might have 26 points before play begins—lacking 4 points for *Repique;* but if he takes the first four tricks *with face cards or ten's,* these 4 points give him *Pique.* If his opponent has scored for a Blank, a Ruff, a Sequence, or a Trio, he is ineligible for either *Pique* or *Repique.*] Here note, that if you can but remember to call for your Picy, or Repicy, before you deal again, you shall lose neither of them, otherwise you must.

[Capet]     He that wins more than his own cards reckons ten, but he that wins all the cards reckons forty, and this is called a *Capet*.

[Penalties &c.]     The rules belonging to this game are these. If the dealer give more cards than his due, whether through mistake or otherwise it lieth in the choice of the elder hand whether he shall deal again or no, or whether it shall be play'd out.

He that forgets to reckon his Blank, Ruff, Sequences, Aces, Kings, or the like, and hath begun to play his cards cannot recall them. So it is with him that showeth not his Ruff before he play his first card, losing absolutely all the advantage thereof.

He that misreckons anything, and hath play'd one of his cards, and his adversary finds at the beginning, middle, or end of the game, that he had not what he reckoned, for his punishment he shall be debar'd from reckoning anything he really hath, and his adversary shall reckon all he hath, yet the other shall make all he can in play. He that takes in more cards than he discardeth is liable to the same penalty.

He that throws up his cards imagining he hath lost the game, mingling them with other cards on the table though afterward he perceive his mistake, yet he is not allowed to take up his cards and play them out.

No man is permitted to discard twice in one dealing.

He that hath a Blank, his Blank shall hinder the other *Picy* and *Repicy,* although he hath nothing to shew but his Blank.

He that hath four Aces, Kings, Queens, etc. dealt him and after he hath discarded one of the four reckons the other three, and the other say to him *it is good;* he is bound to tell the other, if he ask him what Ace, King, Queen, etc. he wants.

If after the cards are cleanly cut, either of the gamesters know the upper card by the backside, notwithstanding this the cards must not be shuffled again. In like manner, if the dealer perceive the other hath cut himself an Ace, and would therefore shuffle again, this is not permitted; and if a card be found faced, it shall be no argument to deal again, but must deal on; but if two be found faced, then may he shuffle again.

Lastly, whosoever is found changing or taking back again any of his cards, he shall lose the game, and be accounted a foul player.

PUTT.   Cotton's *Compleat Gamester,* pp. 62–65.

*Putt* is the ordinary rooking game of every place, and seems by the few cards that are dealt to have no great difficulty in the play, but I am sure there is much craft and cunning in it; of which I shall show as much as I understand.

If you play at two-handed Putt (or if you please you may play at three hands) the best Putt-card deals. [The rank of put cards is trey, deuce, ace, king, queen, and so on down to four, the lowest card.] Having shuffled the cards, the adversary cuts them, then the dealer deals one to his antagonist, and another to himself till they have three apiece: five up or a Putt is commonly the game. The eldest if he hath a good game, and thinks it better than his adversaries, puts to him; if the other will not or dare not see him, he then wins one, but if he will see him they play it out, and he that wins two tricks or all three wins the whole set; but if each win a trick and the third tyed, neither win, because it is trick and tye. [Hoyle did not include Put in his analyses: mathematical calculations cannot be made

with precision because there is no draw or discard and in a two-handed game only six cards are dealt from a full deck of fifty-two.]

Sometimes they play without putting, and then the winner is he that wins most tricks. [Like Poker, Put begins with everyone staking; this is the "pot" won by total tricks, when there is no additional betting as each trick is played.] Here note that in your playing keep up your cards very close; for the least discovery of any one of them is a great advantage to him that sees it.

This game consists very much in daring; for a right gamester will put boldly upon very bad cards sometimes, as upon a five, seven and a nine; the other thinking he hath good cards in his adversaries hand, having very indifferent ones in his own dares not see him, and so by going to stock loseth one. Here note that he that once hath the confidence to put on bad cards cannot recal his putting, by which means he frequently pays for his bravado.

The best Putt-cards are first the Trey, next the Deuce, then the Ace, the rest follow in preheminence thus; the King, the Queen, the Knave, the Ten, and so onwards to the four, which is the meanest card at Putt.

Some of the cheats at Putt are done after this manner. First, for cutting to be sure of a good Putt-card, they use the *Bent,* the *Slick,* and the *Breef;* the Bent is a card bended in play which you cut, the Slick is when beforehand the gamester takes a pack of cards, and with a slick-stone smooths all the Putt-cards, that when he comes to cut to his adversary with his forefinger above and his thumb about the middle, he slides the rest of the cards off that which was slickt, which is done infallibly with much facility; but in this there is required neatness and dexterity for fear of discovery, and then your confidence in this contrivance will be vain and of no effect.

Lastly, the Breef in cutting is very advantagious to him

that cuts, and it is thus done. The cheat provides before-hand a pack of cards, whereof some are broader than others; under some of which he plants in play some good Putt-cards, which though they shuffle never so much they shall rarely separate them; by which means he that cuts (laying his fingers on the broad card) hath surely dealt him a Putt-card.

In dealing these rooks have a trick they call the *Spurr,* and that is, as good cards come into their hands that they may know them again by the outside (and so discover the strength or weakness of their adversaries game) I say some where on the outside they give them a gentle touch with their nail.

Now when they intend to bleed a *Col* to some purpose whom they have set before, they always fix half a score packs of cards before (as I have related in Whist) by slicking them or spurring them, that is, giving them such marks that they shall certainly know every card in the pack, and conse-quently every card that is in his adversaries hand, an advan-tage that cannot well be greater.

But if they are not furnished with such cards, and cannot accomplish their ends by the former indirect means without palpable discovery, then they have accomplices who standing by the innocent Col look over his Game, and discovers what it is to his adversary: and to strengthen their interest by cheating, they frequently carry about them Treys, Deuces, Aces, etc. in their pockets, which they use as need requires, or if not, they will steal them out of the pack whilst they are playing, which is the securest way and freest from discovery.

Lastly, they have one most egregious piece of roguery more, and that is playing the *High-game* at Putt; and this is to be done but once at a set-meeting; and therefore on this depends the absolute overthrow of the Col that plays, or the Col that is a stander by.

This High-game at Putt is thus performed: the rook whilst playing singles out the Deuces and Treys for the last game, and placeth them thus in order, hiding them in his lap or other covert, first a Deuce, then a Trey, next a Deuce, then a Trey, then a Trey and a Trey; now stooping letting fall a card or some other way as he shall think fit, he claps these cards fac'd at the bottom, having shuffled the cards before, and bids his adversary cut, which he nimbly and neatly with both his hands joyns the divided cards, and then the bottom fac'd cards are upwards, and then he deals, and lest there should be a discovery made of the facing, he palms them as much as he can, nimbly passing the last card.

Now do the gamesters smile at the goodness of each others game, one shows his to one, the other, his to another; and cries 'Who would not put at such cards?' The other in as brisk a tone, says, 'Come if you dare.' 'What will you lay of the game?' says the Rook. 'What you dare,' says the Col; then pausing a while the rook seems to consult with his friends, who cry, they know not what to think on't. 'Five pound,' cries a rooking confederate on this gentlemans side. The Col encouraged hereby, cries ten pound more: and thus the rook holds him in play till there be a good sum of money on the board; then answers the Putt of the now ruin'd Cully. They now play; the Col begins with a Deuce, the rook wins that with a Trey; the rook then plays a Deuce, and the Col wins it with his Trey; then he plays his Deuce which is won with a Trey; thus the rook wins the day. This game may be plaid otherways according to fancy: let these and the former cheats be a sufficient warning.

# APPENDIX B. TABLE GAMES

## Eighteenth-Century Rules of Play

**BILLIARDS.** Cotton's *Compleat Gamester*, pp. 12–18.

The gentile, cleanly and most ingenious game at *Billiards* had its first original from Italy, and for the excellency of the recreation is much approved of and plaid by most nations in Europe, especially in England there being few towns of note therein which hath not a publick Billiard-Table, neither are they wanting in many noble and private families in the country, for the recreation of the mind and exercise of the body.

The form of a Billiard-Table is oblong, that is something longer than it is broad; it is rail'd round, which rail or ledge ought to be a little swel'd or stuft with fine flox or cotton: the superficies of the table must be covered with green-cloth, the finer and more freed from knots the better it is: the board must be level'd as exactly as may be, so that a ball may run true upon any part of the table without leaning to any side thereof; but what by reason if ill-season'd boards which are subject to warp, or the floar on which it stands being uneven, or in time by the weight of the table, and the gamesters yielding and giving way, there are very few billiard-tables which are found true; and therefore such which are exactly level'd are highly valuable by a good player; for at a false table it is impossible for him to show the excellency of his art and skill, whereby bunglers many times by knowing the windings and tricks of the table have shamefully beaten a very good gamester, who at a true table would have given him three in five.

But to proceed in the description thereof; at the four corners of the table there are holes, and at each side exactly in the middle one, which are called hazards, and have hanging at the bottoms nets to receive the balls and keep them from falling to the ground when they are hazarded. I have seen at some tables wooden boxes for the hazards, six of them as aforesaid, but they are nothing near so commendable as the former, because a ball struck hard is more apt to fly out of them when struck in.

There is to the table belonging an ivory port, which stands at one end of the table, and an ivory king at the other, two small ivory balls and two sticks; where note if your balls are not compleatly round you can never expect good proof in your play: your sticks ought to be heavy, made of Brasile, Lignum vitae or some other weighty wood, which at the broad end must be tipt with ivory; where note, if the heads happen to be loose, you will never strike a smart stroke, you will easily perceive that defect by the hollow deadness of your stroak and faint running of your ball.

The game is five by day light, or seven if odds be given, and three by candle-light or more according to odds in houses that make a livelihood thereof; but in gentlemens houses there is no such restriction; for the game may justly admit of as many as the gamesters please to make.

For the lead you are to stand on the one side of the table opposite to the king, with your ball laid near the cushon, and your adversary on the other in like posture; and he that with his stick makes his ball come nearest the king leads first.

The leader must have a care that at the first stroke his ball touch not the end of the table leading from the king to the port, but after the first stroke he need not fear to do it, and let him so lead that he may either be in a possibility of passing the next stroke, or so cunningly lie that he may be in a very fair probability of hazarding his adversaries ball, that very stroak he plaid after him.

The first contest is who shall pass first, and in that strife there are frequent opportunities of hazarding one another; and it is very pleasant to observe what policies are used in hindering one another from the pass, as by turning the port with a strong clever stroke; for if you turn it with your stick it must be set right again; but indeed more properly he that doth it should lose one; sometimes it is done (when you see it is impossible to pass) by laying your ball in the port, or before your adversaries, and then all he can do is to pass after you, for fear he should in the interim touch the king and so win the end, you must wait upon him and watch all opportunities to hazard him, or king him; that is, when his ball lyeth in such manner that when you strike his ball may hit down the king, and then you win one.

Here note, that if you should king him, and your ball fly over the table, or else run into a hazard, that then you lose one notwithstanding.

The player ought to have a curious eye, and very good judgment when he either intends to king his adversary's ball, or hazard, in taking or quartering out just so much of the ball as will accomplish either; which observation must be noted in passing on your adversary's ball, or corner of the port. Some I have observed so skilful at this recreation, that if they have had less than a fifth part of a ball they would rarely miss king or hazard.

As this is a cleanly pastime, so there are laws or orders made against lolling slovingly players, that by their forfeitures they may be reduced to regularity and decency; wherefore be careful you lay not your hand on the table when you strike or let your sleeve drag upon it, if you do it is a loss. If you smoak and let the ashes of your pipe fall on the table, whereby oftentimes the cloth is burned, it is a forfeiture, but that should not so much deter you from it as the hindrance piping is to your play.

When you strike a long stroke, hold your stick nearly between your two fore fingers and your thumb, then strike smartly, and by aiming rightly you may when you please either fetch back your adversary's ball when he lyeth fair for a pass, or many times when he lyeth behind the king, and you at the other end of the table you may king him backward.

If you lie close you may use the small end of your stick, or the flat of the big end, raising up one end over your shoulder, which you shall think most convenient for your purpose.

Have a care of raking, for if it be not a forfeiture it is a fault hardly excusable, but if you touch your ball twice it is a loss.

Beware when you jobb your ball through the port with the great end of your stick that you throw it not down, if you do it is a loss, but do it so handsomly that at one stroke without turning the port with your stick you effect your purpose; it is good play to turn the port with your ball, and so hinder your adversary from passing; neither is it amiss if you can to make your adversary a Fornicator, that is having past your self a little way, and the others ball being hardly through the port you put him back again, and it may be quite out of pass.

It argueth policy to lay a long hazard sometimes for your antagonist, whereby he is often entrapped for rashly adventuring at that distance. Thinking to strike your ball into the hazard, which lieth very near it, he frequently runs in himself by reason of that great distance.

There is great art in lying abscond, that is, to lie at bo-peep with your adversary, either subtlely to gain a pass or hazard.

Here note, if your adversary hath not past and lyeth up by the king, you may endeavour to pass again, which if you do, and touch the king, it is two, but if thrown down you lose. Some instead of a king use a string and a ball, and then you need not fear to have the end, if you can pass first;

this is in my judgment bungling play, there being not that curious art of finely touching at a great distance a king that stands very ticklishly.

For your better understanding of the game read the ensuing orders. But there is no better way than practice to make you perfect therein.

[Summary of penalties and points. Also Orders in Verse as the author found them framed for a very ancient billiard table.]

Since recreation is a thing lawful in it self if not abused, I cannot but commend this as the most gentile and innocent of any I know, if rightly used; there being none of those cheats to be plaid at this as at several other games I shall hereafter mention. There is nothing here to be used but pure art; and therefore I shall only caution you to go to play, that you suffer not your self to be over-matcht, and do not when you meet with a better gamester than your self condemn the table, and do not swear as one did playing at nine-pins, this L. N. hath put false pins upon me.

To conclude, I believe this pastime is not so much used of late as formerly, by reason of those spunging caterpillars which swarm where any billiard-tables are set up, who making that single room their shop, kitching and bed-chamber; their shop, for this is the place where they wait for ignorant cullies to be their customers; their kitching, for from hence comes the major part of their provision, drinking and smoaking being their common sustenance; and when they can perswade no more persons to play at the table, they make it their dormitory, and sleep under it; the floor is their feather-bed, the legs of the table their bed-posts, and the table the tester; they dream of nothing but *Hazards,* being never out of them, of *passing,* and *repassing,* which may be fitly applied to their lewd lives, which makes them continually pass from one prison to another till their lives are ended; and there is an end of the game.

HAZZARD. Cotton's *Compleat Gamester,* pp. 82–84.

This game is play'd but with two dice, but there may play at it as many as can stand round the largest round table.

There are two things chiefly to be observed, that is, *Main* and *Chance;* the Chance is the casters, and the Main theirs who are concerned in play with him. There can be no Main thrown above nine and under five; so that five, six, seven, eight and nine are the only Mains and no more which are flung at Hazzard. Chances and *Nicks* are from four to ten, thus four is a Chance to nine, five to eight, six to seven, seven to six, eight to five; and nine and ten a Chance to five, six, seven and eight: in short, four, five, six, seven, eight, nine and ten are Chances to any Main, if any of these Nick it not. Now Nicks are either when the Chance is the same with the Main, as five and five, six and six, seven and seven, and so on, or six and twelve, seven and eleven, eight and twelve; where note, that twelve is out to nine, seven, and five; and eleven is out to nine, eight, six, and five; *Ames-Ace,* and Deuce-Ace, are out to all Mains what ever.

That I may the better illustrate this game, it will not be amiss to give one example for your better information. Seven's the Main, the caster throws five, and that's his Chance, and so hath five to seven; if the caster throw his own Chance he wins all the money was set him, but if he throw seven which was the Main, he must pay as much money as is on the board. If again seven be the Main, and the caster throws eleven, that is a Nick, and sweeps away all the money on the table; but if he throw a Chance, he must wait which will come first; Lastly, if seven be the Main, and the caster throws Ames-Ace, Deuce-Ace or twelve, he is out, but he throw from four to ten he hath a Chance, though they are accounted the worst Chances on the dice, as seven is reputed the best and easiest Main to be flung;

thus it is in eight or six, if either of them be the Main, and the caster throw either four, five, seven, nine, or ten, this is his Chance, which if he throw first, he wins, otherwise loseth; if he throw twelve to eight, or six or the same cast with the Main, he wins; but if Ames-Ace or Deuce-Ace to all he loseth; or if twelve when the Main is either five or nine. Here note, that nothing Nicks five but five, nor nothing nine but nine.

Four and five to seven is judged to have the worst on't, because four (called by the tribe of Nickers little Dick-Fisher) and five have but two Chances, Trey Ace and two Deuces, or Trey Deuce and Quater Ace, whereas Seven hath three Chances, Cinque Deuce, Six Ace, and Quater Trey; in like condition is nine and ten, having but two Chances, six Trey, Cinque and Quater, or six Quater and two Cinques.

Now six and eight one would think should admit of no difference in advantage with seven, but if you will rightly consider the case, and be so vain to make trial thereof, you will find a great advantage in seven over six and eight. 'How can that be,' you will say, hath not six, seven and eight eight equal chances? For example, in six, Quater Deuce, Cinque Ace, and two Treys; in eight, six Deuce, Cinque Trey, and two Quaters, and hath not seven three as aforesaid? It is confest; but pray consider the disadvantage in the doublets, two Treys and two Quaters, and you will find that six Deuce is sooner thrown than two Quaters, and so consequently Cinque Ace or Quater Deuce sooner than two Treys: I saw an old rook once take up a young fellow in a tavern, upon this very score: the bargain was made that the rook should have seven always and the young gentleman six, and throw continually; agreed to play they went, the rook got the first day ten pound, the next day the like sum; and so for six days together losing in all three-score pounds; notwithstanding the gentleman, I am confident, had square dice, and threw them always himself. And farther to confirm

what I alledg'd before, not only this rook, but many more have told me that they desir'd no greater advantage than to have seven always and the caster to have six. Here note, it is the opinion of most that at the first throw the caster hath the worst on't.

Certainly Hazzard is the most bewitching game that is plaid on the dice; for when a man begins to play he knows not when to leave off; and having once accustom'd himself to play at Hazzard he hardly ever after minds any thing else. I have seen an old man about the age of seventy play at an ordinary when his own eyes were so defective, that he was forced to help them with a pair of spectacles; and having an opportunity one day to speak to him, how a man of his years could be so vain and boyish still to mind play; insisting withall upon the folly of that action to hazzard his money when he had not sight enough remaining to discern whether he had won or lost. 'Besides Sir,' said I, 'you cannot but hear how you are derided every time you come to the ordinary;' one says, 'here comes he that cannot rest quiet, but will cry without the rattle of the dice;' another cries, 'certainly such a one plays by the ear; for he cannot see to play.' 'Let them talk what they will," said the gentleman, 'I cannot help it, I have been for above forty years so us'd to play, that should I leave it off now, I were as good stop those issues about me, which have been instrumental in the preservation of my life to this length of time.'

To conclude, happy is he that having been much inclined to this time-spending-money-wasting game, hath took up in time, and resolved for the future never to be concerned with it more; but more happy is he that hath never heard the name thereof.

[It is interesting to note that of all the personalities in modern Craps, only "Little Joe" had an eighteenth-century ancestor—"Little Dick Fisher."]

*A Summary of Hoyle's Calculation of the Betting Odds:*

There are 36 possible number combinations on the two dice:

```
6 of these  total  7 (1-6, 6-1, 2-5, 5-2, 3-4, 4-3)
5  "     "     "   6 (1-5, 5-1, 2-4, 4-2, 3-3)
5  "     "     "   8 (2-6, 6-2, 3-5, 5-3, 4-4)
4  "     "     "   5 (1-4, 4-1, 2-3, 3-2)
4  "     "     "   9 (3-6, 6-3, 4-5, 5-4)
3  "     "     "   4 (1-3, 3-1, 2-2)
3  "     "     "  10 (4-6, 6-4, 5-5)
2  "     "     "   3 (1-2, 2-1)
2  "     "     "  11 (5-6, 6-5)
1  "     "  totals 2 (1-1; this is "Ames-Ace")
1  "     "     "  12 (6-6)
___
36
```

Therefore, a player has 6 chances of throwing a 7, against 5 of throwing a 6, and so on.

Betting odds against the caster are calculated thus:

```
when 7 is the main and  4 is the chance, 6 to 3 or 2 to 1
 "   "  "   "    "    "  5  "   "     "   , 3 to 2
 "   "  "   "    "    "  6  "   "     "   , 6 to 5
 "   "  "   "    "    "  8  "   "     "   , 6 to 5
 "   "  "   "    "    "  9  "   "     "   , 3 to 2
 "   "  "   "    "    " 10  "   "     "   , 2 to 1
 "   6  "   "    "    "  4  "   "     "   , 5 to 3
 "   "  "   "    "    "  5  "   "     "   , 5 to 4
 "   "  "   "    "    "  7  "   "     "   , 5 to 6—caster's advantage
 "   "  "   "    "    "  8  "   "     "   , even
 "   "  "   "    "    "  9  "   "     "   , 5 to 4
 "   "  "   "    "    " 10  "   "     "   , 5 to 3
```

And so on for the other combinations.

If a gambling house adopted these odds as house rules governing the banker's second bet (after the initial throw has determined the caster's chance), then players would be willing to place stakes with the banker or the caster, whatever main and chance might be, because the odds had been adjusted.

# APPENDIX C.   BOARD GAMES

## Eighteenth-Century Rules of Play

### THE ROYALL AND MOST PLEASANT GAME OF THE GOOSE.
Invented at the Consistory in Rome and are printed and sold by John Overton over against St. Sepulchers Church: in London [ca. 1670].

The Rules to be observed in this Game are as followeth

1. As many as please may play with a paire of Dyce and every one stakeing. throw who shall begin.

2. Hee that throws 6 and 3 at the first must goe to the number 26 and if he throws 5 and 4 then to the number 53 for every such advantage adde a stake to the rest.

3. Hee that throws a Goose must double his chance forward from his last place.

4. Hee that throws 6 must pay a stake for his passage over the Bridge and goe to the numer 12.

5. Hee that throws 19 where the Alehouse is must pay a stake and drink till every one has thrown once.

6. Hee that throws 31 where the well is must pay a stake and stay there till every one play twice unlesse some other throw the same by which he is delivered.

7. Hee that throws 42 where the Maze is payes one and returnes back to the number 29.

8. Hee that goeth to 52 where the Prison is must pay one and stay there till some other bring him out.

9. Hee that goeth to 58 where death is must pay one and begin againe.

10. Hee that is overtaken by another must returne to his place that overtooke him and both must pay.

11. Hee that overthroweth the number 63 must turn back againe and counte his throw from the begining.

12. Hee that throweth the just number 63 wineth the Game.

### THE NEW GAME OF HUMAN LIFE (London, 1790)

#### Rules of the Game

The immortal Man, who has existed 84 years, seems worthy by his Talents and Merit to become a Model for the Close of Life, which can end only by Eternity. When we shall arrive at the No. 84 we shall have gain'd all we can by this Game, but if we exceed this number, we must go back as many Points, as we have proceeded beyond it.

The Age of Man is divided into seven periods of twelve years, *viz.* Infancy to Youth, Man-hood, Prime of Life, Sedate middle age, Old age, Decrepitude, and Dotage. He passes through life in a variety of situations which are here arranged in the order they generally succeed each other.

This game, like all others of the same kind, is played with a Totum; each Player spinning twice in his turn the only difference is, that the Players cannot stop at any of the seven ages, but must proceed as many Points beyond, as they have in coming to them. Yet as they may spin at first two Sixes, and consequently would go on to 84, which would be improper, those who have this chance at first, must content themselves with going to the Historian at 39.

The studious boy at 7 shall receive a Stake, and shall proceed to 42, the place of the Orator.

The Negligent boy at 11 shall pay a Stake and shall remain two rounds without spinning.

The Assiduous youth at 15 shall receive two Stakes, and proceed to 55, where he will find the Patriot.

The Trifler at 19 shall pay one Stake, and proceed to the Songster at 38.

The Duellist at 22 shall pay two Stakes, and return to take the place of the Boy at Number 5.

The Complaisant man at 26 shall remain there, and let others play till another comes to take his place, and then he shall go back to the place of his Liberator.

The Prodigal at Number 30 shall pay four Stakes, and go back to the Careless boy at 6.

The married Man at 34, shall receive two Stakes for his Wife's Portion and go to be a good Father at 56.

The Romance Writer at 40 shall pay two Stakes and go back to the mischievious Boy at 5.

The Dramatist at 44 shall pay four Stakes to the Masters of his Art, and shall begin the Game again.

The Benevolent man at 52 shall go to 78, to amuse himself with the Joker.

The Temperate man at 58 shall go to 82, to find the Quiet man.

The Drunkard at 63 shall pay two Stakes, and go back to the Child at 2.

The Patient man at 68, shall receive two Stakes and go to amuse himself with the merry fellow at 80.

The Manhater at 71 shall pay two Stakes, and go back to the Obstinate youth at 16.

The Old beau at 74 shall receive one Stake, and let each of the others play one round.

The Satyrist at 77 shall pay four Stakes, and go back to the Malignant boy at 8.

Lastly, the Tragic Author at 45 shall go the place of the Immortal Man at 84, and win the Game by succeeding him.

## THE UTILITY and MORAL TENDENCY of this GAME.

If Parents who take upon themselves the pleasing Task of Instructing their Children (or others to whom that important Trust may be delegated) will cause them to stop at each Character, and request their attention to a few moral and judicious observations, explanatory of each Character as they proceed and contrast the happiness of a Virtuous and well spent life with the fatal consequences arising from Vicious and Immoral pursuits. This Game may be rendered the most useful and amusing of any that has hitherto been offered to the Public.

## DIRECTIONS for PLAYING.

This Game may be played by any number of Persons at a time; but care must be taken, that each player make use of a different mark to move with, and be provided with at least twelve counters each, and agree how much to value them per dozen. Let us then suppose, that four Gentlemen agree to play a game together, and stake four counters each. A. takes red for his mark, B. green, C. black, and D. white. A. begins and spins 9, and accordingly places his mark upon No. 9, which is the docile boy. B. plays next and spins 7; but (as the rules of the game specify) instead of putting his mark on No. 7, he must receive a counter from the pool, and carry his mark to the orator, at No. 42. C. being next in turn, spins only 2, and puts his mark on the place of the child at No. 2. D. being the last player, spins 11 and goes to the negligent boy; but this being a forfeit, he must pay a counter to the pool, and remain two rounds at No. 11, without playing in his turn.—A. now resumes the totum, and spins 3, which bring him from No. 9, where he was, to No. 12 but this being one of the seven ages, he cannot stop here, for (agreeable to the rules of the game) he must proceed as far beyond the age of youth, as he had to come to it, which being three points, he must of course go to No. 15, the place of the assiduous youth; but instead of that, he must receive two counters from the pool, and go to No. 55, the place of the patriot.—B. now takes the

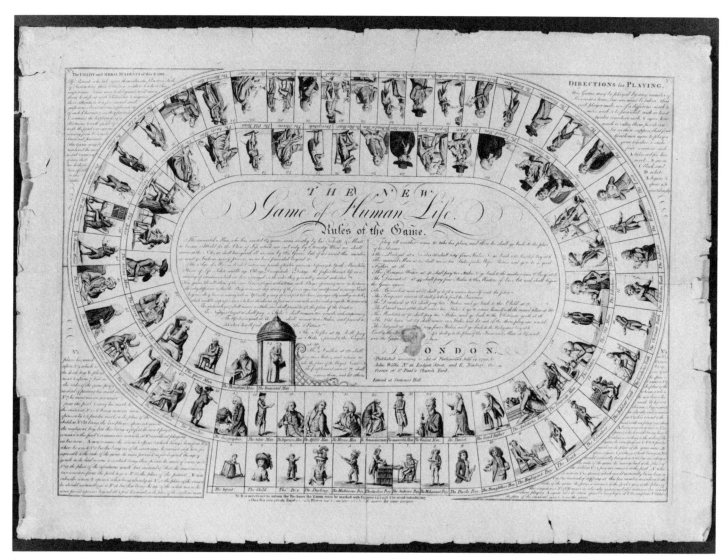

41. *The New Game of Human Life. London, 1790.*

totum and spins 6, when being already at No. 42, the place of the orator, he should naturally go to No. 48, but that being the age of the sedate man, he must proceed 6 points beyond 48, and put his mark on the place of the vigilant man at No. 54. C's. turn being come again, he spins 11, and comes to No. 13 the place of the volunteer, where he now leaves his mark. D. having thrown 11 before, must, as already said, remain at No. 11, this round and the next without playing—thus A. being next in turn, and at No. 55, spins 3 which would bring him to No. 58, but (according to the rules of the game) he must pass on to No. 82, and put his mark on the place of the quiet man.—B. spins again, and fetches 9, which, being at No. 54 would naturally bring him to 63, but (according to the rules of the game) he must go back to the place of the child, at No. 2, and pay two counters to the pool.—C who is now at No. 13, spins 6, which would naturally bring him to No. 19, but instead of stopping at this last number (according to the rules of the game) he pays a counter to the pool, and goes to the place of the songster at No. 38. D. must as already mentioned, also remain this round without playing. A again takes the totum spins 2 and being before at No. 82, compleats No. 84, takes the place of the immortal man and wins the game.

N.B.    It is necessary to inform the Purchaser, the Totum must be marked with Figures 1. 2. 3. 4. 5. 6. and to avoid introducing a Dice Box into private Families, each Player must spin twice which will answer the same purpose.

## NINE-MEN'S MORRIS

Merrils, Three-men's Morris, Six-men's Morris, Ninepenny Morris are a few of the variations of this ancient game. Medieval shepherds marked off the lines of the diagram on the ground and used sticks or pebbles as men.

In Shakespeare's time their game was part of the rural scene: Titania, describing the havoc of heavy rains, said to Oberon:

> The fold stands empty in the drowned field,
> And crows are fatted with the murrain flock;
> The nine men's morris is fill'd up with mud. . . .
> (*A Midsummer Night's Dream,* Act II, scene 1)

Indoors it was a favorite game of patrons of alehouses. Children played both outdoors and indoors, using marbles or pegs, pebbles, buttons, fruit seeds, or counters from other games.

The design of the board is three squares, one within the other, with lines connecting the sides of the squares but not the corners. The points where lines intersect are the spots where men are placed in the play. If flat disks or stones are used as men, only the lines are needed. If pegs or marbles are used, there are small holes at intersecting points, as on a Chinese checker board.

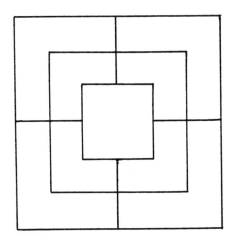

There are two players, each having nine men. The object of the game is to remove from the board all the men belonging to one's opponent. First, each player in turn places his men on the board, one at a time, on any intersection not already occupied. Then each player in turn moves one of his men along the pattern of the lines and in any direction to an adjoining vacant spot—one space usually, but two spaces if both are unoccupied and no corner intervenes. As soon as a player has three men in a row, he may remove any one of his opponent's men except one of those standing in a row of three which the opponent may have already set up. The game is won when a player cannot move—either because his men have been captured or because they are blocked by his opponent's pieces.

The skillful player when placing his men on the board scatters them on all three squares and covers as many corners as possible. Early in the play he sets up a see-saw arrangement, which permits him to open one row of three and form another at the same move; if his opponent cannot break up the see-saw, he soon loses all his men.

FOX AND GEESE

This game is sometimes played on a checkerboard with four geese and a fox. The conventional eighteenth-century game, however, is played with seventeen geese and one fox on a board of this design:

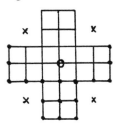

As Strutt explains, "The business of the game is to shut the fox up, so that he cannot move." The fox moves in a straight line in any direction; the geese move only forward or sideways. The fox may jump, as in draughts, and remove the goose from the board, but the geese may not jump the fox. The fox wins the game if he breaks through the line of geese in front of him; he loses if he is cornered and blocked in. The advantage is with the geese if their player is skillful.

In an earlier form of the game there were thirteen geese which could move backward as well as forward and sideways, and an older board had four additional holes where the small x's appear on the diagram. During the nineteenth century two changes were introduced to give the fox a better fighting chance: twenty-two geese opposed two foxes, and diagonal lines were added to the board for the use of the foxes.

Today the Fox and Geese board is used for SOLITAIRE, a game invented on the Continent at the end of the eighteenth century (one tradition says by a prisoner in the Bastille) and known to Strutt only by name. In Solitaire, thirty-two pegs or marbles are placed on the board so that only the fox's starting position is vacant. The player then jumps, removing the peg that was passed over, and continues until only one peg remains on the board. The player wins the game if the last move puts the last peg into the fox hole. Only one peg may be moved at a time, and no peg may jump another unless it stands close to it without an intervening hole.

# NOTES

## Chapter One: Home Entertainments

[1]An early statement of this opinion is Durand of Dauphiné's: "The people [Virginians] spend most of their time visiting each other." *A Huguenot Exile in Virginia,* ed. Gilbert Chinard (New York, 1934), p. 111.

[2]Robert Beverley, *The History and Present State of Virginia,* ed. Louis B. Wright (Chapel Hill, N. C., 1947), pp. 308, 312–313. Although Beverley was well-to-do and socially prominent, his own home was simply furnished. When John Fontaine stopped there in 1715, he found good beds but no curtains, wooden stools but no chairs, yet, he reported, Beverley "lives well." John Fontaine, "Journal," in *Memoirs of a Huguenot Family* . . . , ed. Ann Maury (New York, 1853), p. 265. Early travelers who enjoyed Virginia hospitality and commented on it include: Capt. Peter De Vries, who visited George Menefie in 1632, *Voyages from Holland to America, A. D. 1632–1644,* trans. and ed. Henry C. Murphy (New York, 1853), reprinted in New-York Historical Society, *Collections,* 2nd Ser., III (1857), pp. 1–136; Beauchamp Plantagenet, a guest of Samuel Mathews in 1648, *A Description of the Province of New Albion,* in Peter Force, ed., *Tracts and Other Papers, Relating Principally to the Origin, Settlement, and Progress of the Colonies in North America, from the Discovery of the Country to the Year 1776* (Washington, D. C., 1836–1846), II, No. 7; the author of *A Perfect Description of Virginia,* who visited Mathews and others in 1649, *ibid.,* No. 8; Col. Henry Norwood, who was entertained in several homes on the Eastern Shore and by Ralph Wormeley, Sir William Berkeley, and others in the Tidewater about the year 1650, *A Voyage to Virginia, ibid.,* I, No. 6; and Durand of Dauphiné, a guest of Ralph Wormeley, William Fitzhugh, and others in 1687, *Huguenot Exile,* ed. Chinard. Other seventeenth-century writers, notably William Bullock, John Hammond, and Thomas Glover, made favorable comments on the hospitable spirit of the people but mentioned no specific visits. William Bullock, *Virginia impartially examined* . . . (London, 1649); John Hammond, *Leah and Rachel, or, the Two Fruitful Sisters Virginia, and Mary-Land,* in Force, ed., *Tracts,* III, No. 14; Thomas Glover, *An Account of Virginia . . .*

*Reprinted from the Philosophical transactions of the Royal Society, June 20, 1676* (Oxford, 1904).

[3]For the most discerning comments on Virginians as hosts, see the following eighteenth-century travel accounts: Andrew Burnaby, *Travels Through the Middle Settlements in North-America. In the Years 1759 and 1760. With Observations upon the State of the Colonies,* 2nd ed. (London, 1775); Nicholas Cresswell, *The Journal of Nicholas Cresswell, 1774–1777,* ed. Samuel Thornely (New York, 1924); Ebenezer Hazard, Journal of Journey to the South, 1777–1778, MS, Historical Society of Pennsylvania, Philadelphia, photostat of Virginia portion in Foundation Library, Colonial Williamsburg Foundation, Williamsburg, Va.; Marquis de Chastellux, *Travels in North America, in the Years 1780, 1781, and 1782,* II (London, 1787); Louis Jean Baptiste Silvestre de Robertnier, Journal des guerres faites en Amérique . . . , 1780–1783, MS, Rhode Island Historical Society, Providence, microfilm in Foundation Lib.; Johann David Schoepf, *Travels in the Confederation [1783–1784],* trans. and ed. Alfred J. Morrison (Philadelphia, 1911); J. F. D. Smyth, *A Tour in the United States of America . . . ,* 2 vols. (London, 1784); Noah Webster, "Diary, 1785–1786," in Emily Ellsworth Ford Skeel, ed., *Notes on the Life of Noah Webster,* I (New York, 1912), pp. 122–171; Harry Toulmin, *The Western Country in 1793: Reports on Kentucky and Virginia by Harry Toulmin,* ed. Marion Tinling and Godfrey Davies (San Marino, Calif., 1948); and John Davis, *Travels of Four Years and a Half in the United States of America . . .* (London, 1803).

[4]Hugh Jones, *The Present State of Virginia: From Whence Is Inferred A Short View of Maryland and North Carolina,* ed. Richard L. Morton (Chapel Hill, N. C., 1956), p. 84.

[5]Burnaby, *Travels,* p. 31.

[6]John Bernard, *Retrospections of America, 1797–1811,* ed. Mrs. Bayle Bernard (New York, 1887), p. 146.

[7]Young Robert Hunter, spending the night in Gloucester, confided to his journal: "A courtship is going on at this house. I think it seems to be the principal business in Virginia." *Quebec to Carolina in 1785–1786: Being the Travel Diary and Observations of Robert Hunter, Jr., a Young Merchant of London,* ed. Louis B. Wright and Marion Tinling (San Marino, Calif., 1943), p. 231.

[8]Lucinda Lee, *Journal of a Young Lady of Virginia, 1782,* ed. Emily V. Mason (Baltimore, 1891).

[9]*Ibid.,* p. 37.

[10]*Ibid.,* pp. 41–43.

[11]An extreme example of cousins marrying cousins may be seen in the families of Gov. John Page of Rosewell and Gov. Thomas Nelson of Yorktown. Five children of Gov. Nelson married five sons and daughters of Gov. Page:

1788 Mann Page married Elizabeth Nelson.
1790 William Nelson married Sally Burwell Page.
1795 Thomas Nelson, Jr., married Frances Page.
1803 Robert Nelson married Judith Carter Page.
1806 Francis Page married Susanna Nelson.

These children were double second cousins, Gov. Nelson and Mrs. Page being double first cousins: his mother and her father were Burwell sister and brother, and his father and her mother were Nelson brother and sister. The two common ancestors were "Scotch Tom" Nelson, grandfather of Gov. Nelson and of Frances Burwell Page (Mrs. John Page), whose mother was Sally Nelson, and Nathaniel Burwell of Carter's Creek, whose daughter Elizabeth was Gov. Nelson's mother and whose son Robin was Frances Burwell Page's father. Another common ancestor was Robert "King" Carter: his eldest daughter, Elizabeth, married Nathaniel Burwell of Carter's Creek, and another daughter, Judith, married Mann Page I, Gov. Page's grandfather.

Gov. Nelson's other children further compounded the relationship—two of them married Page cousins of Gov. Page (the North End branch of the family). Another married a Nelson cousin; yet another, a Carter cousin. In Gov. Page's family, too, there were further complications—his sister Judith married her cousin Lewis Burwell, and another sister, Lucy, married Lewis Burwell's cousin Nathaniel.

[12]See Julia Cherry Spruill, *Women's Life and Work in the Southern Colonies* (Chapel Hill, N. C., 1938), p. 23.

[13]One day in the 1770s Dr. Theodorick Bland, looking forward to "a Good Old Xmas," wrote to John Randolph, "With what pleasure I shd. participate with you in the festivity and mirth which generally reigns at this happy season especially when Liberal Minds are met together you need not be told.

Nor shd. my exertions be wanting to add my Quota to the General stock of Good humor, which always predominates at yr. Social Board." Bryan Family Papers, microfilm, Alderman Library, University of Virginia, Charlottesville.

[14]Philip Vickers Fithian, *Journal & Letters of Philip Vickers Fithian, 1773–1774: A Plantation Tutor of the Old Dominion,* ed. Hunter Dickinson Farish (Williamsburg, Va., 1943), entry for Dec. 18, 1773, p. 44.

[15]Sally Cary Fairfax, "Diary of a Little Colonial Girl," *Virginia Magazine of History and Biography,* XI (1903), pp. 212–213.

[16]Sally S. Kennon to Ellen Mordecai, Jan. 15, 1807, *ibid.,* XXXI (1923), p. 188.

[17]Cresswell, *Journal,* ed. Thornely, pp. 52–53.

[18]"Diary of Col. Landon Carter," *William and Mary Quarterly,* 1st Ser., XIII (1904–1905), p. 46.

[19]*Ibid.,* p. 53.

[20]*Ibid.,* p. 162.

[21]*Ibid.,* XIV (1905–1906), p. 250.

[22]Fithian, *Journal,* ed. Farish, entry for Aug. 19, 1774, p. 225.

[23]Hugh Jones wrote in 1724 that Virginians "most commonly" married at home. *Present State of Virginia,* ed. Morton, p. 97.

[24]William Eddis, *Letters from America, Historical and Descriptive . . .* (London, 1792), No. IX, p. 114.

[25]*Virginia Gazette* (Purdie and Dixon), Mar. 14, 1771.

[26]Durand of Dauphiné, *Huguenot Exile,* ed. Chinard, pp. 137–139.

[27]"Journal of Col. James Gordon," *WMQ,* 1st Ser., XI (1902–1903), p. 104.

[28]"Diary of Col. Landon Carter," *ibid.,* XVI (1907–1908), p. 264.

[29]Meredic Moreau de Saint-Méry, *Moreau de St. Méry's American Journey [1793–1798],* trans. and ed. Kenneth Roberts and Anna M. Roberts (Garden City, N. Y., 1947), p. 54.

[30][Mrs. Anne Ritson], *A Poetical Picture of America, Being Observations Made, during a Residence of Several Years, at Alexandria, and Norfolk, in Virginia . . .* (London, 1809), pp. 113–117.

[31]A younger daughter, Lucy, later married Richard's brother Brett on Nov. 21, 1789. "Notes and Queries," *VMHB* (1926), p. 162.

[32]The Church of England prescribed exact regulations for the marriage ceremony: that it be preceded by publication of banns or by special license; that it be performed by an Anglican minister and in church if possible; that the time of day be morning and the time of year between special seasons in the church calendar—Advent, Epiphany, Easter, Pentecost. See George Maclaren Brydon, *Virginia's Mother Church and The Political Conditions Under Which It Grew*, I (Richmond, Va., 1947), pp. 406–407. At first the Virginia General Assembly attempted to enforce these regulations in the colony. In Feb. 1631/32 Act VI limited the hours for marriage ceremonies to between 8 and 12 in the forenoon, and in Sept. 1732 Act III required all sacraments to be administered "in the church except in cases of necessitie." William Waller Hening, ed., *The Statutes at Large; Being a Collection of All the Laws of Virginia, from the First Session of the Legislature, in the Year 1619* (New York, Philadelphia, and Richmond, Va., 1819–1823), I, pp. 156, 181. As settlement spread out from the Jamestown area, enforcement became increasingly difficult. Parishes were very large, and the parish church was an inconvenient distance from the homes of most of the parishioners. Home weddings, funerals, and baptisms gradually became the rule, "necessary" because they were more convenient, and noon became the popular hour for the convenience of guests who had to drive some distance to attend. After the Revolution, as Mrs. Ritson implied, the Virginia clergy—now freed from the restrictions of the Establishment—were allowed great liberty in performing any part of the service and in setting the hour and day for it to be performed.

[33]Hunter, *Quebec to Carolina*, ed. Wright and Tinling, pp. 206–209.

[34]Quoted in John P. Kennedy, *Memoirs of the Life of William Wirt*, I (Philadelphia, 1850), pp. 133–135. An earlier mention of the wedding cake is in William Byrd II's letter to Daniel Parke Custis, Sept. 23, 1742. His daughter Maria had married Landon Carter the day before, and Byrd urged Custis to come to see the happy newlyweds. "If you will come before Sunday," he wrote, "you will be time enough to wish the Partys Joy, and eat a Piece of the Bride Cake." Quoted in Maude H. Woodfin, *Another Secret Diary of William Byrd of Westover, 1739–1741. With Letters & Literary Exercises, 1696–1726*, trans. Marion Tinling (Richmond, Va., 1942), p. 31n.

[35]Diary of Robert Wormeley Carter, 1769, MS, Earl Gregg Swem Library, College of William and Mary, Williamsburg, Va., typescript in Foundation Lib.

[36]The best descriptions of middle-class weddings that I have seen are concerned with the Scotch-Irish in the Shenandoah Valley of Virginia and are based largely on reminiscences. The descriptions are from Samuel Kercheval, *A History of the Valley of Virginia*, 4th ed. (Strasburg, Va., 1925), pp. 60–62, 260–263; and J. Lewis Peyton, *History of Augusta County, Virginia* (Staunton, Va., 1882), pp. 44–46.

[37]Joseph Doddridge, "Notes on the Settlement and Indian Wars of the Western Parts of Virginia and Pennsylvania . . . ," in Kercheval, *History*, p. 262.

[38]Burnaby pronounced them "immoderately fond of dancing" and declared that it was almost their only amusement. *Travels*, p. 35. See also Lewis Beebe Journals, 1799–1801, II, entry for Feb. 28, 1800, MS, Hist. Soc. Pa., microfilm in Foundation Lib.; Cresswell, *Journal*, ed. Thornely, pp. 52–53, 270; Eddis, *Letters*, No. IX; James Franklin, *The Philosophical & Political History of the Thirteen United States of America . . .* (London, 1784), pp. 90–92; Adam Gordon, *Journal of an Officer Who Travelled in America and the West Indies in 1764 and 1765*, in Newton D. Mereness, ed., *Travels in the American Colonies* (New York, 1916), pp. 403–406; Joseph Hadfield, *An Englishman in America, 1785, Being the Diary of Joseph Hadfield*, ed. Douglas S. Robertson (Toronto, 1933), p. 10; John Harrower, Diary, entry for Aug. 28, 1775, MS, Richard Corbin Papers, Foundation Lib.; [Edward Kimber], *Itinerant Observations in America* (Savannah, Ga., 1878), p. 49; Duke de La Rochefoucauld-Liancourt, *Travels through the United States of North America . . .* , II (London, 1799), p. 117; Moreau de St. Méry, *American Journey*, trans. and ed. Roberts and Roberts, pp. 52, 69; [Ritson], *Poetical Picture*, pp. 99–100; de Robertnier, Journal, p. 156; and Evelyn M. Acomb, ed., "The Journal of Baron Von Closen," *WMQ*, 3rd Ser., X (1953), p. 213.

John Kello, writing from Hampton to a London friend in 1755, stated, "Dancing is the chief diversion here, and hunting and racing." Quoted in Mary Newton Stanard, *Colonial Virginia: Its People and Customs* (Philadelphia, 1917), p. 140. Gov. William Gooch shortly after his arrival in Williamsburg wrote to his brother Thomas: "The Gentm. and Ladies here are perfectly well bred, not an ill Dancer in my Govmt." Gooch Letter Book, Dec. 28, 1727, typed copy in Foundation Lib.

[39] Fithian, *Journal,* ed. Farish, entries for Jan. 17–21, 1774, pp. 75–78. Other accounts of balls may be found in the following sources: George Washington's famous description of the "Bread and Butter Ball" in Alexandria, Feb. 15, 1760, in John C. Fitzpatrick, ed., *The Diaries of George Washington, 1748–1799* (Boston, 1925), I, p. 126; Hunter's description of an Alexandria assembly, Nov. 17, 1785, in *Quebec to Carolina,* ed. Wright and Tinling, pp. 198–199; and Cresswell's description of a Negro ball that he attended on May 29, 1774, *Journal,* ed. Thornely, pp. 18–19.

[40] The Reverend Hugh Jones felt that boys at the College of William and Mary should be encouraged to master "the accomplishments of musick, dancing, and fencing." *Present State of Virginia,* ed. Morton, p. 111. The sons of Col. John Spotswood of Newpost were sent to England to school. Their expenses for the two-year period 1762–1764 included regular semiannual fees of £4 4s. to the dancing master. A. G. Grinnon, "Expenses of Virginia Boys at Eton in the Eighteenth Century," *VMHB,* XXV (1917), pp. 182–188. Washington exercised special care in selecting dancing masters for his stepson and nephews. See his letters to [Jonathan Boucher], Apr. 24, 1769, and to the Reverend Stephen Bloomer Balch, June 26, 1785, in John C. Fitzpatrick, ed., *The Writings of George Washington from the Original Manuscript Sources, 1745–1799* (Washington, D. C., 1931–1944), III, p. 499, XXVIII, p. 178. Charles Carter of Cleve provided in his will, 1762, that his two sons then in England "continue at school to learn the languages, Mathematicks, Phylosophy, dancing and fencing till they are well accomplished." His ten daughters were to be "maintained with great frugality and taught to dance." Fairfax Harrison, "The Will of Charles Carter of Cleve," *VMHB,* XXXI (1923), pp. 62, 63. Dancing lessons were even more important

for girls than for boys. William Lee, writing to his London agent Samuel Thorp on Sept. 8, 1785, expressed the hope that his daughter Portia might continue to learn dancing until the last minute before leaving Europe. "Some Notes on 'Green Spring,'" *ibid.,* XXXVIII (1930), p. 47. When Thomas Jefferson was drafting a plan for female education, he urged: "The ornaments, too, and the amusements of life, are entitled to their portion of attention. These, for a female, are dancing, drawing, and music." Jefferson to Nathaniel Burwell, Mar. 14, 1818, in Andrew A. Lipscomb and Albert Ellery Bergh, eds., *The Writings of Thomas Jefferson* (Washington, D. C., 1903), XV, pp. 167–168. The author of *The Complete Letter Writer; or The Art of Correspondence* (Albany, N. Y., 1802), p. 39, defined the "elegant accomplishments" of the female sex as "dress, dancing, music and drawing."

[41] For the history of Williamsburg's first theater, see Hugh F. Rankin, "The Colonial Theatre, Its History and Operations," 1955, typescript in Foundation Lib. Levingston, the Staggs, and the first theater appear in old novels too. See Mary Johnston, *Audrey,* and John Esten Cooke, *The Virginia Comedians.* In 1720 Stagg's itinerary included plantations in the neighborhood of Westover. See Louis B. Wright and Marion Tinling, eds., *The London Diary (1717–1721) and Other Writings* (New York, 1958), pp. 456, 458, 464, 467. Robert "King" Carter, Diary, 1722–1727, MS, Alderman Lib., contains frequent references to Stagg's presence at Corotoman and to payments for his services. See the following entries: May 17, Aug. 2, 22, Oct. 7, 19, 1722, Jan. 25, Feb. 18, Apr. 20, Aug. 31, Sept. 1, Dec. 21, 1723, Feb. 21, Mar. 20, May 30, June 20, Sept. 4, Nov. 27, 1724, Jan. 27, 29, Feb. 22, Mar. 12, Apr. 19, June 28, 1725, Jan. 15, Feb. 4–5, Apr. 9, Sept. 16, 1726, May 19, July 1, 1727. When Carter's daughter Anne was married to Benjamin Harrison in Oct. 1722, Stagg and John Langford had charge of the dancing and music for the wedding festivities; Langford's fee was 5 guineas, and Stagg's "man" received 3 guineas after Stagg had left the plantation. When Carter was in Williamsburg at court in Apr. 1723, he paid Stagg 6 shillings for "his Plays and Ball" and another 30 shillings "entrance" fees for young George Carter and two wards, his grandchildren Carter and Elizabeth Burwell. In May 1727 Carter paid 4½

pistoles for Stagg's assemblies; in July 5 guineas "for his trouble at the ball and for my sons Landon and George" and "for sweetmeats 18/." In 1729 Stagg was still teaching the Burwell children; he received £12 for a year's tutoring, presumably at Carter's Creek, and "also 3 pistoles for their ball doings." Carter to Col. [Mann] Page, June 20, 1729, "King" Carter, Letter Book, 1728–1731, Alderman Lib. Francis Christian's arrangement with Carter's grandson, Robert Carter of Nomini Hall, was similar. See Fithian, *Journal*, ed. Farish, pp. 25, 27, 32–33, 42–46, 88, 163–165, 187, 233, 250–252.

[42]This was good teaching—the sort of "real life situation" so revered by modern educationists, some of whom might even call it "an experience unit of work."

[43]"Libraries in Colonial Virginia," *WMQ*, 1st Ser., III (1894–1895), p. 251.

[44]Microfilm copy in Foundation Lib. The book is engraved throughout and Feuillet's method of notation is thoroughly explained. Weaver kept his promise "to make Mons. Feuillet speak English," and the diagrams might be used today as readily as in the eighteenth century. Indeed, Weaver was an ideal translator, a skillful dancing master who recognized a good thing in his profession when he saw it and shared his find with English colleagues and rivals. And Stagg's choice of Weaver's manual tells us something of *his* proficiency.

[45]Weaver's claims for Feuillet are supported by M. Goussier, author of the article "Chorégraphie" in Denis Diderot, ed., *Encyclopédie ou Dictionnaire Raisonné des Sciences, des Arts et des Métiers* . . . (Paris, 1751–1765), III, pp. 367–373, illustrated in *Planches*, III. Diderot considered Goussier the best French authority on design and mechanics and chose him to supervise all the diagrams for the *Encyclopédie* and to draw those illustrating music. Therefore, Goussier's high opinion of Feuillet's method of diagramming dance steps and patterns together with the corresponding musical notes is a recommendation indeed.

In the second edition of Weaver's translation an appendix showed designs for several popular contredanses—the Rigadoon, the Louver, and the Brittagne—which Stagg probably used for advanced pupils who had mastered the minuet, reels, and simpler country dances. Contredanses or country dances had a definite form at court and in high society in France and in England. (The distinction between contredanse and country dance is not clear in the minds of modern writers. *French contredanses* or *contradances* were probably ancestors of our square dance patterns with four couples—the Quadrille, for example—but the term *country dances* could include a "longways dance" like the Sir Roger de Coverly or Virginia Reel, where the number of couples was indefinite.) For the first part of the tune a set pattern of movements began with a formal bow and went through a series of circles and chains and promenades. For the second part there were special steps and figures to correspond with special dance tunes, like the Rigadoon. Diderot, ed., *Encyclopédie, Supplement* II, s.v. "Contredanse." Contredanses were especially popular because almost any kind of step could be introduced into the second part, and most of the dancing manuals included several hundred appropriate tunes. See *The Compleat Country Dancing Master* (London, 1731) and Giovanni-Andrea Gallini, *Critical Observations on the Art of Dancing* . . . (London, [1770]).

[46]S. Foster Damon, "The History of Square-Dancing," American Antiquarian Society, *Proceedings,* N.S., LXII (1952), pp. 63–74.

[47]Review of *Copley-Pelham Letters*, Massachusetts Historical Society, *Collections*, LXXI, in *WMQ*, 1st Ser., XXIII (1914–1915), p. 222.

[48]Acomb, ed., "Journal of Von Closen," *ibid.*, 3rd Ser., X (1953), p. 213.

[49]"Letters of William Byrd, 2d, of Westover, Va.," *VMHB*, IX (1900), p. 240.

[50]Woodfin, ed., *Another Secret Diary*, entries for July 3, 1740, Jan. 30, Mar. 1, 1741. Dering gave notice in the *Va. Gaz.*, Nov. 25, 1737, that he opened his dancing school at the College of William and Mary on that day; he was teaching gentlemen's sons the art of dancing in the newest French manner, holding classes on Fridays and Saturdays once in three weeks. Advertisements in 1745 and 1746 announced balls and assemblies at the Capitol during meetings of the General Court. In Dec. 1749 he was advertising a similar dancing school in Charleston. Spruill, *Women's Life and Work*, p. 204.

[51]Woodfin, ed., *Another Secret Diary*, entries for Dec. 29, 1739, Feb. 25, 1740, Apr. 10, June 20, 1741. Byrd's regular

exercise, described in the daily statement, "I danced," was some sort of calisthenics.

[52]See his master's advertisement, *Va. Gaz.*, Apr. 6, 1739.

[53]*Ibid.*, Oct. 24, 1751. From 1757 to 1767 a Mr. Covington, dancing master, was paid for teaching Elizabeth Reade of York County. "Education in Colonial Virginia," *WMQ*, 1st Ser., VI (1897–1898), p. 3. John Mercer's ledgers show accounts with "Mr. Covington the Dancing Master" in 1750. Ledgers, 1725–1732, 1741–1750, pp. 120, 131, MS, Bucks County Historical Society, Doylestown, Pa., microfilm in Foundation Lib.

[54]Advertisement, *Va. Gaz.*, Mar. 20, 1752.

[55]Fitzpatrick, ed., *Writings of Washington*, I, p. 79.

[56]William, Chevalier de Peyroney, to George Washington, Sept. 5, 1754, in Stanislaus Murray Hamilton, ed., *Letters to Washington, and Accompanying Papers,* I (Boston, 1898), pp. 39–49.

[57]H. R. McIlwaine and John Pendleton Kennedy, eds., *Journals of the House of Burgesses of Virginia, 1750–1758* (Richmond, Va., 1905–1915), entry for Oct. 25, 1754, p. 219.

[58]See Landon Carter's report to the House on his address to Gov. Dinwiddie in Peyroney's behalf, Aug. 30, 1754, *ibid.*, p. 198.

[59]Washington to Dinwiddie, July 18, 1755, in Fitzpatrick, ed., *Writings of Washington*, I, p. 149. For a full narrative of the battle, see Douglas Southall Freeman, *George Washington: A Biography.* Vol. I: *Young Washington* (New York, 1948), Chap. 11.

[60]Russworm, an accomplished violinist, advertised for music and dancing pupils, offering to teach young gentlemen at Mr. Singleton's house in Williamsburg and young ladies in their own homes. *Va. Gaz.* (Purdie and Dixon), May 16, 1771. Two years later, the *Gazette* announced: "Mr. Francis Russworm, of Nansemond County, who played such a sweet Fiddle, and was a worthy good-tempered Man, had the Misfortune to be drowned a few Days ago in crossing over some Ferry." *Ibid.*, June 24, 1773. In Sept. one of his admirers, Samuel Nelson, praised him in poetry as a social being, brother Mason, and musician. *Ibid.*, Sept. 9, 1773.

[61]Sarah Hallam was the wife of Lewis Hallam, Jr. After he deserted her, she stayed on in Williamsburg with one of her sons, Mirvan Hallam. She had little dramatic talent and seldom appeared on the stage. Apparently she supported her son and herself by operating a boardinghouse and dancing school from the early 1770s until her death in 1792. See Rankin, "Colonial Theatre," pp. 105, 129, 241–242, 247.

[62]The death of William Fearson, dancing master, was reported in the *Va. Gaz.*, May 23, 1777. He was teaching in Williamsburg in 1769, for Anne Blair mentioned him in a letter to her sister, Mrs. George Braxton. Of young Betsy Braxton, who was visiting in the Blair home, Anne wrote: "Betsy is at work for you, I suppose she will tell you tomorrow is Dancing day, for it is in her thoughts by Day and her dreams by night. Mr. Fearson was surprized to find she knew much of the Minuet step, and could not help asking if Miss had never been taught, so you find she is likely to make some progress that way." Anne Blair to Martha [Mary?] Braxton, Aug. 21, 1769, *WMQ*, 1st Ser., XVI (1907–1908), pp. 176–180.

[63]John K'Dore, lately from France, advertised his intention of opening dancing schools in Williamsburg and at King William Courthouse, promising to teach the minuet "in the neatest and newest manner" and also offering instruction in fencing and the French language. *Va. Gaz.* (Dixon and Nicholson), July 17, 1779.

[64]See Fitzpatrick, ed., *Diaries of Washington*, I, pp. 373, 377–378; Fithian, *Journal*, ed. Farish, pp. 25, 27, 32, 33, 42–46, 88, 163–165, 187, 233, 250–252; and "Diary of Col. Landon Carter," *WMQ*, 1st Ser., XIV (1905–1906), p. 41. In Stanard, *Colonial Virginia*, p. 145, is an undated entry for 1774 (not included in the excerpts printed in the *Quarterly*) in which Carter rejoiced because Christian had stopped holding dancing classes in the neighborhood—the schoolboys had been losing two days in every three weeks when they attended the classes.

[65]*Va. Gaz.* (Purdie and Dixon), Dec. 22, 1768.

[66]Quoted in Marie Kimball, *Jefferson: War and Peace, 1776 to 1784* (New York, 1947), p. 20.

[67]The following music teachers were active in Williamsburg. Peter Pelham was the organist at Bruton Church from about 1750 to about 1785. Cuthbert Ogle, at the time of his death in 1755, owned a fiddle and case, a harpsichord, and an

unusually good collection of sheet music. "Libraries in Colonial Virginia," *WMQ*, 1st Ser., III (1894–1895), pp. 250–253. Lyon G. Tyler's often quoted conclusion that Ogle was Williamsburg's most prominent musician before Pelham's arrival seems somewhat strained. Ogle's advertisement in the *Va. Gaz.*, Mar. 28, 1755, suggests that he had just arrived in town. He then *proposed* to teach instrumental music and concluded his offer in these words: "Upon having Encouragement I will fix in any Part of the Country." Less than a month later he was dead. John Singleton, one of the actors in the Hallam group, advertised violin lessons in Williamsburg, Yorktown, Hampton, and Norfolk. *Ibid.*, June 12, 1752. Nearly 20 years later Francis Russworm offered to teach young gentlemen dancing and music at Mr. Singleton's house in Williamsburg. *Ibid.* (Purdie and Dixon), May 16, 1771. Whether Singleton stayed on in Virginia after the Hallam Company left is not known, nor is there a record of his buying a Williamsburg house. In 1771 another musician, William Attwood, offered his services as an instructor in playing the French horn, oboe, and German flute. *Ibid.*, May 23, 1771. Charles Leonard, who died in 1776 at the age of 76, was a native of Cologne, Germany, and was "well known in Virginia for his excellent but capricious performance on the violin." "Personal Notices from 'Virginia Gazette,'" *WMQ*, 1st Ser., XI (1902–1903), p. 94. Jefferson later recalled another violin teacher, Francis Alberti, who came over with a troop of players and afterward taught at Williamsburg. Subsequently Jefferson said, "I got him to come up here [Monticello] and took lessons for several years." Henry S. Randall, *The Life of Thomas Jefferson*, I (New York, 1858), p. 131, quoting Nicholas P. Trist's memoranda. John Stedler (or Stadley), like Francis Christian, is known today from the diaries of Washington and Fithian. See Fitzpatrick, ed., *Diaries of Washington*, I, pp. 257, 265–266, 294, 299, 303, 321–322, 346, 369, 373, 378, 386–387, II, p. 22; and John C. Fitzpatrick, *George Washington, Colonial Traveller, 1732–1775* (Indianapolis, Ind., 1927), pp. 186, 194, 200. These entries mention Stedler's presence at Mount Vernon and Washington's payments to him for teaching music to Mrs. Washington and the Custis children from 1765 to 1771. Fithian spoke well of "this good German," whose tact, simplicity, and good sense made him an agreeable companion. He had taught music in New York and Philadelphia and performed "extremely well" on violin, flute, harpsichord, armonica, and piano, but not on the guitar—Carter himself instructed his daughter Nancy on this instrument. Fithian, *Journal*, ed. Farish, pp. 28, 37, 105, 110, 111, 159–160, 182, 207–208, 222, 246, 248, 266, 267.

[68]Mary R. M. Goodwin, "Musical Instruments of 18th-century Virginia," 1953, typescript in Foundation Lib.

[69]*Va. Gaz.* advertisements for runaway Negroes and slaves for sale often mentioned their ability to play a musical instrument. Jefferson thought they brought the "Banjar" with them from Africa. *Notes on the State of Virginia*, ed. William Peden (Chapel Hill, N. C., 1955), p. 288. John Harrower, tutor in Col. William Daingerfield's household at Belvidera, described the barrafou, a kind of marimba played by one of Col. John Spotswood's Negroes. Diary, Mar. 25, 1775. Smyth, describing the amusements of the Virginia Negro in the period just before the Revolution, wrote: "But instead of retiring to rest, as might naturally be concluded he would be glad to do, he generally sets out from home, and walks six or seven miles in the night, be the weather ever so sultry, to a negroe dance, in which he performs with astonishing agility, and the most vigorous exertions, keeping time and cadence, most exactly, with the music of a banjor (a large hollow instrument with three strings), and a quaqua (somewhat resembling a drum), until he exhausts himself." *Tour*, I, p. 48.

[70]Advertisements in the *Va. Gaz.*, 1765, 1770, 1771.

[71]Fithian, *Journal*, ed. Farish, pp. 49, 90–99, 110, 174, 270.

[72]Blair to Braxton, Aug. 1769, *WMQ*, 1st Ser., XVI (1907–1908), pp. 174–180. Travelers mentioned similar evenings. See Chastellux, *Travels*, II, pp. 130, 149; Hunter, *Quebec to Carolina*, ed. Wright and Tinling, pp. 204–205, 210, 213, 216, 219, 225–226, 229, 241, 246, 251, 291; and Cresswell, *Journal*, ed. Thornely, pp. 18, 19, 30, 48, 57–58, 109, 111, 115, 132.

[73]Fithian carefully noted the difference in his diary entry for Sept. 3, 1774: "I was invited this morning by Captain *Tibbs* to a *Barbecue:* this differs but little from the Fish Feasts, instead of Fish the Dinner is roasted *Pig*, with the proper apendages,

but the Diversion and exercise are the very same at both." Fithian, *Journal,* ed. Farish, p. 240. Other references to fish feasts may be found on pp. 193, 194, 198, 206, 212, 220, 226, 233.

[74]Harrower, Diary, entry for June 11, 1774; Cresswell, *Journal,* ed. Thornely, p. 30; Isaac Weld, *Travels through the States of North America, and the Provinces of Upper and Lower Canada, during the Years 1795, 1796, and 1797,* I (London, 1807), p. 187.

[75]Benjamin Latrobe explained in 1796: In Alexandria one June day "about half-past eight the Philadelphia company of players who are now acting in a barn in the neighborhood came in a body. They had been at a 'drinking party' in the neighbor-hood. Once, in Virginia, these drinking parties had a much more modest name—they were called 'barbecues.' Now they say at once a 'drinking party.'" Benjamin Henry Latrobe, *The Journal of Latrobe: Being the Notes and Sketches of an Architect, Naturalist and Traveler in the United States from 1796 to 1820* (New York, 1905), p. 30.

[76]"Diary of Col. Landon Carter," *WMQ,* 1st Ser., XIII (1904–1905), p. 163.

[77]Henry René D'Allemagne, *Récréations et Passe-Temps* (Paris, [1905]), pp. 211–217. There were restrictions on the choice of proverb—not only those imposed by the limitations of the players' ability and imagination, but stronger ones of good taste. D'Allemagne explained that the game had to be played "avec beaucoup d'à-propos, mais surtout avec discrétion et savoir-vivre."

[78]Wright and Tinling, eds., *London Diary,* pp. 121, 178, 216, 313, 413, 474, 476, 478, 495, 501, 511.

[79]Accomack County Records, Nov. 16, Dec. 18, 1665, Jan. 16, 1665/66, quoted in Ralph T. Whitelaw, *Virginia's Eastern Shore: A History of Northampton and Accomack Counties,* I (Richmond, Va., 1951), pp. 712–713.

[80]Cresswell, *Journal,* ed. Thornely, entry for June 19, 1774, p. 23.

[81]*Va. Gaz.,* Sept. 10, 1736; Thomas Jones to Mrs. Jones, Sept. 17, 1736, "Jones Papers," *VMHB,* XXVI (1918), p. 180. Another performance was planned in 1751. John Blair wrote in his diary on Nov. 18: "This evening Mr. Pr[est]on to prevent

the young gentlemen at the college from playing at a rehearsal in the dormit'y, how they could act Cato privately among themselves, did himself, they say, act the Drun[ke]n Peasant; but his tearing down the curtains is to me very surprising." "Diary of John Blair," *WMQ,* 1st Ser., VIII (1899–1900), p. 15.

[82]*Va. Gaz.* (Purdie and Dixon), May 21, 1767.

[83]Washington to [Sally Cary Fairfax], Sept. 25, 1758, in Fitzpatrick, ed., *Writings of Washington,* II, p. 293. This Sally Cary Fairfax was the wife of George William of Belvoir; the little girl of the same name, quoted on p. 4, was William Fairfax's granddaughter.

[84]George Farquhar wrote *The Beaux' Stratagem* in 1707; it immediately became popular in London playhouses, and it was presented in Williamsburg in 1736. Throughout the colonial period it appeared on American stages—in Annapolis, New York, Philadelphia, and Charleston—from the 1730s through the 1770s. See Susan S. Armstrong, "A Repertoire of the American Colonial Theatre," 1955, typescript in Foundation Lib. *The Belle's Stratagem* does not appear in any list of eighteenth-century plays available in the Department of Research. Since Farquhar died shortly after writing *The Beaux' Stratagem,* he is not a likely author of the sequel. Perhaps this was an anonymous effort to profit from the popularity of Farquhar's comedy, perhaps Mr. Pinkard adapted the title of Farquhar's play to suit his audience, or perhaps Lucinda got the title wrong.

[85]Lee, *Journal,* ed. Mason, pp. 27, 54.

[86]For examples in the year 1709, see Louis B. Wright and Marion Tinling, eds., *The Secret Diary of William Byrd of Westover, 1709–1712* (Richmond, Va., 1941), entries for Mar. 26, Apr. 5, 6, 7, Nov. 22, 24.

[87]William Byrd, *A Progress to the Mines, in the Year 1732,* in John Spencer Bassett, ed., *The Writings of "Colonel William Byrd of Westover in Virginia, Esqr."* (New York, 1901), p. 341.

[88]Anonymous essay, *Va. Gaz.* (Purdie and Dixon), Mar. 28, 1771. The viciousness of novel reading was much discussed in England. When Fanny Burney wrote *Evelina,* she carefully defended her book in the preface: "Perhaps were it possible to effect the total extirpation of novels, our young ladies in

general, and boarding-school damsels in particular, might profit by their annihilation; but since the distemper they have spread seems incurable, since their contagion bids defiance to the medicine of advice or reprehension, and since they are found to baffle all the mental art of physic, save what is prescribed by the slow regimen of time, and bitter diet of Experience, surely all attempts to contribute to the number of those which may be read, if not with advantage, at least without injury, ought rather to be encouraged than contemned." 2nd ed. (London, 1779), reprint edition, ed. Sir Frank D. Mackinnon (Oxford, 1930), p. x. While John Davis was tutoring the Ball children at Pohoke, about 1798, he was especially interested in forming the literary tastes of the eldest daughter, Virginia, whose favorite book was a translation of Bernardin de St. Pierre's *Paul and Virginia*. Davis, *Travels*, p. 363. Virginia men usually read for information rather than amusement; their reading time was limited, and romances seldom appealed to them. *Tristram Shandy*, as fiction, was an exception; it is not a typical romance because the emphasis is on characters associated with Tristram and not on the plot.

[89]Few of these romances have survived to our time, and in contemporary book lists they are hard to distinguish from popular biography because the title is usually a *History* of the main character. For a list of novels advertised in the *Va. Gaz.* and other southern newspapers, see Spruill, *Women's Life and Work*, p. 230n.

[90]Other titles mentioned were *Victoria*, a new novel, and *Malvern Dale*, something like *Evelina*, although not so "pretty." Lee, *Journal*, ed. Mason, pp. 12, 17, 25, 48–49. These two titles have not been identified.

[91]Hunter, *Quebec to Carolina*, ed. Wright and Tinling, passim.

[92]Elizabeth Ambler Carrington to her sister Nancy [1810], "An Old Virginia Correspondence," *Atlantic Monthly*, LXXXIV (1899), p. 547.

[93]James Parker to Charles Steuart, Sept. 29, 1774, Charles Steuart Letter Books, 1751–1763, MS 5028, fols. 265–266, Hist. Soc. Pa., microfilm in Foundation Lib.

Chapter Two: Games

[1]An example is John Mercer's self-explanatory ledger entry of an account with Col. George Braxton: "To a Wager you laid me at Capt. Robt. Brooke's house before Mr. James Reid, Willm. Brooke etc, Six guineas to one that Colo. Spotswood would not during the reign of K. George that now is, procure a Commission as Chief or Lieut. Govr. of Virginia. £7.16–." Ledger, 1725–1732, p. 61. For other examples, see Philip Alexander Bruce, *Social Life in Virginia in the Seventeenth Century*, 2nd ed. (Lynchburg, Va., 1927), Chap. 16.

[2]John Ashton, *The History of Gambling in England* (London, 1898), p. 156.

[3]. Horace Walpole to Sir William Hamilton, June 19, 1774, quoted in Wilmarth Sheldon Lewis, *Three Tours through London in the Years 1748, 1776, 1791* (New Haven, Conn., 1952), p. 61.

[4]For brief descriptions of the London gambling scene, see Cyril Hughes Hartmann, ed., *Games and Gamesters of the Restoration* (London, 1930), introduction; Lewis, *Three Tours*, pp. 61–62; T. S. Ashton, *An Economic History of England: The 18th Century* (London, 1955), pp. 24–26; and Dorothy Marshall, "Manners, Morals, and Domestic Pastimes," in A. S. Turberville, ed., *Johnson's England: An Account of the Life & Manners of his Age*, I (Oxford, 1933), pp. 354–355.

[5]"Letters of the Byrd Family," *VMHB*, XXXVII (1929), p. 310.

[6]"Some Notes from 'The Memorial of Benjamin Ogle Tayloe,' " *Tyler's Quarterly Historical and Genealogical Magazine*, II (1920), pp. 82–83.

[7]"Journal of a French Traveller in the Colonies, 1765," *American Historical Review*, XXVI (1901), p. 741.

[8]Stanard, *Colonial Virginia*, p. 149.

[9]William Nelson to Samuel Athawes, May 16, 1771, Nelson Letterbook, 1766–1775, pp. 199–201, Virginia State Library, Richmond, microfilm in Foundation Lib.

[10]*Maryland Gazette* (Annapolis), Dec. 27, 1753.

[11]See, for example, William Byrd II's smug account of cheating at piquet, undetected by his wife, in Wright and Tinling, eds., *Secret Diary*, p. 75.

[12]George Webb's summary in *The Office and Authority of a Justice of Peace* . . . (Williamsburg, Va., 1736), pp. 165–168.

[13]"Journal of the Meetings of the President and Masters of William and Mary College," *WMQ*, 1st Ser., II (1893–1894), pp. 55–56, XVI (1907–1908), p. 247, XXII (1913–1914), p. 288.

[14]For typical acts of the Assembly, see Hening, ed., *Statutes*, I, p. 114, III, pp. 360, 397, IV, pp. 214–218, V, pp. 102, 229–231, VI, pp. 76–81.

[15]*Va. Gaz.* (Purdie and Dixon), Oct. 7, 1773.

[16]Anne Staunton to Thomas Gooch, Feb. 25, 1728/29, Gooch Letter Book, p. 152.

[17]Martha Jefferson once lost 1s. 3d. at cards. Thomas Jefferson's MS Account Book, n.d., cited in William Eleroy Curtis, *The True Thomas Jefferson* (Philadelphia, 1901), p. 317. Washington's account books show occasional losses to ladies. Twice at Mount Vernon in Feb. 1749 Mrs. Anne Washington (wife of Maj. Lawrence Washington) won small sums at whist, and at Belvoir in the spring of 1755 Mrs. Ann Spearing won 4s. 6d., 3s. 9d., and 1s. 6d. from him. Fitzpatrick, *George Washington*, pp. 20, 68, 69.

[18]In 1749 Lady Mary Montagu summarized: "Your new fashioned game of *brag* was the genteel amusement when I was a girl; *crimp* succeeded to that, and *basset* and *hazard* employed the town when I left it to go to Constantinople. At my return, I found them all at *commerce*, which gave place to *quadrille*, and that to *whist*; but the rage of play has been ever the same, and will be so among the idle of both sexes." Quoted in Marshall, "Manners, Morals, and Domestic Pastimes," in Turberville, ed., *Johnson's England*, I, p. 358.

[19]Wright and Tinling, eds., *London Diary*, passim.

[20]Mrs. Taylor to William Byrd, Jan. 8, 1742, "Letters of the Byrd Family," *VMHB*, XXXVII (1929), p. 113.

[21]Jules Verne, *The Tour of the World in Eighty Days* (New York, n.d.), pp. 3, 15, 18–24, 32–33, 55–60, 70, 127, 236–238, 246–249, 310.

[22]See advertisements of books for sale in the *Va. Gaz.* Several inventories of private libraries listed them, and Daniel Parke Custis had both titles. "Catalogue of the Library of Daniel Parke Custis," *VMHB*, XVII (1909), pp. 404–412. The surviving Virginia Gazette Day Books, 1750–1752, 1764–1765, show the following sales of Hoyle, which was popular at those periods: to Dr. Peter Hay, David Galloway, Nathaniel Walthoe, and Dr. James Carter in 1751; to James Lyle, Hon. Peter Randolph, William Willis, Robert Tucker, Jr., John Tazewell, David Mason, and John Connelly in 1764; and to John Tunstall in 1765. MS, Alderman Lib., photostats in Foundation Lib.

[23]The 3rd, 4th, and 5th editions (1709, 1721, 1725) emphasized card games; the sales noted above were probably eighteenth-century editions. A recent reprint is in Hartmann, ed., *Games and Gamesters*.

[24]The Bodleian copy of the first edition is the only one known to exist. The College of William and Mary has an 11th edition, *Mr. Hoyle's Games of Whist, Quadrille, Piquet, Chess, and Back-gammon, Complete. In which are contained, the Method of Playing and Betting, at Those Games, upon equal, or advantageous Terms. Including also, the Laws of the Several Games* (London, n.d. [1750–1760]). Individual titles in the volume describe Hoyle's method:

(1) "A Short Treatise on the Game of Whist. Containing The Laws of the Game: and also Some Rules, whereby a Beginner may, with due Attention to them, attain to the Playing it well. Calculations for those who will bet the Odds on any Points of the Score of the Game then playing and depending. Cases stated, to shew what may be effected by a very good Player in critical Parts of the Game. References to Cases, viz. at the End of the Rule, you are directed how to find them. Calculations, directing with moral Certainty, how to play well any Hand or Game, by shewing the Chances of your Partner's having 1, 2, or 3 certain Cards. With Variety of Cases added in the Appendix. By Edmond Hoyle, Gent. The Laws of the Game, and an Explanation of the Calculations which are necessary to be understood by those who would play it well. And also, A Dictionary for Whist, which resolves almost all the critical Cases that may happen at the Game. To which is added, An Artificial Memory: Or, an easy Method of assisting the Memory of those that play at the Game of Whist. And several Cases, not hitherto published."
(2) "A Short Treatise on the Game of Quadrille; Shewing The Odds of winning or losing most Games that are com-

monly played; either by calling a King, or by playing *Sans Prendre*. To which are added, The Laws of the Game. The Third Edition. By Edmond Hoyle, Gent."

(3) "A Short Treatise On the Game of Piquet; Directing, with moral Certainty, how to discard any Hand to Advantage, by shewing the Chances of taking in any one, two, three, four, or five certain Cards. Computations for those who Bet their Money at the Game. Also the Laws of the Game. To which are added, Some Rules and Observations for playing well at Chess. The Third Edition. By Edmond Hoyle, Gent."

(4) "A Short Treatise On the Game of Back-gammon. Containing A Table of the thirty-six Chances, with Directions how to find out the Odds of being hit, upon single, or double Dice. Rules whereby a Beginner may, with due Attention to them, attain playing it well. The several Stages for carrying your Men home, in order to lose no Point. How to find out who is forwardest to win a Hit. Cases stated for Back-Games, with Directions how to play for one. Cases stated, how to know when you may have the better of saving a Gammon by running. Variety of Cases of Curiosity and Instruction. The Laws of the Game. The Fourth Edition. By Edmond Hoyle, Gent."

[25]William Byrd, *The Secret History of the Line,* Mar. 25, 1728, in William K. Boyd, ed., *William Byrd's Histories of the Dividing Line betwixt Virginia and North Carolina* (Raleigh, N. C., 1929), p. 91. For card playing at Westover, see Wright and Tinling, eds., *Secret Diary;* Woodfin, ed., *Another Secret Diary;* and Wright and Tinling, eds., *London Diary,* pp. 382ff.

[26]*Va. Gaz.,* May 16, 1751.

[27]"Diary of Col. Landon Carter," *WMQ,* 1st Ser., XIV (1905–1906), p. 248.

[28]Charles Cotton, *The Compleat Gamester or, Instructions How to Play at Billiards, Trucks, Bowls, and Chess* . . . (1674), in Hartmann, ed., *Games and Gamesters,* pp. 55–58. Since the rules of play were so well known, Cotton was "unwilling to speak any thing more of them than this, that there may be a great deal of art used in dealing and playing at these games which differ very little one from the other." In his time, each hand consisted of 12 cards. In whist, deuces were removed

from the pack. In ruff and slam there was a widow of 4 cards, which was given to the player holding the ace of trumps.

[29]Byrd played ombre, and Washington purchased quadrille counters. These games used a 40-card deck (with 8s, 9s, and 10s discarded). See Cotton, *Compleat Gamester,* in Hartmann, ed., *Games and Gamesters,* pp. 47–51. Spanish names for special cards reveal the origin of the games: the best or "killing" cards are *Matadors—Spadillo* (ace of spades), *Basto* (ace of clubs), and *Mallillio* (black deuce or red seven).

[30]It was played in England from the sixteenth century into the twentieth. For eighteenth-century rules of play, see Appendix.

[31]Near the present-day Toano, about 10 or 12 miles northwest of Williamsburg.

[32]Daniel Fisher's Journal, 1750–1755, published as "The Fisher History" in Louise Pecquet du Bellet, *Some Prominent Virginia Families,* II (Lynchburg, Va., 1907), p. 788.

[33]Norfolk County Deed Book, No. 9, p. 163, summarized in Thomas J. Wertenbaker, *Norfolk: Historic Southern Port* (Durham, N. C., 1931), p. 20.

[34]*South Carolina Gazette* (Charleston), Jan. 15, 1732.

[35]Fithian, *Journal,* ed. Farish, p. 140.

[36]Cotton, *Compleat Gamester,* in Hartmann, ed., *Games and Gamesters,* p. 62. See Appendix for his essay.

[37]Stanard, *Colonial Virginia,* p. 148. Soane got into trouble with horse racing, too. See Chap. 3.

[38]York County, Deeds, Orders, Wills, No. 7 (1684–1687), p. 143, microfilm in Foundation Lib.

[39]Henrico County Minute Book, 1682–1701, p. 279, Va. State Lib.

[40]The *Oxford English Dictionary* traces the origin of the name to the French word *lanturelu,* the meaningless refrain of a song popular in the seventeenth century.

[41]"Loo-table" is now a trade name for this kind of gaming table. One on display at Colonial Williamsburg, an English piece dated about 1760, has a tilt-top with an embossed leather surface and seven "fish ponds." Colonial Williamsburg owns two other card tables with counter grooves; they are square and each has four pits. Robert Wormeley Carter often recorded his winnings and losses at cards of all kinds in terms of so many

fish, usually valued at sixpence each. See his diaries, 1764–1792, especially entries for Aug. 1765. Separate volumes variously owned, typescript copies in Foundation Lib.

[42]See Appendix for rules of play. A similar game, bragg, is closer to modern poker and is more interesting than loo. Although it was popular in eighteenth-century England, I have found no account of its being played in Virginia. Cotton's rules for playing bragg are so explicit that modern readers can easily follow them. See Appendix, pp. 120–122.

[43]*Va. Gaz.* (Purdie and Dixon), Nov. 10, 1768.

[44]Fitzpatrick, *George Washington,* p. 20. In later account books Washington entered sums won and lost "at Cards" without specifying the games he was playing. See Ledger A, 1750–1772, and Ledger B, 1772–1793, MS, Library of Congress, microfilm in Foundation Lib. In Ledger B, p. 48, he summarized his "Cards and Other Play" account (excluding horse racing bets) for the years 1772, 1773, and 1774: lost £78.5.9., won £72.2.6.

[45]Mercer, Ledger, 1725–1732, p. 140.

[46]"Historical and Genealogical Notes and Queries," *VMHB,* XVI (1908), p. 89.

[47]"Diary of Col. Landon Carter," *WMQ,* 1st Ser., XVI (1905–1906), p. 250.

[48]The exception was a game of Nov. 4, 1780, when Giberne won $46 from Wormeley Carter at piquet.

[49]See R. W. Carter's diaries, especially those for the period 1764–1780, passim.

[50]Mercer, Ledger, 1725–1732, pp. 35, 114.

[51]See Appendix for Cotton's rules. In the modern six-card game we cut the deck for the "starter" instead of turning it up from the top of the stack of undealt cards, and we count the hand after play instead of before. Rules for three-handed cribbage may be found in any modern Hoyle.

[52]William P. Palmer, ed., *Calendar of Virginia State Papers and Other Manuscripts Preserved in the Capitol at Richmond* (Richmond, Va., 1875–1893), IX, p. 41.

[53]"Robert Bailey," *Tyler's Quarterly,* III (1921), p. 54.

[54]Weld, *Travels,* I, p. 191.

[55]Latrobe to Thomas Blackburn, Apr. 21, 1796, quoted in Talbot Hamlin, *Benjamin Henry Latrobe* (New York, 1955), pp. 71–72.

[56]Wright and Tinling, eds., *London Diary,* passim; Wright and Tinling, eds., *Secret Diary,* passim. In London Byrd played commerce, slam, faro, and ace of hearts and often indulged in the betting at various fashionable clubs, in the Spanish ambassador's home, and on the Walk at Tunbridge Wells. But not in Virginia.

[57]See Appendix for Cotton's rules.

[58]Cotton, *Compleat Gamester,* in Hartmann, ed., *Games and Gamesters,* p. 24.

[59]Richard Seymour, *The Compleat Gamester: In Three Parts . . . ,* 5th ed. (London, 1734), p. 125.

[60]Hoyle, *Mr. Hoyle's Games,* pp. 155ff.

[61]Jefferson's account books show purchases in 1769, 1778, 1783, 1784, and 1786. These MSS are variously owned; photostatic copies are in the Alderman Lib.

[62]Jefferson to Jack Walker, Sept. 3, 1769, in Julian P. Boyd et al., eds., *The Papers of Thomas Jefferson,* I (Princeton, N. J., 1950), p. 32. The letter was a Latin stunt reading "Ferto etiam, ut ante tibi praecepi, tabulam scaccariam. Oculus feram viros." See also Jefferson's reference to "music, chess, or merriments of family companions," in the famous letter on books for a small library to Robert Skipwith, Aug. 3, 1771, *ibid.,* p. 78.

[63]York County, Wills and Inventories, No. 22 (1771–1783), pp. 83, 89.

[64]*Ibid.,* p. 467. Further research *should* reveal other sets, but no other inventory I have seen included them. The same thing is true of the letters, account books, county records, diaries, and travel accounts examined. Neither boards nor men were advertised in the *Va. Gaz.* The Day Books, however, have one curious entry—Nathaniel Walthoe on Aug. 3, 1751, was debited for "Hoyle on Chess" at 2/–. Hoyle's Games usually sold for 5/– or 7/6; no separate publication of Hoyle on chess alone has been found in bibliographies consulted.

[65]Stanard, *Colonial Virginia,* p. 328.

[66]Joseph Strutt, *The Sports and Pastimes of the People of England . . . ,* new ed. enl. by J. Charles Cox (London, 1903), pp. 255–256. The draughts now played in most continental

countries is the Polish game of 100 squares, introduced into France in the 1720s.

[67]For a sampling of these, see the card index to York County records, Foundation Lib., where 20 backgammon tables are listed, together with other references to the game.

[68]Stanard, *Colonial Virginia*, p. 149.

[69]Jefferson, Account Book, 1770, pp. 9, 15.

[70]See the inventory printed in "Carter Papers," *VMHB*, VI (1898), p. 145.

[71]Cotton, *Compleat Gamester*, in Hartmann, ed., *Games and Gamesters*, pp. 74–79. See also Strutt, *Sports and Pastimes*, pp. 247–248.

[72]Cotton, *Compleat Gamester*, in Hartmann, ed., *Games and Gamesters*, p. 82.

[73]See Appendix for Cotton's rules and for a summary of Hoyle's table of chances. To calculate the odds in craps, all one need know is that there are:

6 combinations for 7,
5 combinations for 6 and 8,
4 combinations for 5 and 9,
3 combinations for 4 and 10,
2 combinations for 3 and 11, and
1 combination for 2 and 12.

The game has undergone other changes, of course, notably in making 12 a crap number. The colorful language of the game reflects the interests of the players and the localities and social groups where it is most popular. A convenient description of later developments in the house game of hazard may be found in the *Encyclopedia Britannica*.

[74]Dice games were unlawful for workingmen and servants in all the Virginia statutes from 1619 on.

[75]*Va. Gaz.*, June 9, 1738.

[76]George Holden was a brother-in-law of Dudley Digges and of James Hubard of Williamsburg, usher of the grammar school in 1755. His wife, Elizabeth Hubard Holden, was a daughter of Mathew Hubard, clerk of the York court. John James Hughlett is difficult to identify precisely. He had large landholdings, which at one time included Portobello, on the north side of Queen's Creek near Williamsburg. During the 1740s there was rarely a meeting of the York court when he did not have one or more civil suits on the docket—and he usually won the suit.

[77]*Holden* v. *Hughlett*, tried June 16, 1746. York County, Land Causes (1746–1769), pp. 1–7 at back of book.

[78]Stanard, *Colonial Virginia*, p. 149.

[79]Cotton, *Compleat Gamester*, in Hartmann, ed., *Games and Gamesters*, p. 119.

[80]Mercer, Ledger, 1741–1750, p. 91.

[81]Wright and Tinling, eds., *Secret Diary*, p. 442.

[82]Strutt, *Sports and Pastimes*, p. 322.

[83]D'Allemagne, *Récréations et Passe-Temps*, pp. 82–95. Illustrations include several beautifully carved boxes of delicately engraved dominoes from his collection. Most of these are seventeenth- or eighteenth-century pieces of Italian workmanship in ivory, bone, and wood. They resemble the carved wooden box owned by Colonial Williamsburg (Accession No. 1956-579) which seems to be English because the name "J. Bell" and the date "1716" are cut into the wood of the box, although too crudely to be the work of the artisan who carved the box itself. D'Allemagne was interested in the history of the game, and after rejecting theories of its Hebrew, Greek, or Chinese origin, concluded that it probably developed in medieval convents and monasteries. The name, he thought, came from the resemblance of the black and white of the tiles to the sixteenth-century hooded habit, the domino, or else from the expression customarily used by the player of the last tile to announce the end of the game—"Benedicamus Domino" or "Gratias Domino."

[84]Furniture inventories of ordinaries and private estates usually included them; advertisements of ordinaries for sale often described the good condition of billiard tables as important selling points. See E. G. Swem, comp., *Virginia Historical Index* (Roanoke, Va., 1934–1936); Lester J. Cappon and Stella F. Duff, comps., *Virginia Gazette Index, 1736–1780* (Williamsburg, Va., 1950); and card index to York County records and *Va. Gaz.*, Foundation Lib.

[85]Cotton, *Compleat Gamester*, in Hartmann, ed., *Games and Gamesters*, p. 12.

[86]Strutt, *Sports and Pastimes*, p. 239. Pl. 31 and p. 219 show and explain an old print of bowls driven by a bat through

a wicket, somewhat like the nineteenth-century development in England called croquet; this game already had the latter name in France in the eighteenth century.

[87]Cotton, *Compleat Gamester,* in Hartmann, ed., *Games and Gamesters,* pp. 12–13. For illustrated instructions for making the table and equipment, see Diderot, ed., *Encyclopédie,* II, s.v. "Belouses," X, s.v. "Masse, terme de billard," XIII, s.v. "Queue, paumier," XV, s.v. "Table de billard," and *Planches,* VIII, s.v. "Paumier," pls. 4–5.

[88]See Appendix for Cotton's rules. By mid-century French billiards was popular in England; port and king were removed, and the stick resembled a modern cue, although the leather tip was not invented until the nineteenth century. Yet Diderot's directions and illustrations clearly call for port and king. Perhaps the name "French billiards," as used in the 1734 edition of the *Compleat Gamester,* did not mean "billiards as it is played in France."

[89]Wright and Tinling, eds., *Secret Diary,* passim; Wright and Tinling, eds., *London Diary,* passim; Woodfin, ed., *Another Secret Diary,* passim.

[90]His account books, cited in Fitzpatrick, ed., *George Washington,* pp. 16, 67, 68, 81, 85, 108, show that he played at Williamsburg, Fredericksburg, and Belvoir, and at ordinaries en route to and from Winchester.

[91]Stanard, *Colonial Virginia,* p. 149.

[92]Sarah N. Randolph, *The Domestic Life of Thomas Jefferson. Compiled from Family Letters and Reminiscences* (New York, 1871), p. 332.

[93]Fithian, *Journal,* ed. Farish, p. 146.

[94]The collection of lottery tickets that belongs to Mr. Philip G. Nordell of Ambler, Pa., one of the best in the country, contains several Virginia items.

[95]Not everyone held a winning ticket, of course. The *Va. Gaz.,* Apr. 24, 1752, once printed the following soliloquy for the amusement of readers who had lots:

*A Meditation: or Contemplation, by an unsuccessful Adventurer in a Late Lottery,*

Why frets my Soul because of a Blank! or why doth it lament at having missed of a Prize? Suppose I had got one of the Ten Thousands, what then?—Why then, slap dash down at a Blow, with the whole Catalogue of my Wants. But soft—Would not the Destruction of those Wants be the Generation of others; and the Destruction of these the Generation of more? and so on?—As sure as a Gun.—At this Rate, what would be gained by a Ten Thousand Pound Prize?—Nothing—Or, what have I lost by a Blank?—Nothing at all.—Why then, a Blank is as good as a Ten Thousand Pound Prize.—Who then in their Wits can doubt it? and consequently better than an Inferior Prize.—As plain as a Pike Staff. Then what are they who rejoice at a Prize?—Prize Fools. And what are they who grieve at a Blank?—Blank Fools.—*Sing tan-tara-ra-ra, Fools all, Fools all, etc.*

[96]Rules of play as detailed in an advertising broadside, "From Paris. The Public are respectfully informed that The Fashionable and Interesting Game of Loto, May be had Here" (London, n.d.), copy in Foundation Lib. The Colonial Williamsburg Department of Collections has two beautifully decorated sets of lotto cards—one Italian, the other French—and a French lotto bag, together with a set of numbered slips rolled into small squills and inserted in separate little wooden capsules, which are placed in the bag for drawing.

[97]Wright and Tinling, eds., *London Diary,* p. 411.

[98]Curtis, *The True Jefferson,* p. 317. For Jefferson's famous "Thoughts on Lotteries," see Lipscomb and Bergh, eds., *Writings of Jefferson,* XVII, pp. 448ff.

[99]Strutt, *Sports and Pastimes,* p. 266.

[100]The morning following the game he claimed 700 pounds. Henrico County Records, Deeds and Wills, 1677–1692, p. 224, Va. State Lib. In another suit in the Henrico court Pygott paid gambling losses at cards. *Ibid.,* p. 28.

[101]*Oxford English Dictionary;* Strutt, *Sports and Pastimes,* p. 268.

[102]See Chap. 3, pp. 80–81.

[103]Fitzpatrick, ed., *Writings of Washington,* IV, pp. 1–2.

[104]See Jay B. Hubbell and Douglass Adair, "Robert Munford's *The Candidates,*" *WMQ,* 3rd Ser., V (1948), pp. 217–257, for the use of this word.

[105]*Va. Gaz.* (Rind), June 29, 1769.

[106]The French collector of antiques, Henry René D'Allemagne, had nearly 100 Goose boards. His book, *Le Noble Jeu*

*de l'Oie en France, de 1640 à 1950* (Paris, 1950), is lavishly illustrated with colored plates of the rare items in his collection, and the text relates the history of the game in France.

[107]Fredericksburg District Court Records, File 312, Nov. 9, 1755, microfilm in Foundation Lib.

[108]R. W. Carter, Diary, Apr. 6, 1765.

[109]There were a number of adaptations of the Game of the Goose that were designed for instruction as well as pleasure. D'Allemagne's collection includes 30 or 40 different kinds of boards, many of them clearly educational in intent. Some teach geography, others history, philosophy, mythology, the French classics, mathematics, botany, zoology, and astronomy. For an example of educational boards, see *The New Game of Human Life* (London, 1790). It is obviously a literal translation of a French board that appeared about 1775. Mounted on linen like a map, it is folded and enclosed in a slipcase, which pronounces it "the most Agreeable and Rational Recreation ever Invented for Youth of both Sexes." For other examples of English boards, see F. R. B. Whitehouse, *Table Games of Georgian and Victorian Days* (London, 1951). These include, besides an early version of the Goose, The Royall Pass-Tyme of Cupid, or The New and Most Pleasant Game of the Snake, in which the track is the coiled body of a large snake and cupids serve as geese. There is also an instructional game, A Journey Through Europe, or The Play of Geography, in which the picture is a map and the track a series of lines joining cities; hazards and rewards are determined by conventional tourist activities at each stop.

[110]The following proprietors in Williamsburg advertised both dressed and undressed imported dolls, some with glass eyes and hair wigs, in the *Va. Gaz.*: Sarah Pitt (1769, 1770, 1771); Mary Dickinson (1771); Margaret Hunter (1772, 1773); Catherine Rathell (1774, 1775); and John Carter (1774). Other merchants who advertised a variety of imported toys doubtless carried dolls in stock. Samuel and Henry Dixon ordered a list of toys that included a dozen dressed dolls and a dozen dressed dolls with glass eyes from John Norton on Jan. 2, 1774; these were not advertised in the *Gazette*. John Norton and Sons Papers, 1750–1902, Foundation Lib.

[111]Washington's papers contain the only orders I have seen that were addressed to toy manufacturers. In 1759 and 1760 he dealt directly with Unwin and Wigglesworth, toymaker, of London. Fitzpatrick, ed., *Writings of Washington,* II, pp. 335, 342.

[112]The most common description used in orders and advertisements was the phrase "Fash. drest."

[113]Extract from an account book of Thomas Davis, 1783–1785, *VMHB,* XVII (1909), p. 103.

[114]Blair to Braxton, Aug. 1769, *WMQ,* 1st Ser., XVI (1907–1908), p. 177. Anne explained to the child's mother: "I have had Hair put on Miss Dolly, but find it is not in my power of complying with my promise in giving her silk for a Sacque and Coat; some of our pretty Gang, broke open a Trunk in my absence and has stolen several thing's one of which the Silk makes a part—so imagine Betsy will petition you for some."

[115]Fitzpatrick, ed., *Writings of Washington,* II, pp. 335, 342.

[116]This is my own impression gathered from conversation with Mr. and Mrs. R. C. Mathes, doll collectors, in Escondido, Calif.

[117]*Va. Gaz.* (Rind), Apr. 19, 1770, Oct. 17, 1771; *ibid.* (Dixon and Hunter), Nov. 11, 1773. Francis Norton, in London, sent to his Virginia niece, John Hatley Norton's daughter, a set of small china "for her amusement." Francis Norton to John Hatley Norton, Sept. 6, 1774, in Frances Norton Mason, ed., *John Norton & Sons, Merchants of London and Virginia . . .* (Richmond, Va., 1937), p. 374.

[118]Fitzpatrick, ed., *Writings of Washington,* II, pp. 335, 342.

[119]Unidentified toys in "curious" assortments were advertised for sale in Williamsburg by George Wells, John Greenhow, James Craig, Sarah Pitt, Jane and Margaret Hunter, Frances Webb, Mary Dickinson, and Catherine Rathell. The Norfolk merchants Balfour and Barraud had tortoise and enameled toys for sale in 1766. The problem of identifying toys from merchants' advertisements is complicated by the fact that *toys* also included frivolous luxuries like fans, thimbles, buckles, powder boxes, scissors, and inkstands. Vivien Greene, *English Dolls' Houses of the Eighteenth and Nineteenth Centuries* (London, 1955), p. 51. It will be noticed that Williamsburg milliners advertised toys more often than did other merchants. There are the following orders for toys in the Norton Papers: Aug. 24, 1768, George Wilson, York County, ordered toy fiddles, mar-

bles, dressed babies, and dolls with glass eyes; July 22, 1772, James Wilkins, Northampton, ordered toy fiddles, Jew's harps, and an assortment of toys; Jan. 2, 1774, Samuel and Henry Dixon [Williamsburg], ordered tops and string, marbles, Jew's harps, toy fiddles, toy watches, basket rattles, dressed dolls, and dolls with glass eyes; Aug. 30, 1774, Mrs. John Norton in London asked permission of her son John Hatley to send a coral and bells to her new grandchild. In the Skipwith Papers, Swem Lib., there is an order of Lady Skipwith to William Moon, apothecary, dated Nov. 1799. It included a doll, a windmill, two cups and balls, a fox and geese board, and a "Suple Jack" (either a top or a dancing man on a stick that was operated by a string). In the Richard Blow Papers, Box 5, Swem Lib., is an invoice to Donald and Burton, London, July 11, 1788, that included a dozen toy watches. In Box 30 an invoice of Hodgson, Nicholson and Thompson, Feb. 9, 1796, included a thousand marbles. A runaway convict servant, Philip Vaughan, advertised for in the *Va. Gaz.* (Rind), June 1, 1769, had a toy watch in his pocket.

[120]Sarah Pitt advertised bilbo-catchers in the *Va. Gaz.* (Rind), Nov. 8, 1770. The cups and balls in Lady Skipwith's order were this same toy.

[121]R. W. Carter, Diary, May 1, 1765, shows that he paid 40 shillings for coral and rattles. The *Oxford English Dictionary* gives examples of the name in use from the early seventeenth century to the mid-nineteenth.

[122]A popular book for children, which could be purchased at the Printing Office in Williamsburg, was *A Little Pretty Pocket-Book, Intended for the Instruction and Amusement of Little Master Tommy, and Pretty Miss Polly.* Of the 1st edition, 1744, no copy is known today. A copy of the 1787 edition printed in Worcester, Mass., is in the New York Public Library; Colonial Williamsburg owns a facsimile. On pp. 24–55 are illustrations, one to a page, showing children playing 32 games. Below each picture is a four-line poem about the game, and, below that, a statement of the moral lesson the game teaches. Other contemporary pictures and descriptions may be found in Strutt, *Sports and Pastimes;* Henry René D'Allemagne, *Sports et Jeux d'Adresse* (Paris, [1903]); and D'Allemagne, *Récréations et Passe-Temps.*

[123]Lee, *Journal,* ed. Mason, p. 35.

[124]Fithian, *Journal,* ed. Farish, p. 45.

[125]*Ibid.,* pp. 68, 249, 254, 282.

[126]Fairfax, "Diary," *VMHB,* XI (1903), p. 213.

[127]See Lady Skipwith's order for a fox and geese board. Skipwith Papers. See also pp. 132, 136 for diagrams of boards and rules of play.

[128]Wright and Tinling, eds., *London Diary,* July 28, 1720, p. 433.

[129]R. W. Carter, Diary, Apr. 26, 1780.

[130]Fairfax, "Diary," *VMHB,* XI (1903), p. 213.

[131]Thomas Jones to Mrs. Jones [Aug.] 6, 1728, "Jones Papers," *ibid.,* XXVI (1918), p. 170.

[132]*Va. Gaz.* (Purdie and Dixon), June 1, 1769.

[133]Byrd, *Progress to the Mines,* in Bassett, ed., *Writings of Byrd,* pp. 356–357.

[134]Mrs. Frances Baylor to John Baylor, May 25, 1770, *VMHB,* XXI (1913), p. 90.

[135]William J. Hinke, trans. and ed., "Report of the Journey of Francis Louis Michel from Berne, Switzerland, to Virginia, October 2, 1701–December 1, 1702," *ibid.,* XXIV (1916), p. 39.

[136]Norton Papers.

[137]*Ibid.,* June 12, 1773.

## Chapter Three: Sports and Outdoor Games

[1]Smyth, *Tour,* I, p. 23.

[2]Hinke, trans. and ed., "Report of the Journey of Michel," *VMHB,* XXIV (1916), pp. 21, 36.

[3]This point is illustrated by the position of the horse thief in both societies. The convicted felons who most consistently received the death sentence in colonial Virginia were horse thieves. For statements of attitude, see acts of the General Assembly in 1744 and 1748 in Hening, ed., *Statutes,* V, p. 247, VI, p. 124.

[4]Hinke, trans. and ed., "Report of the Journey of Michel," *VMHB,* XXIV (1916), p. 21.

[5]*A Letter from Mr. John Clayton Rector of Crofton at Wake-*

*field in Yorkshire, to the Royal Society, May 12, 1688 . . .* , in Force, ed., *Tracts,* III, No. 12, p. 35.

[6]Jones, *Present State of Virginia,* ed. Morton, p. 84.

[7][Kimber], *Itinerant Observations,* p. 49.

[8]Smyth, *Tour,* I, p. 23.

[9]Boyd, ed., *William Byrd's Histories,* p. 266.

[10]J. P. Brissot de Warville, *New Travels in the United States of America. Performed in 1788,* trans. Joel Barlow (New York, 1792), p. 237. Nearly all travelers said the same thing, but not so concisely.

[11]Jones, *Present State of Virginia,* ed. Morton, p. 84.

[12]Weld, *Travels,* I, pp. 186–187.

[13]Bernard, *Retrospections of America,* ed. Bernard, p. 154.

[14]Parts of the story are related by Bruce, *Social Life in Virginia,* pp. 212–213, using Henrico Records, 1688–1697, p. 147, and Henrico Minute Book, 1682–1701, p. 268. The testimony of Randolph and Harrison is on p. 147 of the Order Book, 1678–1693. In the same volume, pp. 340–341, is a brief record of the trial, a list of jurors, and their decision in favor of Soane. Blair's testimony does not appear in any extant volume of court records for the year 1690; there is no Minute Book in the library's holdings, and therefore Blair's testimony is taken from Bruce, who probably used a volume no longer extant. For similar cases in the Henrico Records, see William G. Stanard, "Racing in Colonial Virginia," *VMHB,* II (1895), pp. 293–305.

[15]Further evidence of the impossibility of withdrawing from such a wager is in a letter from Napier to Soane dated a week before the race, also entered in Henrico Minute Book: "I have sent the bearer [Littlebury Eppes] for my horse and desire you to draw the race you being at no trouble with your horse which is all from Yor. lov: Cos: and fr'd." Henry Randolph endorsed the communication with a memorandum that the note was delivered to Soane in his presence three days before the date of the race. No one involved in the suit seemed to feel that Soane should have granted Napier's request despite the circumstance that no horse of Soane's was concerned; he was backing Eppes's sorrel.

[16]Bruce, *Social Life in Virginia,* Chap. 17.

[17]This description of the track, like the account of racing procedure that follows, is taken from details revealed in county court records of suits similar to the Soane-Napier dispute. Note the similarity of quarter racing a century later as described by Bernard. See p. 56.

[18]See the much quoted case of James Bullock, the York County tailor who was fined 100 pounds of tobacco for presuming to participate in a "sport only for Gentlemen." York County, Deeds, Orders, Wills, No. 5 (1672–1694), p. 34, microfilm in Foundation Lib. Another interesting point about this race was an agreement formally signed by Bullock's gentleman opponent to allow his horse to "runn out of the way that Bullock's mare might win." This "apparent Cheate" was punished by an hour in the stocks.

[19]An act of the Assembly in 1710 regulating ordinaries forbade "setting up booths, arbours, and stalls, at court-houses, race-fields, general-musters and other public places, where . . . the looser sort of people resort, get drunk, and commit many irregularities." Hening, ed., *Statutes,* III, p. 536. Public announcements were sometimes ordered for race meetings, like those at church and court. For an instance of this in 1705, see "Papers Relating to the Administration of Governor Nicholson . . . ," *VMHB,* VIII (1900), p. 130.

[20]Fairfax Harrison, "The Equine F F Vs," *VMHB,* XXXV (1927), p. 367.

[21]John Hervey, *Racing in America: 1665–1865,* I (New York, 1944), p. 22.

[22]*Ibid.,* pp. 24–25.

[23]Smyth, *Tour,* I, p. 23.

[24]Thomas Anburey, *Travels through the Interior Parts of America . . . ,* II (London, 1789), p. 227.

[25]Bernard, *Retrospections of America,* ed. Bernard, pp. 155–156.

[26][Ritson], *Poetical Picture,* pp. 79–80.

[27]Partial results are in Harrison, "The Equine F F Vs," *VMHB,* XXXV (1927), pp. 329–370.

[28]*Ibid.,* p. 331.

[29]Schoepf, *Travels,* II, p. 65.

[30]Harrison, "The Equine F F Vs," *VMHB,* XXXV (1927), p. 333.

[31]Hervey, *Racing in America,* I, pp. 57, 281–284.

32Summary, *ibid.,* pp. 80–81.

33Hervey's selection, guided by Harrison. The details in the biographical sketches that follow are taken largely from material *ibid.,* pp. 68–76.

34For advertisements in the *Va. Gaz.,* 1751–1753, see Cappon and Duff, comps., *Virginia Gazette Index,* II, p. 1203. The Va. Gaz. Day Book, 1750–1752, has an entry for Apr. 1751 charging Morton 5/ for advertising Traveller in the Apr. 25 issue.

35See advertisements for the years 1766–1780 in Cappon and Duff, comps., *Virginia Gazette Index,* I, p. 615.

36The first *American Stud Book,* published in 1833, is dominated by Janus descendants, probably because the author, Patrick Nesbet Edgar, lived in the Southside and collected there some of the fabulous stories that make up a Janus cult.

37See advertisements for the years 1766–1780 in Cappon and Duff, comps., *Virginia Gazette Index,* I, p. 384.

38Smyth, *Tour,* I, p. 21.

39Harrison, "The Equine F F Vs," *VMHB,* XXXV (1927), p. 364.

40The loss of the early *Va. Gazettes* and the absence of other specific data leave the time of the changeover open to speculation. Harrison dates it in 1739 with the Williamsburg fair of that year. Hervey and other sport experts use the arrival of Bulle Rock as the time marker. Certainly the Gooch era of prosperity is significant.

41Advertisements and news reports in *Va. Gazettes* record horse racing in the following places in the years indicated: Aquia, 1768, 1769, 1770, 1771, 1773, 1774; Dudley's Ferry, 1751, 1752; Dumfries, 1774; Fredericksburg, 1751, 1766, 1770, 1773, 1774; Gloucester, 1740; Hanover, 1736, 1737; King and Queen, 1752; King William, 1746; Leedstown, 1746, 1751, 1752, 1756, 1757, 1765, 1769, 1770, 1773, 1776; Port Royal, 1774, 1776; Portsmouth, 1774; Richmond, 1755, 1765, 1773, 1774, 1777; Richmond County, 1768; Ruffin's Ferry, 1776; Warwick, 1772, 1773; Yorktown, 1745, 1752, 1755, 1779. The following tracks are noted in other newspapers, diaries, and journals: Alexandria and Falmouth, Washington's diaries; Fredericksburg, diaries of Fithian, Harrower, and Lee; Richmond County, Fithian's journal; Tappa-hannock, Hunter's diary and the *Fredericksburg Gazette;* Norfolk, Mrs. Ritson's poetry; Smithfield, Hazard's diary; Surry County, Byrd's diary. Latrobe and Weld attended races near Petersburg in 1796; John Randolph's MS notes from newspapers now lost record races at Warwick and Richmond Courthouse in 1760; and the *Md. Gaz.* reported Virginia turf events from time to time, notably the Gloucester race of 1752. For bibliographical data on these diaries and journals, see Jane Carson, "Travelers in Tidewater Virginia, 1700–1800: A Bibliography," 1956, typescript in Foundation Lib. Details in the following descriptions were taken from all these sources.

42Smyth, *Tour,* I, p. 20.

43*Ibid.,* Chap. 4.

44See diaries cited in n. 41.

45Smyth, *Tour,* I, p. 21.

46Bernard, *Retrospections of America,* ed. Bernard, pp. 154–155.

47John Lawrence, *The History and Delineation of the Horse, in All His Varieties* (1809), quoted in E. D. Cuming, "Sports and Games," in Turberville, ed., *Johnson's England,* I, p. 263.

48*Va. Gaz.* (Rind), Aug. 4, 1768.

49Fithian, *Journal,* ed. Farish, entry for Nov. 25, 1773, p. 32.

50Hunter, *Quebec to Carolina,* ed. Wright and Tinling, p. 252.

51Fithian, *Journal,* ed. Farish, p. 245.

52*Md. Gaz.,* Dec. 21, 1752.

53Hervey, *Racing,* I, p. 94.

54The blood of ten of her foals has "suffused the entire American breeding fabric," and today her name appears, often again and again, in the pedigrees of most American thoroughbreds. Among her most famous descendants in the colonial period were Lightfoot's Partner, Lee's Mark Anthony, Willie Jones's Spadille, Selim, and Washington's Magnolio. She is still honored in Maryland. In 1926 the Maryland State Fair inaugurated the Selima Stakes for two-year-old fillies with a $30,000 challenge cup, and the present owner of Belair, a horse breeder, has erected a bronze tablet to her there. *Ibid.,* pp. 92–95. Hervey used data about Selima and Othello and their descendants collected by Fairfax Harrison and printed in *The Belair Stud, 1747–1761* (Richmond, Va., 1929).

[55]Fitzpatrick, ed., *George Washington*, passim.

[56]An entry in his Ledger A on May 26, 1769, shows 12 shillings paid to Robert Sanford for riding one of his horses in what seems to have been a pacing race at Accotinck; no other instance of the kind has been found. There is an apocryphal story of a match race between Washington's Magnolio and a roan colt of Jefferson's, which has been traced to Thomas Peter, a Georgetown merchant who married a daughter of John Parke Custis. The year was about 1790; the occasion, the Alexandria Jockey Club races; the winner, Jefferson's colt. Hervey, *Racing*, I, p. 117. In spite of the fact that Peter should have known if the story was true, it seems doubtful. Jefferson kept no race-horses and was not interested in horse racing; his account books show only one instance of his attending a race—in 1768—where he spent money for bumbo and cakes, not bets.

[57]The *Va. Gaz.* recorded races at Aquia, Dumfries, Fredericksburg, Port Royal, Portsmouth, and Richmond.

[58]*Va. Gaz.* (Purdie and Dixon), Feb. 10, 17, 1774.

[59]R. W. Carter, Diary, Oct. 3, 1774.

[60]*Va. Gaz.* (Purdie and Dixon), Apr. 7, 28, 1774.

[61]*Ibid.*, June 9, 1774.

[62]*Ibid.*, Oct. 20, 1774.

[63]Wright and Tinling, eds., *London Diary*, p. 436.

[64]*Ibid.*, pp. 527–528.

[65]Fithian, *Journal*, ed. Farish, p. 264.

[66]Hunter, *Quebec to Carolina*, ed. Wright and Tinling, pp. 251–252.

[67]Fithian, *Journal*, ed. Farish, pp. 198, 200–204.

[68]For examples, see Palmer, ed., *Calendar of Virginia State Papers*, I, p. 1; and Hening, ed., *Statutes*, III, pp. 309, 310, 312, IV, pp. 515–516, V, pp. 408–431.

[69]For the law of 1640, see Hening, ed., *Statutes*, I, p. 228.

[70]*Ibid.*, p. 199.

[71]Beverley, *History and Present State of Virginia*, ed. Wright, p. 308.

[72]John Clayton to Samuel Durrent, Mar. 21, 1739, *VMHB*, VII (1899), pp. 172–174.

[73]*Ibid.*

[74]Beverley, *History and Present State of Virginia*, ed. Wright, p. 308.

[75]*Ibid.*, p. 309.

[76]Hening, ed., *Statutes*, I, p. 462; revision in Palmer, ed., *Calendar of Virginia State Papers*, I, p. 96.

[77]For the period 1691–1772, see Hening, ed., *Statutes*, III, p. 69, V, pp. 60–62, 431, VII, pp. 412–413, VIII, pp. 591–594.

[78]William Lee to Richard Eggleston, Aug. 24, 1785, "Some Notes on 'Green Spring,' " *VMHB*, XXXVIII (1930), p. 46.

[79]Fitzpatrick, ed., *Writings of Washington*, XXIX, pp. 295–296, XXXII, p. 109, XXXVII, pp. 194–195.

[80]Washington to the Mr. Chichesters, Apr. 25, 1799, *ibid.*, XXXVII, pp. 194–195.

[81]Act of 1632 in Hening, ed., *Statutes*, I, p. 199. For later statutes, see II, p. 67, III, p. 282.

[82]Jones, *Present State of Virginia*, ed. Morton, p. 85.

[83]*Letter from Clayton* in Force, ed., *Tracts*, III, No. 12, p. 38.

[84]Beverley, *History and Present State of Virginia*, ed. Wright, p. 309.

[85]Clayton to Durrent, Mar. 21, 1739, *VMHB*, VII (1899), pp. 172–174.

[86]Dixon Wecter, *The Saga of American Society: A Record of Social Aspiration, 1607–1937* (New York, 1937), p. 444. Wecter's information came from Allen Potts, *Fox Hunting in America* (Washington, D. C., 1912). Mrs. Potts, née Gertrude Rives, an ardent fox hunter early in this century, was a descendant of Dr. Walker and lived at Castle Hill.

[87]Thomas Jett to Capt. John Anderson, July 20, 1770, "Letter Book of Thomas Jett," *WMQ*, 1st Ser., XXI (1912–1913), p. 89. See also John Norton to John Hatley Norton, Apr. 1, 1768, Norton Papers.

[88]Hunter, *Quebec to Carolina*, ed. Wright and Tinling, p. 245.

[89]In 1905 a match contest between American and English foxhounds was organized by Henry Worcester Smith, founder of the hunt clubs at Warrenton, Middleburg, and Casanova.

The American pack won the $2,000 purse. Wecter, *Saga of American Society,* p. 445.

[90]William H. Gaines, Jr., "John Peel in Virginia: Fox Hunting in the Old Dominion, Frolicsome and Fashionable," *Virginia Cavalcade,* III (1953), pp. 22–27.

[91]Wecter, *Saga of American Society,* pp. 444–445.

[92]Beverley, *History and Present State of Virginia,* ed. Wright, p. 309.

[93]*Ibid.,* p. 310.

[94]George Edie's phrase from *The Art of English Shooting* (1777) is quoted by Cuming, "Sports and Games," in Turberville, ed., *Johnson's England,* I, p. 369.

[95]Clayton to Durrent, Mar. 21, 1739, *VMHB,* VII (1899), pp. 172–174.

[96]Nets were still being used at the end of the century. Hunter spent several days helping the lovely Catherine McCall make a net to catch partridges with. Hunter, *Quebec to Carolina,* ed. Wright and Tinling, p. 243.

[97]Burnaby, *Travels,* pp. 42–43. Cf. pheasant hunting in Virginia mountains, described in Chastellux, *Travels,* II, pp. 72–74.

[98]Beverley, *History and Present State of Virginia,* ed. Wright, p. 312. Virginians today have similar experiences with Chincoteague ponies.

[99]Clayton's letter to Durrent is the first known mention of riding to hounds in the English tradition. Fairfax Harrison, "The Genesis of Foxhunting in Virginia," *VMHB,* XXXVII (1929), p. 156.

[100]The distinction is made by David Bruce Fitzgerald, "An Old Virginia Fox Hunt," *Lippincott's Monthly Magazine,* LVIII (1896), pp. 824–828.

[101]Fairfax's letter is printed with a date of 1768 in Stanard, *Colonial Virginia,* p. 259.

[102]Fitzpatrick, ed., *Diaries of Washington,* I, pp. 245–252.

[103]Beebe, Journals, II, entry dated Feb. 28, 1800.

[104]Acomb, ed., "Journal of Von Closen," *WMQ,* 3rd Ser., X (1953), p. 214.

[105]Bernard, *Retrospections of America,* ed. Bernard, pp. 156–157.

[106]*Ibid.,* pp. 157–159.

[107]For shooting matches in Williamsburg in 1692 and 1702, see "Extracts from the Records of Surry County," *WMQ,* 1st Ser., XI (1902–1903), p. 87; and Hinke, trans. and ed., "Report of the Journey of Michel," *VMHB,* XXIV (1916), p. 129.

[108]Wright and Tinling, eds., *Secret Diary,* entries for Dec. 5, 1709, Feb. 21, Mar. 27, 1710, Nov. 13, Dec. 29, 1711, Jan. 1, Mar. 10, 1712; Wright and Tinling, eds., *London Diary,* entries for May 29, June 20, 24, 1720.

[109]*Va. Gaz.,* July 8, 1737.

[110]Beverley, *History and Present State of Virginia,* ed. Wright, p. 310.

[111]*Ibid.,* pp. 148–149.

[112]Chastellux, *Travels,* II, pp. 169–170.

[113]Aug. 3, 1769, Aug. 24, 1770, Sept. 24, 1771, Norton Papers.

[114]Hening, ed., *Statutes,* V, p. 102. For similar laws later, see *ibid.,* VI, p. 76, X, p. 205.

[115]Jones, *Present State of Virginia,* ed. Morton, p. 84.

[116]Cuming, "Sports and Games," in Turberville, ed., *Johnson's England,* I, pp. 372–374.

[117]An unidentified tavern, probably on Francis Street in James City County.

[118]*Va. Gaz.,* Feb. 14, 1751.

[119]"Diary of Blair," *WMQ,* 1st Ser., VII (1898–1899), p. 136.

[120]Woodfin, ed., *Another Secret Diary,* entry for Mar. 26, 1740, p. 50.

[121]Fitzpatrick, ed., *Diaries of Washington,* I, p. 36.

[122]*Va. Gaz.,* Feb. 27, 1752.

[123]*Ibid.,* May 23, 1755.

[124]*Ibid.* (Purdie and Dixon), Mar. 17, 1768.

[125]*Ibid.* (Rind), Apr. 14, 1768.

[126]R. W. Carter, Diary, May 2, 7, 1768.

[127]*Va. Gaz.* (Purdie and Dixon), Feb. 22, 1770.

[128]*Ibid.* (Rind), Apr. 19, 1770.

[129]*Ibid.* (Purdie and Dixon), May 24, 1770.

[130]*Ibid.,* Aug. 15, 1771.

[131]*Ibid.,* May 28, 1772.

[132]*Ibid.* (Rind), Apr. 1, 1773.

133*Ibid.* (Purdie and Dixon), Apr. 22, May 27, 1773.

134*Ibid.* (Rind), May 12, 1774.

135R. W. Carter, Diary, Apr. 23, 1774, balancing an account with Reuben Beale, refers to £3.4.0 borrowed earlier "at the Cock fight at Hobbshole."

136Fithian, *Journal,* ed. Farish, pp. 121–122.

137*Ibid.,* entry for Apr. 10, 1774, p. 128.

138*Ibid.,* entry for Sept. 15, 1774, p. 250.

139Hazard, Journal of Journey, entry for June 10, 1777.

140Acomb, ed., "Journal of Von Closen," *WMQ,* 3rd Ser., X (1953), p. 215.

141Chastellux, *Travels,* II, pp. 28–32.

142Winslow C. Watson, ed., *Men and Times of the Revolution; or, Memoirs of Elkanah Watson, including Journals of Travels in Europe and America, from 1777 to 1842* (New York, 1856), pp. 261–262. Other postwar travelers who mentioned the popularity of the sport at taverns throughout the state include Moreau de St. Méry, *American Journey,* trans. and ed. Roberts and Roberts, p. 329; J. R., *The Port Folio: or A View of the Manners and Customs of Various Countries,* II (London, 1812), p. 103; Smyth, *Tour,* I, p. 66; and Weld, *Travels,* I, p. 192.

143Quoted in Cuming, "Sports and Games," in Turberville, ed., *Johnson's England,* I, pp. 373–374.

144*Encyclopedia Britannica,* s.v. "Cock-fighting or Cocking."

145I have seen no evidence of the use of churchyards and church buildings here, as was the custom in Wales, where wakes and religious holidays—Shrove Tuesday, Easter week, Whitsun Tuesday—were favorite occasions for cockfights. Virginia did follow the time schedule popular in England, however.

146Cuming, "Sports and Games," in Turberville, ed., *Johnson's England,* I, p. 373.

147*Ibid.*

148Card file of Virginia libraries in Foundation Lib. For comments on the books, see Louis B. Wright, *The First Gentlemen of Virginia: Intellectual Qualities of the Early Colonial Ruling Class* (San Marino, Calif., 1940), pp. 207, 228, 244.

149Cotton, *Compleat Gamester,* in Hartmann, ed., *Games and Gamesters,* pp. 100–112.

150*Va. Gaz.* (Purdie and Dixon), July 2, 1772.

151"By a pistole won of me about Hedgman's wrestling with and throwing Fra: Dade, £1/1/8," account with William Brent, May 1731, in Mercer, Ledger, 1725–1732, p. 119.

152This is the conventional order in critical statements of lower-class tastes. See also the diatribe against gaming in the *Va. Gaz.,* May 29, 1752.

153Chastellux, *Travels,* II, p. 192n. Other travelers registered similar reactions. Isaac Weld, for example, said they fought like wild beasts. Early in the nineteenth century a similar contest on the Kentucky frontier was described by Thomas Ashe, *Travels in America, Performed in 1806,* quoted in John Allen Krout, *Annals of American Sport,* in Ralph Henry Gabriel, ed., *The Pageant of America: A Pictorial History of the United States,* XV (New Haven, Conn., 1929), p. 28.

154Anburey, *Travels,* II, pp. 217–218.

155*Ibid.,* pp. 201–202.

156Hening, ed., *Statutes,* VI, p. 250, VIII, p. 520.

157William Gooch to the bishop of London, July 8, 1735, in G. Maclaren Brydon, ed., "The Virginia Clergy," *VMHB,* XXXII (1924), p. 332.

158Fithian, *Journal,* ed. Farish, p. 212.

159Cuming, "Sports and Games," in Turberville, ed., *Johnson's England,* I, pp. 376–378.

160*Va. Gaz.,* Mar. 20, 1752, supplement.

161*Ibid.* (Dixon), July 17, Nov. 13, 1779. That same year the *Gazette* announced the death of Claudius Peter Cary, fencing master.

162John Brown, student at the College of William and Mary, to William Preston, Feb. 15, 1780, *WMQ,* 1st Ser., IX (1900–1901), p. 76.

163Harrison, ed., "Will of Charles Carter," *VMHB,* XXXI (1923), p. 62.

164Lyon G. Tyler, "Early Presidents of William and Mary," *WMQ,* 1st Ser., I (1892–1893), p. 65.

165Wright and Tinling, eds., *Secret Diary,* entry for Apr. 25, 1709.

166Thomas Hughes, *Tom Brown's School Days,* 6th ed. (Boston, 1895), pp. 32–34.

167Cuming, "Sports and Games," in Turberville, ed., *Johnson's England,* I, p. 381.

168Wright and Tinling, eds., *London Diary,* entries for July

16, Sept. 8, 9, 10, 11, 15, 17, 18, 20, 22, 23, 24, 1718, June 18, 20, 29, 1719.

[169]Wesley Frank Craven, *The Southern Colonies in the Seventeenth Century, 1607-1689*, in Wendell Holmes Stephenson and E. Merton Coulter, eds., *A History of the South*, I (Baton Rouge, La., 1949), p. 108.

[170]Deposition of Robert West, Nov. 28, 1636, in Susie M. Ames, ed., *County Court Records of Accomack-Northampton, Virginia, 1632-1640* (Washington, D. C., 1954), p. 61. Two years earlier, when he was 26, Ward testified in a slander case, saying that he had heard Marie Drew, the defendant, call Joane Butler, the plaintiff, a "carted hoare." *Ibid.*, pp. 22–23. Two years later, in 1638, he was sued for nonpayment of the governor's rents. *Ibid.*, pp. 119–120.

[171]Northampton County Records, 1689–1698, cited in Bruce, *Social Life in Virginia*, p. 189.

[172]Bruce states that "all the taverns" had them, but presents no evidence beyond a few examples. *Ibid.*, p. 188.

[173]Henrico County Records, pp. 191–192.

[174]Bruce, *Social Life in Virginia*, p. 189n.

[175]York County, Orders and Wills, No. 15 (1716–1720), p. 88.

[176]York County, Wills and Inventories, No. 18 (1732–1740), p. 57.

[177]*Ibid.*, p. 206.

[178]"Fisher History," in du Bellet, *Some Prominent Virginia Families*, p. 788.

[179]John S. Charles, "Recollections of Williamsburg, as it appeared at the beginning of the Civil War and just previous thereto, with some incidents in the life of its citizens," MS, 1928, Foundation Lib.

[180]York County, Deeds, Bonds, No. 3 (1713–1729), pp. 204–206; York County, Orders, Wills, No. 16 (1720–1729), pp. 222, 230.

[181]Wright and Tinling, eds., *London Diary*, pp. 399, 525, 526.

[182]Jones, *Present State of Virginia*, ed. Morton, p. 70.

[183]George Gilmer to the mayor of Williamsburg etc., Dec. 16, 1745, York County, Deeds, No. 5 (1741–1754), pp. 153–154.

[184]Wright and Tinling, eds., *London Diary*, pp. 507, 510, 527.

[185]Woodfin, ed., *Another Secret Diary*, pp. 3–14, 66–96, 148–181.

[186]Fithian, *Journal*, ed. Farish, p. 109.

[187]British rules for playing the game revived there in the nineteenth century may be found in E. J. Linney, *A History of the Game of Bowls* (London, 1933), Chap. 10. Chap. 11 gives directions for maintaining the green.

[188]Strutt, *Sports and Pastimes*, p. 220.

[189]Hartmann, ed., *Games and Gamesters*, p. 22.

[190]*Ibid.*, p. 24.

[191]Quoted in Strutt, *Sports and Pastimes*, p. 217.

[192]*Ibid.*, pp. 63–64.

[193]Quoted in Mary Newton Stanard, *John Marshall: An Address . . .* (Richmond, Va., [1913]), p. 32.

[194]Mercer, Ledger, 1725–1732, pp. 17, 18, 25, 39, 67.

[195]Thomas Jefferson, Memorandum Book, 1769, pp. 21, 25, MS, Lib. Cong., photostat in Alderman Lib.

[196]Young Bowyer became tithable in 1763 and in 1765 received a permit to build a kitchen, 20 feet by 16, adjoining the old jail. Lyman Chalkley, ed., *Chronicles of the Scotch-Irish Settlement in Virginia, Extracted from the Original Court Records of Augusta County, 1745–1800*, I (Rosslyn, Va., 1912), pp. 109, 122. For payment to Bowyer for punch and entertainment, see Jefferson, Memorandum Book, June 23, 1769.

[197]Charles E. Kemper, "The Birth-Place of Bishop Madison," *WMQ*, 2nd Ser., II (1922), p. 185.

[198]Memoirs of Thomas Jefferson Randolph, pp. 12–13, Edgehill-Randolph Papers, MS, Alderman Lib., cited in Dumas Malone, *Jefferson and His Time*. Vol. I: *Jefferson the Virginian* (Boston, 1948), p. 118.

[199]Wright and Tinling, eds., *Secret Diary*, entries for Apr. 25, May 6, Nov. 28, 1709, Feb. 1, 20, 22, 25, Mar. 4, 10, 15, 17, 22, 23, 27, 28, 1710.

[200]Cuming, "Sports and Games," in Turberville, ed., *Johnson's England*, I, p. 378.

[201]*Ibid.*

[202]Strutt, *Sports and Pastimes*, pp. 102–103.

[203]*Ibid.,* p. 101. See also *A Little Pretty Pocket-Book,* pp. 41, 44.

[204]Reference to cricket, Nov. 13, 1802, published in Norfolk *Herald,* Dec. 2, 1802, quoted in Wertenbaker, *Norfolk,* p. 134. Boys in the middle and northern colonies played bandy on ice and called it "shinny." They made their own rules and used any kind of puck—barrel bung, knob of wood, and the like. Krout, *Annals of American Sport,* pp. 271–272.

[205][Ritson], *Poetical Picture,* p. 147.

[206]Aug. 19, 1758, Augusta County Records, abstracted in Chalkley, ed., *Chronicles,* I, p. 82.

[207]David Yancey to [David Watson], June 6, 1795, *VMHB,* XXX (1922), p. 224.

[208]Strutt, *Sports and Pastimes,* p. 82. But the game was not adopted in English public schools until well into the nineteenth century. Cuming, "Sports and Games," in Turberville, ed., *Johnson's England,* I, p. 382.

[209]Strutt, *Sports and Pastimes,* p. 82.

[210]Nov. 22, 1750, York County, Wills, Inventories, No. 20 (1745–1759), p. 200.

[211]Strutt, *Sports and Pastimes,* p. 243.

[212]Jan. 26, 1742, Gibson-Maynadier Papers, 1740–1752, Maryland Historical Society, Baltimore, microfilm in Foundation Lib.

[213]*Ibid.,* torn invoice [May? 1741].

[214]See advertisements in the *Va. Gaz.* (Rind), Oct. 26, Nov. 2, 1769, Nov. 8, 1770; *ibid.* (Purdie and Dixon), July 25, 1766.

[215][July 25, 1766], Norton Papers.

[216]Fithian, *Journal,* ed. Farish, pp. 73, 75.

[217]Wright and Tinling, eds., *Secret Diary,* Dec. 28, 29, 1709.

[218]Byrd, *A Journey to the Land of Eden: Anno 1733,* in Bassett, ed., *Writings of Byrd,* p. 305.

[219]Albert Henry Smyth, ed., *The Writings of Benjamin Franklin* (New York, 1905–1907), I, p. 285, V, pp. 542–550; Melchisédech Thévenot, *The Art of Swimming, Illustrated by Forty Copper-plate Cuts, which Represent the different Postures necessary to be used in that Art, with Advice for Bathing* (London, 1789). Thévenot's book is a curious collection of suggestions for beginners about practical ways to avoid the dangers of swimming—especially about how to keep clear of entangling weeds and mud. Chap. 17, "To Swim like a Dog," and Chap. 27, "To cut the Nails of the Toes in the Water," are the most useful parts of the treatise for modern readers. The author considered Indians (Asian, probably) and Negroes the best swimmers and divers of his time, for they were the great pearl fishers, and the Chinese were not much inferior to them in this sort of exercise. Thévenot was most noted as an authority on the Orient, where he had spent much of his life.

[220]Because they had no big rivers in their country, the Choctaw had never learned to swim and therefore lost an engagement with the Creek in 1779. John Rodgers to Gov. Henry Lee, Feb. 8, 1792, in Palmer, ed., *Calendar of Virginia State Papers,* V, p. 440.

## Chapter Four: Publick Times and Public Occasions in Williamsburg

[1]Rutherfoord Goodwin, *A Brief & True Report Concerning Williamsburg in Virginia,* 3rd ed. (Williamsburg, Va., 1941), pp. 35–37.

[2]The account of the ceremony is taken from details in the text of the "Treaty between Virginia and the Indians, 1677," *VMHB,* XIV (1907), pp. 289–296.

[3]Councillors who lived close enough to attend the conference included Nathaniel Bacon the Elder, Philip Ludwell, Thomas Swann, William Cole, Richard Lee, John Bridges, John Bray, Thomas Ballard, and possibly Ralph Wormeley, Sir Henry Chicheley, Nicholas Spencer, and Maj. Robert Beverley. Berkeley stated in 1671 that the Council normally had 16 members. The list suggested here is taken from the names of those who attended meetings of the General Court in Mar. 1676 and in 1680. In Apr. 1676 Sir William complained to Thomas Ludwell, who was then in England, that Chicheley and Spencer were seldom available for consultation because they lived "too remote" from Green Spring.

[4]This is the description of her dress when she appeared before the General Assembly in Jamestown the year before.

Charles Campbell, *History of the Colony and Ancient Dominion of Virginia* (Philadelphia, 1860), p. 295.

[5]The formal request for them, signed by Berry and Morrison, estimated the cost at £120. Colonial Entry Book No. 18, pp. 264–271, W. N. Sainsbury abstract, *VMHB*, XXII (1914), p. 141. At least one of the crowns was made and delivered. It is now owned by the Association for the Preservation of Virginia Antiquities. It was on display at the Virginia Historical Society in 1907 and at the John Marshall House in 1914. For a photograph, see Mary Newton Stanard, *The Story of Virginia's First Century* (Philadelphia, 1928), facing p. 296.

[6]For a facsimile of their signatures, see "Treaty," *VMHB,* XIV (1907), p. 296.

[7]H. R. McIlwaine, ed., *Executive Journals of the Council of Colonial Virginia* (Richmond, Va., 1925–1966), II, pp. 250, 253–255.

[8]Hinke. trans. and ed., "Report of the Journey of Michel," *VMHB*, XXIV (1916), pp. 126–134. In England, too, fireworks did not always go off properly. Horace Walpole thought the elaborate series celebrating the Peace of 1748 "by no means answered the expense, the length of preparation, and the expectation that had been raised. . . . The rockets, and whatever was thrown up into the air, succeeded mighty well; but the wheels, and all that was to compose the principal part, were pitiful and ill-conducted, with no changes of coloured fires and shapes: the illumination was mean, and lighted so slowly that scarce anybody had patience to wait the finishing and then, what contributed to the awkwardness of the whole, was the right pavilion catching fire and being burnt down in the middle of the show. . . . Very little mischief was done, and but two persons killed: at Paris, there were forty killed and near three hundred wounded, by a dispute between the French and Italians in the management, who, quarreling for precedence in lighting the fires, both lighted at once and blew up the whole." Walpole to Horace Mann, May 3, 1749, in W. S. Lewis, ed., *A Selection of the Letters of Horace Walpole*, I (New York, 1926), pp. 52–54. For a description of fireworks at Ranelagh, together with a listing of the 24 pieces used there in 1764, see Strutt, *Sports and Pastimes*, pp. 298–299.

[9]Spotswood to Board of Trade, Oct. 25, 1714, in R. A. Brock, ed., *The Official Letters of Alexander Spotswood*, Virginia Historical Society, *Collections*, N.S., II (1882), p. 76.

[10]McIlwaine, ed., *Executive Journals*, III, pp. 378–380.

[11]This order was carried out in Lancaster County on Oct. 9. On that day Carter recorded, "About 12 T. Edwards, the Doctor, my two sons went to the proclaiming the King. Carried with them 6 gallons rum sugar, 12 bottles Madera." "King" Carter, Diary.

[12]*Ibid.*

[13]McIlwaine, ed., *Executive Journals*, IV, p. 149.

[14]Carter to William Robertson, Sept. 2, 1727, Robert "King" Carter Letterbook, 1727–1728, p. 71, Alderman Lib.

[15]Palmer, ed., *Calendar of Virginia State Papers,* I, pp. 211–212.

[16]W. Gooch to T. Gooch, Sept. 18, 1727, Feb. 18, 1728, pp. 1, 5, Gooch Letter Book.

[17]Carter to [John Carter], May 15, 1727, Robert "King" Carter Letterbooks, 1723–1729, Va. Hist. Soc.

[18]Carter to [Robertson], May 15, 1727, *ibid.*, pp. 56–57.

[19]W. Gooch to T. Gooch, Sept. 18, Dec. 28, 1727, Feb. 18, 1728, pp. 1, 3, 5, Gooch Letter Book.

[20]Fauquier to the Board of Trade, Feb. 17, 1761, in McIlwaine and Kennedy, eds., *Journals of Burgesses, 1758–1761,* p. 293. The governor used this "slender appearance of Councillors" as an argument for the expediency of having at least five members of the Council chosen from the gentlemen who lived "near at hand."

[21]For the ceremonies attending the arrival of Nott (1705), Spotswood (1710), Drysdale (1722), and Dinwiddie (1751), see McIlwaine, ed., *Executive Journals*, III, pp. 23–25, 247, IV, p. 20, V, pp. 371–372. Spotswood's arrival is also described in Wright and Tinling, eds., *Secret Diary*, pp. 194–195. Dinwiddie's arrival is described in the *Va. Gaz.*, Nov. 21, 1751, and in "Diary of Blair," *WMQ*, 1st Ser., VII (1898–1899), pp. 148, 153, VIII (1899–1900), p. 15. Fauquier's ceremonies seemed hurried; his commission was read but Loudoun's was not. The governor and councillors who were present took the prescribed oaths and then proceeded to regular business. See Council Journal, June 5, 1758, C.O. 5/1429, fol. 176, Public Record Office, microfilm, Virginia Colonial Records Project, Founda-

tion Lib. Fauquier's arrival on June 5, 1758, was reported to the Board of Trade by Blair in a letter of June 20, and by Fauquier himself on June 11. C.O. 5/1329, fols. 70–72, 75–76, *ibid*. No *Va. Gaz.* for this time is extant, and no diary or private letter describing a dinner or ball has been found.

[22]*Va. Gaz.* (Purdie and Dixon), Oct. 27, 1768.

[23]William Reynolds to Mrs. Courtenay Norton, Oct. 19, 1771, in Mason, ed., *John Norton & Sons,* p. 202. Reynolds crossed the bay with him and introduced him at York.

[24]*Va. Gaz.* (Purdie and Dixon), Sept. 26, 1771.

[25]*Ibid*. (Rind), Mar. 10, 1774; *ibid*. (Purdie and Dixon), Mar. 3, May 26, 1774.

[26]Lewis Burwell, acting governor in 1751, did better by the populace. Blair's diary entry for Oct. 30 reads: "The Presdt. kept the birthday in an extra[ordinar]y manner by adding to his elegant entertainment for the ladies and gentn. a purce of 50 pistoles to be distributed amongst the poor by Mr. Dawson." "Diary of Blair," *WMQ,* 1st Ser., VIII (1899–1900), p. 14.

[27]The queen and other members of the royal family sometimes received similar honors. After 1766, George III's accession date (Oct. 25) was celebrated instead of his birthday (June 4) to coincide with the fall meeting of the General Assembly. Newspaper accounts of ceremonies may be found in the *Va. Gaz.,* Nov. 5, 1736, Jan. 21, Nov. 4, 1737, Nov. 3, 1738, Nov. 2, 1739, Nov. 7, 1745, Nov. 14, 1755; *ibid*. (Purdie and Dixon), June 6, 1766, Oct. 29, 1767, May 25, 1769, June 7, 1770, Oct. 31, 1771, Oct. 29, 1772, Oct. 28, 1773; *ibid*. (Pinkney), Jan. 19, 1775. See also the *Pennsylvania Gazette* (Philadelphia), Nov. 14, 1771; Jones to Jones, Nov. 10, 1736, "Jones Papers," *VMHB,* XXVI (1918), pp. 286–287; Dinwiddie to John Hanbury, Mar. 12 [1754], in R. A. Brock, ed., *The Official Records of Robert Dinwiddie . . . ,* Va. Hist. Soc., *Collections,* N.S., III (1883), p. 102; Fitzpatrick, ed., *Diaries of Washington,* I, p. 326; and "Journal of a French Traveller," *AHR,* XXVI (1901), p. 745.

[28]Brock, ed., *Letters of Spotswood,* II, p. 284.

[29]*Va. Gaz.,* Nov. 17, 1752. Other ceremonial visits of Indian dignitaries are recorded in "Diary of Blair," July 27, Aug. 14–17, 1751, *WMQ,* 1st Ser., VIII (1899–1900), pp. 9–

11; Burnaby, *Travels,* Appendix III; and Hazard, Journal of Journey, May 31, 1777.

[30]Byrd, *Secret History of the Line,* in Boyd, ed., *William Byrd's Histories,* pp. 238, 249. Byrd's version reads: "This being his Majesty's Birth Day we drank his Health in a Dram of excellent Cherry Brandy, but cou'd not afford one Drop for the Queen and the Roial Issue. We therefore remember'd them in Water as clear as our Wishes."

[31]*Va. Gaz.,* July 18, 1746.

[32]*Ibid*. (Purdie and Dixon), June 20, 1766.

[33]*Ibid.,* Oct. 31, 1777.

[34]John Page to George Weedon, Oct. 1777, Weedon Papers, 1777–1786, American Philosophical Society, Philadelphia.

[35]Acomb, ed., "Journal of Von Closen," *WMQ,* 3rd Ser., X (1953), p. 213.

[36]*Va. Gaz.* (Rind), Dec. 14, 1769. The story was picked up and reprinted in other colonies and in London. See *Pa. Gaz.,* Jan. 4, 1770; *S. C. Gaz.,* Feb. 15, 1770; and *Va. Gaz.* (Purdie and Dixon), Apr. 19, 1770, under London dateline.

[37]*Va. Gaz.* (Purdie and Dixon), Dec. 28, 1769.

[38]J. L. Hammond and B. Hammond, "Poverty, Crime, Philanthropy," in Turberville, ed., *Johnson's England,* I, pp. 321–322.

[39]For full details of the career of this 22-year-old coiner, see Hugh F. Rankin, "Criminal Jurisdiction of the General Court," 1958, typescript in Foundation Lib.

[40]*Md. Gaz.,* May 10, 1753.

[41]Arthur P. Scott's attempt in *Criminal Law in Virginia* (Chicago, 1930) is the only one that I have seen. Its value is limited because he did not use all the *Gazettes* available 30 years ago, and more have been found since that time.

[42]My figures in both lists include *Md. Gaz.* reports with Williamsburg headlines, used when the *Va. Gaz.* from which they were picked up has disappeared, but no thorough search of the files of the Maryland paper has been made.

[43]In London at about the same time it has been estimated that more than half the criminals sentenced to death actually went to the gallows; nearly all the reprieved were transported to America—usually to Virginia or Maryland. The Hammonds'

conclusion is based on figures for the 20 years before 1772. "Poverty, Crime, Philanthropy," in Turberville, ed., *Johnson's England,* I, p. 322. Scott found three transportations from colonial Virginia—none of them in the eighteenth century. It is interesting to note that most of the robbers convicted in eighteenth-century Virginia were transported felons.

⁴⁴*Va. Gaz.,* Nov. 23, 1739.

⁴⁵Watson, ed., *Men and Times of the Revolution,* p. 43.

⁴⁶Rankin, "Colonial Theatre," p. 280. Williamsburg's first theater building—the first in British America—was completed about 1718 and remained in sporadic use until 1745, when it was remodeled for the hustings court. We have almost no information about performances there. William Byrd, for example, tells us that he "went to the play" three nights while he was in Williamsburg in the spring of 1721, but furnishes no hint about what the performances were or where they were given. Wright and Tinling, eds., *London Diary,* pp. 522, 525. Even when public plays by townspeople or college students were advertised in the early issues of the *Va. Gaz.* (from 1736), there is no direct evidence that this building on Palace green was used. Certainly it was never a financial success, and it is reasonable to deduce lack of support. William Hugh Grove, an Englishman who saw it in about 1731, made this marginal comment about the theater in his diary: "There was a Playhouse managed by Bowes but having little to do is dropped." Diary, 1698–1732, Travels in Great Britain and the Netherlands and in America, Alderman Lib., photostat of Williamsburg and Yorktown portions, 1731–1732, in Foundation Lib.

⁴⁷*Va. Gaz.,* Sept. 26, 1751.

⁴⁸*Gentleman's Magazine,* XX (1750), p. 524.

⁴⁹*Va. Gaz.,* Apr. 17, 1752.

⁵⁰*Ibid.,* June 2, 1752.

⁵¹*Ibid.,* Sept. 22, 1752. When the opening was announced Aug. 21, a large attendance was expected, and ladies were advised to send their servants early to reserve their seats.

⁵²Dr. George Gilmer to Walter King, Nov. 1752, George Gilmer Letterbook, 1752–1757, Va. Hist. Soc., MS copy by R. A. Brock in Foundation Lib.

⁵³Rankin, "Colonial Theatre," pp. 82–83.

⁵⁴For an example, see *The Court Mercurie,* No. 10 (London, 1644), copy in the McGregor Collection, Alderman Lib.

⁵⁵Hallam had died in Jamaica, his widow had married Douglass, and a few remnants of the Hallam troupe stayed on with the new manager, who retained the name "a Company of Comedians from London."

⁵⁶Washington, Ledger A, pp. 108, 143. William Allason also bought tickets on Oct. 2. Account Book, William Allason Papers, Va. State Lib.

⁵⁷Washington, Ledger A, pp. 147, 160.

⁵⁸Rankin, "Colonial Theatre," pp. 135–184.

⁵⁹*Va. Gaz.* (Purdie and Dixon), Mar. 31, 1768.

⁶⁰Jefferson, Account Book, 1768, p. 39.

⁶¹The announcement of the performance in the *Va. Gaz.* (Purdie and Dixon), May 31, 1768, quoted prices at 7/6, 5/–, and 3/9. For speculations about the lobby refreshment bar, see Rankin, "Colonial Theatre," p. 259.

⁶²*Va. Gaz.* (Purdie and Dixon), May 31, Apr. 7, 1768.

⁶³*Ibid.,* Apr. 14, 1768.

⁶⁴Jefferson, Account Book, 1768, pp. 39–40.

⁶⁵Fitzpatrick, ed., *Diaries of Washington,* I, p. 266; Washington, Ledger A, May 1, 1768, p. 269.

⁶⁶He spent 5/– at the playhouse. Jefferson, Account Book, 1768, p. 40.

⁶⁷Washington, Ledger A, p. 269.

⁶⁸"Pd. at playhouse 5/–." Jefferson, Account Book, 1768, p. 40. He left town a few days later, but returned about the 24th.

⁶⁹*Va. Gaz.* (Purdie and Dixon), May 12, 1768.

⁷⁰*Ibid.,* May 19, 1768. Identification of author and date of some of these plays may be found in Armstrong, "Repertoire."

⁷¹Jefferson, Account Book, 1768, p. 43.

⁷²*Va. Gaz.* (Purdie and Dixon), May 26, 1768. Colonial Williamsburg owns a playbill for this performance.

⁷³Jefferson, Account Book, 1768, p. 43. On May 5, 1769, for example, the account reads: "Pd. Pelham for playing an organ 2/6; pd. Sexton 1/3; pd. at Charlton's for arrack 5/–." This was doubtless a full evening's entertainment for himself and friends.

⁷⁴Jefferson, Account Book, 1769, p. 22. The tickets cost

7/6. He evidently forgot to take his change from a pound note, for the next day he received 12/6 "cash overpd. at puppet show."

[75]Advertisement, *Va. Gaz.* (Purdie and Dixon), Apr. 13, 1769. These puppets were not marionettes, but wire puppets—jointed figures operated with a single wire from above or behind. David Clay Jenkins, "Peter Gardiner's Puppets, Magic, & Perspectives in Williamsburg, 1769–1772," p. 26, 1958, typescript in Foundation Lib.

[76]Gardiner pointedly assured his readers that none of these shows was an optic box (or raree show) but would "appear publick on the stage," and he doubtless used the regular stage equipment—grooves in the floor for his scenery and the cat-walks for operating his puppets. For conjectures about how these spectacles were made, see Paul McPharlin, *The Puppet Theatre in America: A History* (New York, 1949), Chap. 4.

[77]Jefferson, Account Book, 1769, p. 22. Washington did not go to the theater this spring; he arrived in town May 3 and left May 20, having been present for all sessions of the General Assembly, which met from May 8 through May 17.

[78]Advertisement, *Va. Gaz.* (Purdie and Dixon), Apr. 20, 1769.

[79]Jefferson, Account Book, 1769, Oct. 23, Nov. 2, p. 33.

[80]An advertisement in the *Va. Gaz.* (Purdie and Dixon) June 14, 1770, announced their arrival and the opening feature. No other newspaper announcements of the season's repertoire were made.

[81]McIlwaine and Kennedy, eds., *Journals of Burgesses, 1770–1772,* pp. 5–109.

[82]Washington, Ledger A, p. 318; Fitzpatrick, ed., *Diaries of Washington,* I, pp. 378–380.

[83]Jonathan Bouchier, ed., *Reminiscences of an American Loyalist, 1738–1789* . . . (Boston, 1925), p. 66. The ode was printed in the *Md. Gaz.,* Sept. 6, 1770.

[84]Jefferson, "Accounts," in back of *Virginia Almanac, 1770,* pp. 7–8, photostat in Alderman Lib.

[85]*Ibid.,* pp. 13–15.

[86]Hudson Muse to Thomas Muse, Apr. 19, 1771, *WMQ,* 1st Ser., II (1893–1894), pp. 239–241.

[87]*Va. Gaz.* (Purdie and Dixon), Apr. 25, 1771.

[88]Washington, Ledger A, p. 337, shows that he paid 10/– for tickets on May 2, 37/6 on May 7, and 5/– on May 8. He recorded attendance on May 2 and 8 in his diary.

[89]*Va. Gaz.* (Purdie and Dixon), May 16, 1771. Colonial Williamsburg owns a playbill for the Fredericksburg performance on May 28, 1771. Washington bought tickets there on July 23.

[90]*Ibid.,* Oct. 17, 24, 1771.

[91]*Ibid.,* Nov. 7, 21, Dec. 19, 1771.

[92]Washington, Ledger A, p. 345; Fitzpatrick, ed., *Diaries of Washington,* II, pp. 38–49.

[93]McIlwaine and Kennedy, eds., *Journals of Burgesses, 1770–1772,* pp. 153–317.

[94]*Va. Gaz.* (Purdie and Dixon), Mar. 12, 1772.

[95]Washington, Ledger B, p. 5; Fitzpatrick, ed., *Diaries of Washington,* II, pp. 56–59.

[96]*Va. Gaz.* (Purdie and Dixon), Apr. 2, 1772.

[97]*Ibid.,* Apr. 9, 16, 23, May 7, 1772.

[98]William Reynolds to George F. Norton, May 23, 1772, William Reynolds Letterbook, 1771–1785, I, p. 16, Lib. Cong., microfilm in Foundation Lib.

[99]The closing date at the end of the Apr. court had been announced and repeated in notices of Apr. 9, 16, and 23.

[100]Catherine wheels, Italian candles, sea fountains, and sunflowers with the appearance of the sun and moon in their full luster. This was probably the Italian fireless illusion called "giuoco di luce." An example may be seen in the Cooper Union Museum for the Arts of Decoration, New York City. McPharlin, *Puppet Theatre,* p. 52.

[101]*Va. Gaz.* (Rind), Nov. 19, 1772.

[102]Washington, Ledger B, p. 61; Fitzpatrick, ed., *Diaries of Washington,* II, pp. 84–87.

[103]The only waxworks advertised in Williamsburg was shown at Mr. John Lockley's in 1775—a "curious Piece of Waxwork, representing Venus relating to Adonis the Story of Hippomines and Atalanta." *Va. Gaz.* (Dixon and Hunter), Nov. 4, 1775. Robert Wormeley Carter paid 2/6 to see a puppet show in Williamsburg on May 6, 1774; this show has not been identified. R. W. Carter, Diary, 1774.

[104]*Va. Gaz.,* Sept. 19, 1755.

[105]*Ibid.,* Sept. 5, 1755.

[106]*Ibid.,* Oct. 3, 10, 1755.

[107]*Ibid.* (Purdie and Dixon), Oct. 10, 1766.

[108]Whitfield J. Bell, Jr., "A Note on Franklin & His Lightning Rod," introduction to Charles Woodmason, *A Poetical Epistle from Charles Woodmason, Esq. to Benjamin Franklin, Esq. of Philadelphia; On His Experiments and Discoveries in Electricity* [1753] (Richmond, Va., 1954), p. 2.

[109]*Va. Gaz.* (Purdie and Dixon), Jan. 8, 1767.

[110]Rankin, "Colonial Theatre," p. 141.

[111]See *ibid.,* p. 328, for a copy of the syllabus, printed in the *New-York Journal or General Advertiser* (New York City), July 16, 1767, as Douglass delivered it.

[112]*Va. Gaz.* (Purdie and Dixon), Feb. 25, Apr. 23, 1773.

[113]*Ibid.,* May 13, 1773.

[114]Jefferson, Account Book, 1773, entry for May 5, p. 8.

[115]*Va. Gaz.* (Purdie and Dixon), June 3, 1773.

[116]*Ibid.,* Oct. 22, 1772.

[117]*Ibid.,* Dec. 17, 1772, Mar. 17, 1774.

[118]*Ibid.,* May 26, 1774.

[119]Durand of Dauphiné, *Huguenot Exile,* ed. Chinard, p. 158. Fitzhugh "sent for" these performers, who may have been indentured servants (as many modern historians classify them) but more probably were not. Durand does not say where they came from.

[120]*Va. Gaz.,* Apr. 21, 1738.

[121]R. W. Carter, Diary, Nov. 4, 1774.

[122]Mary Goodwin, "Eighteenth-century Fairs," 1955, typescript in Foundation Lib.

[123]Jefferson, Memorandum Book, 1768, p. 39, 1769, pp. 21, 32.

[124]*Va. Gaz.,* Sept. 10, 17, 1736.

[125]Jones to Jones, Sept. 17, 1736, "Jones Papers," *VMHB,* XXVI (1918), pp. 180–181.

[126]Letter signed "Arabella Sly," Oct. 15, 1736.

[127]"Diary of Blair," Nov. 16, 1751, *WMQ,* 1st Ser., VIII (1899–1900), p. 15.

[128]Hazard, Journal of Journey, June 4, 5, 1777.

[129]Blair to Braxton, Aug. [?] 1769, *WMQ,* 1st Ser., XVI (1907–1908), pp. 174–180.

[130]"Journal of Alexander Macaulay," Feb. 25, 1783, *ibid.,* XI (1902–1903), p. 186.

[131]"A Letter to the Rev. Jedediah Morse . . ." [1795], *ibid.,* II (1893–1894), pp. 191–192.

[132]Jefferson, Memorandum Book, 1768, pp. 40, 43, 1769, p. 23, 1777, p. 38.

[133]Washington, Ledger A, pp. 34, 208, 249, Ledger B, p. 4.

[134]The name has survived in a very different kind of instrument—the mouth organ we call a harmonica.

[135]Robert Carter of Nomini Hall to John M. Jordan, May 23, 1764, Robert Carter Letterbooks, 1761–1769, I, pp. 4–5, Foundation Lib.

[136]For a description of the eighteenth-century instrument, see Francis W. Galpin, *Old English Instruments of Music: Their History and Character* (Chicago, 1911), pp. 265–266, illustration, pl. 50.

[137]Fithian, *Journal,* ed. Farish, pp. 39, 49, 208. The music master, Mr. Stadley, also played it Aug. 12, 1774.

[138] *Va. Gaz.* (Rind), Dec. 11, 1766. For advertisements of similar concerts in towns other than Williamsburg, see Cappon and Duff, comps., *Virginia Gazette Index,* I, s.v. "Concerts."

[139]It was ensemble playing of this kind at the Palace when he was a student at the College of William and Mary that Jefferson recalled: "The Governor was musical also [i.e., as well as a philosophical conversationalist and charming host] and a good performer, and associated me with two or three other amateurs in his weekly concerts." Jefferson to L. H. Girardin, Jan. 15, 1815, in Lipscomb and Bergh, eds., *Writings of Jefferson,* XIV, p. 232.

[140]"Diary of Blair," *WMQ,* 1st Ser., VII (1898–1899), pp. 135, 142, 145, 152.

[141]"Diary of Col. Landon Carter," *ibid.,* XIII (1904–1905), p. 159.

[142]Wright and Tinling, eds., *Secret Diary,* entries for Apr. 19, 23, 26, Oct. 24, 31, 1709.

[143]Officially the governor's niece and hostess, but gossip said his mistress.

[144]Wright and Tinling, eds., *Secret Diary,* entries for Feb. 6, 7, 1711. Mrs. Byrd's behavior and appearance pleased her

husband as well as the governor. This was the occasion for the famous argument about whether she should pluck her eyebrows; she lost and gave in gracefully.

[145]*Ibid.,* entries for Nov. 14, 16, 1711.

[146]*Ibid.,* entry for Nov. 2, 1711.

[147]Wright and Tinling, eds., *London Diary,* entries for Apr. 5, 6, 1720.

[148]*Ibid.,* entries for Oct. 20, 26, Nov. 4, 1720.

[149]On Nov. 24 Commissary Blair substituted for the governor as host. *Ibid.,* entries for Oct. 21, Nov. 3, 10, 17, 24, Dec. 12, 1720.

[150]*Ibid.,* entry for Oct. 21, 1720. Anne Carter later married Benjamin Harrison.

[151]Woodfin, ed., *Another Secret Diary,* p. 107.

[152]Advertisements in the *Va. Gaz.,* Feb. 25, Apr. 22, Oct. 7, 14, 21, 1737, Mar. 24, 31, Oct. 13, 1738, Apr. 20, 1739.

[153]*Ibid.,* Mar. 28, Oct. 10, 1745, Sept. 11, 1746.

[154]*Ibid.,* Oct. 24, 1751.

[155]*Ibid.,* Apr. 11, 1751, Feb. 27, Mar. 5, 1752. The Va. Gaz. Day Book, 1750–1752, notes charges for both advertisements and tickets all three years, except in the case of Mrs. Shields, who did not advertise in 1752—probably because she married Wetherburn late in 1751. One hundred tickets was the usual number ordered at a time.

[156]Marshall, "Manners, Morals, and Domestic Pastimes," in Turberville, ed., *Johnson's England,* I, pp. 130–131, 258.

[157]Washington, Ledger A, pp. 24, 34, 55, 62, 299, Ledger B, p. 112; Fitzpatrick, ed., *Diaries of Washington,* I, p. 379. Jefferson's accounts do not include either subscriptions or tickets; when he danced with Belinda in the Apollo Room it was doubtless a private ball.

[158]Smyth, *Tour,* I, p. 20.

[159]*Va. Gaz.,* July 1, 1737.

[160]Wright and Tinling, eds., *Secret Diary,* p. 244.

[161]Woodfin, ed., *Another Secret Diary,* pp. 60, 63, 107.

[162]*Va. Gaz.,* Nov. 30, Dec. 7, 14, 1739.

[163]*Ibid.* (Purdie and Dixon), Apr. 25, Oct. 24, 1766, Apr. 23, Oct. 29, 1767, May 5, Oct. 27, 1768, Apr. 27, 1769.

[164]He noted these payments, sometimes two or three at a time, on Nov. 3, 1759, Apr. 25, Nov. 3, 1760, May 31, 1763, Apr. 16, 25, Nov. 24, 1764, May 2, Dec. 10, 1766, Oct. 20, 1767, May 3, 1769, June 1, 1770. Washington, Ledger A, pp. 62, 89, 108, 160, 176, 189, 231, 237, 255, 290, 318.

[165]*Ibid.,* p. 55.

[166]*Va. Gaz.* (Rind), Feb. 19, 1767.

[167]Mary R. M. Goodwin, "The Coffee-house of the 17th and 18th Centuries," 1956, typescript in Foundation Lib.

[168]Not only in Williamsburg, but also in Norfolk by mid-century and in Fredericksburg in 1777. *Ibid.,* pp. 10–13.

[169]Wright and Tinling, eds., *Secret Diary,* p. 50.

[170]On Nov. 6, 1711, he wrote: "I stayed and wrote at the capitol till about 5 o'clock because it rained so hard that I could not get away. However at last I ran through it to the coffee-house, where I sat an hour before anybody came." *Ibid.*

[171]Col. William Churchill and others roomed there, and on rare occasions Byrd dined there.

[172]At Henry Cary's house for most of this period.

[173]Wright and Tinling, eds., *London Diary,* entry for May 5, 1720.

[174]On one occasion, June 11, 1740, he stayed long enough to read news.

[175]Washington, Ledger A, p. 290.

[176]Fitzpatrick, ed., *Diaries of Washington,* II, p. 104.

[177]Jefferson, Memorandum Book, 1769, p. 33.

[178]*Ibid.,* p. 22.

[179]Jefferson, notes in *Virginia Almanac, 1773,* p. 8.

[180]In 1765 the Frenchman called it a tavern and Fauquier referred to it as a coffeehouse. See Goodwin, "Coffee-house," pp. 24–25.

[181]Page, notes in *Virginia Almanac, 1774,* Foundation Lib.

[182]R. W. Carter, Diary, 1766.

[183]Miscellaneous papers relating to the estate of Richard King, Jones Papers, 1649–1889, Lib. Cong., microfilm in Foundation Lib.

# BIBLIOGRAPHY

## Primary Sources

### *Manuscripts*

Allason, William. Papers. Virginia State Library, Richmond.

Beebe, Louis. Journals, 1776–1801. 3 vols. Historical Society of Pennsylvania, Philadelphia.

Blow, Richard. Papers. Earl Gregg Swem Library, College of William and Mary, Williamsburg, Va.

Bryan Family. Papers. Microfilm. Alderman Library, University of Virginia, Charlottesville.

Carter, Landon. Diary, 1752–1755, 1763–1778. Excerpts printed in "Diary of Col. Landon Carter," *William and Mary Quarterly,* 1st Ser., XIII–XXI (1904–1913).

Carter, Robert "King." Diary, 1722–1727. Alderman Lib.

———. Letterbooks, 1723–1724, 1727–1728, 1728–1731, 1731–1732. Alderman Lib.

———. Letterbooks, 1723–1729. Virginia Historical Society, Richmond.

Carter, Robert, of Nomini Hall. Letterbooks, 1761–1764, 1764–1768, 1769. Colonial Williamsburg Foundation Library, Williamsburg, Va.

Carter, Robert Wormeley. Diaries, 1764–1792. Diaries for 1764, 1765, William L. Clements Library, University of Michigan, Ann Arbor; for 1766, 1768, 1769, 1777, 1780, 1781, 1784–1787, 1790–1792, Swem Lib.; for 1774, American Antiquarian Society, Worcester, Mass.; for 1776, Foundation Lib.

Charles, John S. Recollections of Williamsburg, as it appeared at the beginning of the Civil War and just previous thereto, with some incidents in the life of its citizens. Foundation Lib.

Fredericksburg District Court Records. Fredericksburg, Va.

Gibson-Maynadier Papers. 1740–1752. Maryland Historical Society, Baltimore.

Gilmer, George. Letterbook, 1752–1757. Privately owned; copy in Foundation Lib.

Gooch, William. Letter Book, 1727–1751. Privately owned; copy in Foundation Lib.

Grove, William Hugh. Diary, 1698–1732, Travels in Great Britain and the Netherlands and in America. Alderman Lib.

Harrower, John. "Diary, 1773–1776." Richard Corbin Papers, Foundation Lib.

Hazard, Ebenezer. "Journal of Journey to the South, 1777–1778." MS, Hist. Soc. Penn. Photostat of Virginia portion in Foundation Lib.

Henrico County Records. Deeds and Wills, 1677–1692. Va. State Lib.

Jefferson, Thomas. Account Books, 1767–1782. Account books for 1767–1770, 1773, 1779–1782, Library of Congress; for 1771, 1772, 1774, 1776–1778, Massachusetts Historical Society, Boston; for 1775, Huntington Library, San Marino, Calif. Copies in Alderman Lib.

———. Memorandum Books, 1768, 1769. Lib. Cong.

Jones Papers. 1649–1889. Lib. Cong. Microfilm in Foundation Lib.

Mercer, John. "Ledgers, 1725–1732, 1741–1750." MS, Bucks County Historical Society, Doylestown, Pa. Microfilm in Foundation Lib.

Nelson, William. Letterbook, 1766–1775. Va. State Lib.

Norton, John, and Sons. Papers, 1750–1902. Foundation Lib.

Public Record Office. C. O. 5/1329, 5/1429.

Reynolds, William. Letterbook, 1771–1785. Lib. Cong.

De Robertnier, Louis Jean Baptiste Silvestre. Journal des guerres faites en Amérique pendans les années, 1780, 1781, 1782, 1783 avec quelques dissertations sur les moeurs & coutumes des américains, 1780–1783. Rhode Island Historical Society, Providence. Microfilm in Foundation Lib.

Skipwith Papers. Swem Lib.

Steuart, Charles. Letter Books, 1751–1763. Hist. Soc. Pa. Microfilm in Foundation Lib.

———. Papers, 1747–1797. National Library of Scotland.

Virginia Gazette Day Books. 1750–1752, 1764–1765. Alderman Lib.

Washington, George. Ledger A, 1750–1772; Ledger B, 1772–1793. Lib. Cong.

York County Records. York County Clerk's Office.


*Printed Sources*

Acomb, Evelyn M., ed. "The Journal of Baron Von Closen." *WMQ,* 3rd Ser., X (April 1953), pp. 196–236.

Ames, Susie M., ed. *County Court Records of Accomack-Northampton, Virginia, 1632–1640.* Washington, D. C.: American Historical Association, 1954.

Anburey, Thomas. *Travels through the Interior Parts of America . . .* 2 vols. London: printed for W. Lane, 1789.

Bassett, John Spencer, ed. *The Writings of "Colonel William Byrd of Westover in Virginia, Esqr."* New York: Doubleday, Page & Co., 1901.

Bernard, John. *Retrospections of America, 1797–1811.* Edited by Mrs. Bayle Bernard. New York: Harper and Brothers, 1887.

Beverley, Robert. *The History and Present State of Virginia.* Edited by Louis B. Wright. Chapel Hill, N. C.: University of North Carolina Press, 1947.

Blair, John. "Diary of John Blair." *WMQ,* 1st Ser., VII (January 1899), pp. 133–153; VIII (July 1899), pp. 1–17.

Boucher, Jonathan. *Reminiscences of an American Loyalist, 1738–1789, Being the Autobiography of the Revd. Jonathan Boucher, Rector of Annapolis in Maryland and afterwards Vicar of Epsom, Surrey, England.* Edited by Jonathan Bouchier. Boston: Houghton Mifflin Co., 1925.

Boyd, Julian P., et. al. *The Papers of Thomas Jefferson.* 19 vols. to date. Princeton, N. J.: Princeton University Press, 1950–  .

Boyd, William K., ed. *William Byrd's Histories of the Dividing Line betwixt Virginia and North Carolina.* Raleigh, N. C.: North Carolina Historical Commission, 1929.

Brissot de Warville, J. P. *New Travels in the United States of America. Performed in 1788.* Translated by Joel Barlow. New York: printed by T. and J. Swords, 1792.

Brock, R. A. *The Official Records of Robert Dinwiddie, Lieutenant-Governor of the Colony of Virginia, 1751–1758.* 2 vols. Richmond, Va.: Virginia Historical Society, 1883–1884.

Brock, R. A., ed. *The Official Letters of Alexander Spotswood, Lieutenant-Governor of the Colony of Virginia, 1710–1722.* 2 vols. Richmond, Va.: Virginia Historical Society, 1882, 1885.

Bullock, William. *Virginia Impartially Examined, and Left to Publick View, to be Considered by All Judicious and Honest Men.* London: printed by J. Hammond, 1649.

Burnaby, Andrew. *Travels through the Middle Settlements in North-America. In the Years 1759 and 1760. With Observations upon the State of the Colonies.* 2nd ed. London: T. Payne, 1775.

Burney, Frances. *Evelina; or, The History of a Young Lady's Entrance into the World.* 2nd ed. London, 1779. Reprint edition edited by Sir Frank D. Mackinnon. Oxford: Clarendon Press, 1930.

Carrington, Elizabeth. "An Old Virginia Correspondence." *Atlantic Monthly,* LXXXIV (October 1899), pp. 535–549.

Chalkley, Lyman, ed. *Chronicles of the Scotch–Irish Settlement in Virginia, Extracted from the Original Court Records of Augusta County, 1745–1800.* 3 vols. Rosslyn, Va.: Commonwealth Printing Co., 1912.

Chastellux, Marquis de. *Travels in North America, in the Years 1780, 1781, and 1782.* Translated from the French by an English Gentleman . . . with Notes by the Translator. 2 vols. London: G. G. J. & J. Robinson, 1787.

*The Compleat Country Dancing Master.* London: John Walsh, 1731.

*The Complete Letter Writer; or The Art of Correspondence.* Albany, N. Y.: C. R. and G. Webster, 1802.

Cresswell, Nicholas. *The Journal of Nicholas Cresswell, 1774–1777.* New York: Dial Press, 1924.

Davis, John. *Travels of Four Years and a Half in the United States of America during 1798, 1799, 1800, 1801, and 1802.* London: T. Ostell and T. Hurst, 1803.

De Vries, David Peterson. *Voyages from Holland to America, A. D. 1632 to 1644.* Translated and edited by Henry C. Murphy. New York: privately printed by James Lenox, 1853. Reprinted in New-York Historical Society, *Collections*, 2nd Ser., III (1857), pp. 1–136.

Diderot, Denis, ed. *Encyclopédie ou Dictionnaire Raisonné des Sciences, des Arts et des Métiers . . .* 35 vols. Paris: Briasson, 1751–1765.

Du Bellet, Louise Pecquet. *Some Prominent Virginia Families.* Vol. II. Lynchburg, Va.: J. P. Bell, 1907.

Durand of Dauphiné. *A Huguenot Exile in Virginia; or, Voyages of a Frenchman Exiled for His Religion, with a Description of Virginia & Maryland.* Edited by Gilbert Chinard. New York: Press of the Pioneers, 1934.

Eddis, William. *Letters from America, Historical and Descriptive; Comprising Occurrences from 1769, to 1777, inclusive.* London: printed for the author, 1792.

Fairfax, Sally Cary. "Diary of a Little Colonial Girl." *Virginia Magazine of History and Biography,* XI (October 1903), pp. 212–214.

Fithian, Philip Vickers. *Journal & Letters of Philip Vickers Fithian, 1773–1774: A Plantation Tutor of the Old Dominion.* Edited by Hunter Dickinson Farish. Williamsburg, Va.: Colonial Williamsburg, 1943.

Fitzpatrick, John C. *George Washington, Colonial Traveller, 1732–1775.* Indianapolis, Ind.: Bobbs-Merrill Co., 1927.

Fitzpatrick, John C., ed. *The Diaries of George Washington, 1748–1799.* 4 vols. Boston: Houghton Mifflin Co. for the Mount Vernon Ladies' Association, 1925.

———. *The Writings of George Washington from the Original Manuscript Sources, 1745–1799.* 39 vols. Washington, D. C.: U. S. Government Printing Office, 1931–1944.

Fontaine, John. "Journal" in Ann Maury, ed., *Memoirs of a Huguenot Family: Translated and Compiled from the Original Autobiography of the Rev. James Fontaine, and Other Family Manuscripts.* New York: George P. Putnam & Co., 1853.

Force, Peter, ed. *Tracts and Other Papers, Relating Principally to the Origin, Settlement, and Progress of the Colonies in North America, from the Discovery of the Country to the Year 1776.* 4 vols. Washington, D. C.: printed by P. Force, 1836–1846.

Franklin, James. *The Philosophical & Political History of the Thirteen United States of America . . .* London: J. Hinton & W. Adams, 1784.

Gallini, Giovanni-Andrea. *Critical Observations on the Art of Dancing . . .* London: printed for the author [1770].

Glover, Thomas. *An Account of Virginia, Its Scituation, Temperature, Productions, Inhabitants and Their Manner of Planting and Ordering Tobacco &c. Reprinted from the Philosophical Transactions of the Royal Society, June 20, 1676.* Oxford: Printer to the University, 1904.

Gordon, James. "Journal of Col. James Gordon, of Lancaster County, Va.," *WMQ,* 1st Ser., XI (October 1902), pp. 98–112; (January 1903), pp. 195–205; (April 1903), pp. 217–236; XII (July 1903), pp. 1–12.

Hadfield, Joseph. *An Englishman in America, 1785, Being the Diary of Joseph Hadfield.* Edited by Douglas S. Robertson. Toronto: Hunter-Rose Co., 1933.

Hamilton, Stanislas Murray, ed. *Letters to Washington, and Accompanying Papers.* 5 vols. Boston: Houghton Mifflin Co., 1898–1902.

Hartmann, Cyril Hughes, ed. *Games and Gamesters of the Restoration*. London: G. Routledge and Sons, 1930.

Hening, William Waller, ed. *The Statutes at Large; Being a Collection of All the Laws of Virginia, from the First Session of the Legislature, in the Year 1619*. 13 vols. Philadelphia, New York, and Richmond, Va.: printed for the author, 1810–1823.

Hinke, William J., trans. and ed. "Report of the Journey of Francis Louis Michel from Berne, Switzerland, to Virginia, October 2, 1701–December 1, 1702," *Virginia Magazine of History and Biography*, XXIV (January 1916), pp. 1–43; (April 1916), pp. 113–141; (June 1916), pp. 275–303.

Hoyle, Edmond. *Mr. Hoyle's Games of Whist, Quadrille, Piquet, Chess and Back-gammon, Complete. In which are contained, the Method of Playing and Betting at Those Games, upon equal, or advantageous Terms. Including the Laws of Several Games*. 11th ed. London: printed for Thomas Osborne and others, n.d. [1750–1760].

Hughes, Thomas. *Tom Brown's School Days*. 6th ed. Boston: Houghton Mifflin Co., 1895.

Hunter, Robert, Jr. *Quebec to Carolina in 1785–1786: Being the Travel Diary and Observations of Robert Hunter, Jr., a Young Merchant of London*. Edited by Louis B. Wright and Marion Tinling. San Marino, Calif.: Huntington Library, 1943.

Jefferson, Thomas. *Notes on the State of Virginia*. Edited by William Peden. Chapel Hill, N. C.: University of North Carolina Press, 1955.

Jones, Hugh. *The Present State of Virginia: From Whence Is Inferred A Short View of Maryland and North Carolina*. Edited by Richard L. Morton. Chapel Hill, N. C.: University of North Carolina Press, 1956.

"Journal of a French Traveller in the Colonies, 1765." *American Historical Review*, XXVI (July 1921), pp. 726–747; XXVII (October 1921), pp. 70–89.

[Kimber, Edward]. *Itinerant Observations in America*. Savannah, Ga.: J. H. Estill, 1878.

La Rochefoucauld-Liancourt, Duke de. *Travels through the United States of North America, the Country of the Iroquois, and Upper Canada, in the Years 1795, 1796, and 1797*. 2 vols. London: R. Phillips, 1799.

Latrobe, Benjamin Henry. *The Journal of Latrobe: Being the Notes and Sketches of an Architect, Naturalist and Traveler in the United States from 1796 to 1820*. New York: D. Appleton and Co., 1905.

Lee, Lucinda. *Journal of a Young Lady of Virginia, 1782*. Edited by Emily V. Mason. Baltimore: John Murphy and Co., 1891.

Lewis, W. S., ed. *A Selection of the Letters of Horace Walpole*. 2 vols. New York: Harper and Brothers, 1926.

Lipscomb, Andrew A., and Albert Ellery Bergh, eds. *The Writings of Thomas Jefferson*. Washington, D. C.: Thomas Jefferson Memorial Association, 1903–1904.

*A Little Pretty Pocket-Book, Intended for the Instruction and Amusement of Little Master Tommy, and Pretty Miss Polly*. Worcester, Mass.: Isaiah Thomas, 1787.

McIlwaine, H. R., ed. *Executive Journals of the Council of Colonial Virginia*. 6 vols. Richmond, Va.: Superintendent of Public Printing, 1925–1966.

McIlwaine, H. R., and John Pendleton Kennedy, eds. *Journals of the House of Burgesses of Virginia*. 13 vols. Richmond, Va.: n.p., 1905–1915.

Mason, Frances Norton, ed. *John Norton & Sons, Merchants of London and Virginia: Being the Papers from Their Counting House for the Years 1750 to 1795*. Richmond, Va.: Dietz Press, 1937.

Mereness, Newton D., ed., *Travels in the American Colonies*. New York: Macmillan Co., 1916.

Moreau de Saint-Méry, Mederic. *Moreau de St. Méry's American Journey [1793–1798]*. Translated and edited by Kenneth Roberts and Anna M. Roberts. Garden City, N. Y.: Doubleday and Co., 1947.

Munford, Robert. "The Candidates" in Jay B. Hubbell and Douglass Adair, "Robert Munford's *The Candidates*," *WMQ*, 3rd Ser., V (April 1948), pp. 217–257.

Palmer, William P., ed. *Calendar of Virginia State Papers and other manuscripts, 1652–1781: preserved in the Capitol at Richmond.* 11 vols. Richmond, Va.: Virginia State Library, 1875–1893. New York: Reprint, 1968.

R., J. *The Port Folio: or A View of the Manners and Customs of Various Countries: Interspersed with Anecdotes of Former Times.* 2 vols. London: Dean and Schultze, 1812.

Randolph, Sarah N. *The Domestic Life of Thomas Jefferson. Compiled from Family Letters and Reminiscences.* New York: Harper and Brothers, 1871.

[Ritson, Mrs. Anne]. *A Poetical Picture of America, Being Observations Made, during a Residence of Several Years, at Alexandria, and Norfolk, in Virginia . . . from the Years 1799 to 1807.* London: printed for the author, 1809.

Schoepf, Johann David. *Travels in the Confederation [1783–1784].* 2 vols. Translated and edited by Alfred J. Morrison. Philadelphia: William J. Campbell, 1911.

Seymour, Richard. *The Compleat Gamester: In Three Parts . . .* 5th ed. London: E. Curll and J. Wilford, 1734.

Skeel, Emily Ellsworth Ford, ed. "Diary, 1785–1786," in *Notes on the Life of Noah Webster.* 2 vols. New York: privately printed, 1912.

Smyth, Albert Henry, ed. *The Writings of Benjamin Franklin.* 10 vols. New York: Macmillan Co., 1905–1907.

Smyth, J. F. D. *A Tour in the United States of America . . .* 2 vols. London: G. Robinson, 1784.

Thévénot, Melchisedech. *The Art of Swimming, Illustrated by Forty Copper-plate Cuts, which Represent the different Postures necessary to be used in that Art, with Advice for Bathing. By Monsieur Thevenot. Done out of French . . .* 3rd ed. London: John Lever, 1789.

Toulmin, Harry. *The Western Country in 1793: Reports on Kentucky and Virginia by Harry Toulmin.* Edited by Marion Tinling and Godfrey Davies. San Marino, Calif.: Huntington Library, 1948.

Verne, Jules. *The Tour of the World in Eighty Days.* New York: A. L. Burt Co., n.d.

Watson, Winslow C., ed. *Men and Times of the Revolution; or, Memoirs of Elkanah Watson, including Journals of Travels in Europe and America, from 1777 to 1842.* New York: Dana and Co., 1856.

Weaver, John, trans. *Orchesography or the Art of Dancing by Characters and Demonstrative Figures . . . Being an Exact and Just Translation from the French of Monsieur Feuillet.* 2nd ed. London: John Walsh [ca. 1715].

Webb, George. *The Office and Authority of a Justice of Peace.* Williamsburg, Va.: William Parks, 1736.

Weld, Isaac. *Travels through the States of North America, and the Provinces of Upper and Lower Canada, during the Years 1795, 1796, and 1797.* 2 vols. 4th ed. London: John Stockdale, 1807.

Woodfin, Maude H., ed. *Another Secret Diary of William Byrd of Westover, 1739–1741. With Letters & Literary Exercises, 1696–1726.* Translated by Marion Tinling. Richmond, Va.: Dietz Press, 1942.

Woodmason, Charles. *A Poetical Epistle to Benjamin Franklin, Esq. of Philadelphia; On His Experiments and Discoveries in Electricity.* [1753] Introduction by Whitfield J. Bell, Jr. Richmond, Va.: William Byrd Press, 1954.

Wright, Louis B., and Marion Tinling, eds. *The London Diary (1717–1721) and Other Writings.* New York: Oxford University Press, 1958.

———. *The Secret Diary of William Byrd of Westover, 1709–1712.* Richmond, Va.: Dietz Press, 1941.

*Newspapers and Periodicals*

*The Court Mercurie,* No. 10. London, 1644. McGregor Collection, Alderman Lib.

*Gentlemen's Magazine and Historical Chronicle.* 44 vols. London, 1731–1774.

*Maryland Gazette* (Annapolis). 1727–1734, 1745–1774.

*Pennsylvania Gazette* (Philadelphia). 1738–1774.

*South Carolina Gazette* (Charleston). 1732–1775.

*Virginia Gazette* (Parks, Hunter, Royle, Purdie, Purdie and Dixon, Dixon and Hunter, Rind, Pinkney). (Williamsburg). 1736–1780.


Secondary Sources

Armstrong, Susan S. "A Retrospective of the American Colonial Theatre." 1955. Typescript in Department of Research, Colonial Williamsburg.

Ashton, John. *The History of Gambling in England.* London: Duckworth & Co., 1898.

Ashton, T. S. *An Economic History of England: The 18th Century.* London: Methuen & Co., 1955.

Bruce, Philip Alexander. *Social Life in Virginia in the Seventeenth Century.* 2nd ed. Lynchburg, Va.: Bell, 1927.

Brydon, George Maclaren. *Virginia's Mother Church . . . and the Political Conditions under Which It Grew.* 2 vols. Richmond, Va.: Virginia Historical Society, 1947–1952.

Campbell, Charles. *History of the Colony and Ancient Dominion of Virginia.* Philadelphia: J. B. Lippincott, 1860.

Cappon, Lester J., and Stella F. Duff, comps. *Virginia Gazette Index, 1736–1780.* 2 vols. Williamsburg, Va.: Institute of Early American History and Culture, 1950.

*Cassell's Complete Book of Sports and Pastimes: Being a Compendium of Outdoor and Indoor Amusements.* London: Cassell & Co., n.d.

Craven, Wesley Frank. *The Southern Colonies in the Seventeenth Century, 1607–1689.* Vol. I of *A History of the South,* Wendell Holmes Stephenson and E. Merton Coulter, eds. Baton Rouge, La.: Louisiana State University Press, 1949.

Curtis, William E. *The True Thomas Jefferson.* Philadelphia: J. B. Lippincott, 1901.

D'Allemagne, Henry René. *Le Noble Jeu de l'Oie en France, de 1640 à 1950.* Paris: Libraire Grund, 1905.

———. *Récréations et Passe-Temps.* Paris: Hachette & Cie. [1905].

———. *Sports et Jeux d'Adresse.* Paris: Hachette & Cie. [1903].

Damon, S. Foster. "The History of Square-Dancing." American Antiquarian Society, *Proceedings,* N. S., LXII (1952), pp. 63–74.

Ewing, William C. *The Sports of Colonial Williamsburg.* Richmond, Va.: Dietz Press, 1937.

Fitzgerald, David Bruce. "An Old Virginia Fox Hunt." *Lippincott's Monthly Magazine,* LVIII (1896), pp. 824–828.

Freeman, Douglas Southall. *George Washington: A Biography.* 7 vols. New York: Charles Scribner's Sons, 1948–1957.

Gaines, William H., Jr. "John Peel in Virginia: Fox Hunting in the Old Dominion, Frolicsome and Fashionable." *Virginia Cavalcade,* III (Autumn 1953), pp. 22–27.

Galpin, Francis W. *Old English Instruments of Music: Their History and Character.* Chicago: A. C. McClurg & Co., 1911.

Goodwin, Mary R. M. "The Coffee-house of the Seventeenth and Eighteenth Centuries." 1956. Typescript in Foundation Lib.

———. "Musical Instruments of Eighteenth-Century Virginia." 1953. Typescript in Foundation Lib.

Goodwin, Rutherfoord. *A Brief & True Report Concerning Williamsburg in Virginia.* 3rd ed. Williamsburg, Va.: Colonial Williamsburg, 1941.

Greene, Vivien. *English Dolls' Houses of the Eighteenth and Nineteenth Centuries.* London: Batsford, 1955.

Hamlin, Talbot. *Benjamin Henry Latrobe.* New York: Oxford University Press, 1955.

Harrison, Fairfax. *The Belair Stud, 1747–1761.* Richmond, Va.: Old Dominion Press, 1929.

———. "The Equine F F Vs." *VMHB,* XXXV (October 1927), pp. 329–370.

———. "The Genesis of Foxhunting in Virginia." *VMHB,* XXXVII (April 1929), pp. 155–157.

Hervey, John. *Racing in America, 1665–1865.* 2 vols. New York: privately printed for the Jockey Club, 1944.

Jenkins, David Clay. "Peter Gardiner's Puppets, Magic, & Perspectives in Williamsburg, 1769–1772." 1958. Typescript in Foundation Lib.

Kennedy, John P. *Memoirs of the Life of William Wirt.* 2 vols. New and rev. ed. Philadelphia: Lee and Blanchard, 1850.

Kercheval, Samuel. *A History of the Valley of Virginia.* 4th ed. Strasburg, Va.: Shenandoah Publishing House, 1925.

Kimball, Marie. *Jefferson: War and Peace, 1776 to 1784.* New York: Coward-McCann, 1947.

Krout, John Allen. *Annals of American Sport.* In Ralph H. Gabriel, ed., *The Pageant of America: A Pictorial History of the United States,* XV. New Haven, Conn.: Yale University Press, 1929.

Lewis, Wilmarth Sheldon. *Three Tours through London in the Years 1748, 1776, 1791.* New Haven, Conn.: Yale University Press, 1952.

Linney, E. J. *A History of the Game of Bowls.* London: Laurie, 1933.

McPharlin, Paul. *The Puppet Theatre in America: A History.* New York: Harper, 1949.

Malone, Dumas. *Jefferson and His Time.* Vol. I: *Jefferson the Virginian.* Boston: Little, Brown and Co., 1948.

Marshall, Dorothy. *English People in the Eighteenth Century.* New York: Longmans, Green and Co., 1956.

Peyton, John L. *History of Augusta County, Virginia.* Staunton, Va.: S. M. Yost and Son, 1882.

Randall, Henry S. *The Life of Thomas Jefferson.* 3 vols. New York: Derby & Jackson, 1858.

Rankin, Hugh F. "The Colonial Theatre, Its History and Operations." 1955. Typescript in Foundation Lib.

———. "Criminal Jurisdiction of the General Court." 1958. Typescript in Foundation Lib.

Scott, Arthur P. *Criminal Law in Virginia.* Chicago: University of Chicago Press, 1930.

Spruill, Julia Cherry. *Women's Life and Work in the Southern Colonies.* Chapel Hill, N. C.: University of North Carolina Press, 1938.

Stanard, Mary Newton. *Colonial Virginia: Its People and Customs.* Philadelphia: J. B. Lippincott Co., 1917.

———. *John Marshall: An Address . . . Read before the Association for the Preservation of Virginia Antiquities at the Opening of the John Marshall House, March 27, 1913.* 3rd ed. Richmond, Va.: Whittet and Shepperson, 1913.

———. *The Story of Virginia's First Century.* Philadelphia: J. B. Lippincott Co., 1928.

Stanard, William G. "Racing in Colonial Virginia." *VMHB,* II (January 1895), pp. 293–305.

Strutt, Joseph. *The Sports and Pastimes of the People of England from the Earliest Period.* New ed., enl., by J. Charles Cox. London: Methuen & Co., 1903.

Swem, E. G., comp. *Virginia Historical Index.* 2 vols. Roanoke, Va.: Stone Printing and Manufacturing Co., 1934–1936.

Turberville, A. S., ed. *Johnson's England: An Account of the Life & Manners of His Age.* 2 vols. Oxford: Clarendon Press, 1933.

Tyler, Lyon Gardiner. *Williamsburg, The Old Colonial Capital.* Richmond, Va.: Whittet and Shepperson, 1907.

Wecter, Dixon. *The Saga of American Society: A Record of Social Aspiration, 1607–1937.* New York: Charles Scribner's Sons, 1937.

Wertenbaker, Thomas J. *Norfolk: Historic Southern Port*. Durham, N. C.: Duke University Press, 1931.

Whitehouse, F. R. B. *Table Games of Georgian and Victorian Days*. London: Peter Garnett, 1951.

Whitelaw, Ralph T. *Virginia's Eastern Shore: A History of North-ampton and Accomack Counties*. 2 vols. Richmond, Va.: Virginia Historical Society, 1951.

Wright, Louis B. *The First Gentlemen of Virginia: Intellectual Qualities of the Early Colonial Ruling Class*. San Marino, Calif.: Huntington Library, 1940.

# Index

Index

# Index

## Index